W9-CIL-882

THE INDELIBLE FAMILY

By Mel Roman and William Haddad
  The Disposable Parent

By Mel Roman and Sara Blackburn
  Family Secrets

By Patricia E. Raley
  Making Love

THE
INDELIBLE
FAMILY

❀◆❀◆❀

Mel Roman, Ph. D. and Patricia E. Raley

RAWSON, WADE PUBLISHERS, INC.
New York

Library of Congress Cataloging in Publication Data

Roman, Mel.
  The indelible family.

  Bibliography: p.
  Includes index.
  1. Family. 2. Life cycle, Human. I. Raley,
Patricia E., joint author. II. Title.
HQ734.R72   306.8   78-64812
  ISBN 0-89256-093-2

Published simultaneously in Canada
by McClelland and Stewart, Ltd.

Composition by American–Stratford
Graphic Services, Inc., Brattleboro, Vermont
Printed and bound by R. R. Donnelley & Sons,
Crawfordsville, Indiana

Designed by Jacques Chazaud

First Edition

For Merle
For Ron
and for all our families

❀◆❀

Acknowledgments

Without Charlotte Sheedy this book would never have been. She thought of it, brought us together, stood by us, encouraged us, and beyond all that she lived in and believed in this book to the point of its being her book, too.

Without Eleanor Rawson this book would never have been what we wanted. Her fierce interest in the concept, her patience and excitement as it evolved, her help in setting its direction all made it possible for us to create the book we had in us.

Without Sharon Morgan editing and Barry Greif researching this book would never have been finished.

Without our relatives, friends, students, and colleagues this book would never have been complete. We owe special thanks to those who gave so much of their own experience to enrich ours.

❀◆❀

Contents

PART I

❀◆❀◆❀

ALL
IN THE
FAMILY

Family Matters

W e come from conventional families. We lived with mothers, fathers, sisters, and brothers, and we had other relatives nearby. Although one of us grew up in a big-city, immigrant Jewish family and the other in a small-town, settled Episcopalian family, our families' ideals, values, and expectations for themselves and for us were very much alike. And very much like those of other families a generation or two ago.

Today, we're each a part of what used to be called nonconventional families. Trish Raley is a childfree, married working woman, and Mel Roman has been divorced, remarried, and widowed. Trish is the first woman in her family to have a career and to choose to remain childfree. Mel is the first man in his family to divorce and to become part of a blended family with stepchildren and stepparents. We are both examples of what has been called the death of the family. But our families and, we believe, families in general are very much alive.

This book is about families—how they persist; how they endure. In spite of the great upheaval in society and the continual reorganization of the family into new forms—dual career, blended, single parent, single person—we are all related to our families in ways that have not been appreciated, understood, or even recognized. The survival of the family as an institution and its importance in our individual lives are results of largely unconscious processes by which we re-create some variations on our own original families. Whether or not our family was close, we carry a shared heritage. The more we know about this heritage and its powerful motivations for repetition, the freer we are to create the kinds of families we want in the future.

There seems to be a great demand now for continuity and intimacy in family life because so many other aspects of our lives are transient or alienating. We change jobs, homes, and communities, but we do not change families. Yet, many people find family life less than satisfying—partly because their expectations are so high and partly because so little is known about the changing nature of families. The extreme mobility in modern society is not a sign that the family is breaking up but, rather, that it is opening up. Our investigations indicate that new family forms are as important for the socialization of children and the stabilization of adults as the more traditional forms were in the past. The key is to understand how families—all families—work.

If you are wondering whether the group of people you live with is a family, consider how their behavior might affect your self-image. Family used to mean those related by blood or marriage, but today, families (and extended families in particular) may be composed of groups of friends who rely on one another for help with child-rearing, for advice, and for emotional and perhaps financial support. A scandal or problem involving any one of these people could evoke your sympathy and concern, but if it also affects the way you see yourself, if it raises doubts about your own reliability or place in the world, then you are "related" in a family way to that person. When your image of yourself is truly tested you find out who your family is.

No matter what form your family takes or who is in it, the family as a group will have growing pains. And these growing pains, to the surprise of most families, are much like the growing pains of every other family. Families of all sorts go through a cycle of development that is remarkably similar to the cycle of development for all other families, especially families with children. In other words, tell us who is in your family, how long you have been a family, what your ages are, and we'll tell you what kinds of problems you are grappling with and how your heritage or history may be interfering with solutions and finer family feelings.

This developmental cycle is made up of seven stages that are characterized and shaped by the very normal and predictable events all families face, such as marriage, birth, death, aging, adolescence, retirement. Within the various stages, families must make decisions about these issues—decisions that affect each individual family member as well as the family group as a whole. And the decision-making process determines the family personality and reveals the family heritage, for it is during these periods of change in the family structure that history rushes in.

In the past, all families went through all stages of the family life cycle together. That is, the same group of people faced each stage together, from marriage to birth to aging to death. Now, each stage can be experienced in a different setting, in a different family group. One young woman who traced her family life cycle found that she was part of a nuclear family when she was an infant, a single-parent family after her parents divorced, a blended family when her mother married a man who had custody of his two children, a single-person family after she graduated from college, and a cohabiting family since she had been living with the man she would probably marry. To each new family she brought the skills of the former family, but because she went through different stages with each different group there were always new things to learn.

The cycle that we refer to in the phrase "family life cycle" is not the same as a circle. A cycle is a series of stages that we move through, but we do not go full circle or end up in the same place from which we started. A couple whose children leave home will be a couple as they were before they had children, but they will not be the same couple. A person who has been married before will enter a second marriage with information unavailable to him or her the first time around. But he or she will be a different person this time, with a different partner and different needs. Dealing with crises or ordinary everyday events will give families experience in problem solving that will follow them into the next stage, but it may not help them anticipate the problems. A main purpose of this book is to illuminate the actual challenges of normal growth.

Just What This Family Life Cycle Is

Families grow just as individuals do. They pass through stages that are predictable, explicable, and desirable. Some periods of the family life cycle are very easy for some families and devastating for others. The life cycle of any one particular family is related to that of all families, but especially to the families of origin of its founding members. We don't spring out of the air fully formed. We are all rooted to a vast underground network of family relationships, family patterns, family rules, and roles that are evident in the family personality and the family system. And we carry this network with us into any new family we form. The family we grew up in, the family that teaches us more than we'll ever know, is our family of origin. And when we leave to make our own way in the world or to marry, we attempt to re-create that family in some way.

The family life cycle really begins when we marry and form a new family. In that first stage, and in the six other developmental stages that follow, we begin to develop our own family systems and a unique family identity. Although we will be examining each stage in great detail, the following overview offers a glimpse at the decisions, crises, and tasks that make up the family life cycle.

In Stage One, "Conjugal Blitz," the new couple goes through a period of adjustment that can last from several weeks to several years as they learn how to get along as a twosome, assimilate their differences, and build on their strengths. Their task in this stage is to establish their identity as a mutually supportive and autonomous family.

In Stage Two, "The Dynastic Imperative," the couple faces a major decision—whether or not to have a baby, whether or not to add a new member to the family group. The decision-making process itself, as well as the anticipation of a new family member should the couple choose to have a child, creates complex changes in the family's dynamics. Furthermore, the context in which pregnancy does or does not occur can reveal a great deal about the couple and their family system.

In Stage Three, "And Baby Makes Three," the new parents must redefine their family. They are no longer a family of two, and the addition of a third member affects the parents' relationship in many unforeseen and unexpected ways. It's an exhausting period for parents, both emotionally and physically, as they struggle to meet the baby's needs. Allegiances may begin to shift—from husband to baby, from wife to baby—and the ensuing emotional readjustments can drain parents' energy even further.

Stage Four, "The Best Years of Our Lives," begins when the children enter school. This can be an extremely happy period for many families because children become active participants in family life. They are eager to please their parents, they need less care, and they can take on some responsibilities in the home. But it can be a period of tremendous conflict as well, as the outside world infiltrates the tight family circle, perhaps for the first time. As children form relationships with peers and teachers, and as parents return to work or school or change careers, the family is exposed to outside influences and values that will affect their relationships and development. Even in families without children, adults begin to reevaluate their marriages as they become restless with one another and more involved in careers or outside activities.

In Stage Five, "Rebels With a Cause," the adolescent's struggles to establish a personal and sexual identity reverberate throughout the entire family. Adults begin to question their own identities, values, and beliefs, and they worry about what they have or have not accomplished during their lives and what they can do in the future. Childfree couples may also enter a period of self-doubt, fostered by their sudden awareness that many of their youthful dreams remain unrealized.

In Stage Six, "Letting Go and Taking Off," adult children begin to form families of their own. Both parents and children must deal with the difficult issues of separation and autonomy as the children move away, either literally or figuratively, to begin their own lives. The entire family must rally to ease the pain of separation for both generations, and they must begin to integrate the children's new families into the family of origin. Furthermore, both parents and nonparents become preoccupied with aging, especially if they have to assume care for their own aging or ill parents.

Stage Seven, "Curtain Calls," covers the various unpredictable events that can occur at any time in the family life cycle, such as divorce and death. Although the events themselves are unpredictable, what is predictable is the family's reaction—all families invariably view these events as the end of the family. But, in fact, the family endures; it changes, but it continues. And the family's task in Stage Seven is to deal with those changes and create new patterns and a new family identity.

The Family System

Systems abound in nature. There is the solar system, the circulatory system, the weather system. And man has followed up with systems of government, subway systems, computer systems. The system model fits families, too, for like any system, the family is interdependent and interactive. That is, all members of the family are part of the system, and the system influences all members of the family. Even the baby who cannot yet talk is affected by the expectations and values of the family. The family, in turn, is affected by the way in which the baby does or does not fit into the family system. In some ways the system will change to accommodate the baby, and in other ways the baby will change to fit the system.

It is the purpose of systems to maintain internal equilibrium despite external change. The human body, for example, works to maintain a constant temperature in spite of infection or variations in outside temperature. Similarly, the family system operates to regulate family emotions and behavior despite differences in individual family members and changes in the family's external situation. Thus, if someone in the family loses a job, some family members will go to work and other family members will take over new responsibilities in order to support and stabilize the family. The work of the family will be redistributed. If two family members are fighting, a third may intervene to stop the fight and reestablish the status quo. It is when we cannot redistribute the work or maintain the status quo that we have problems. Because we are not aware that we each operate as part of a group, we sometimes fail to recognize that everything that happens in family life is connected to everything else. The problems of one are the problems of all.

Often, a family member who is in trouble, who is suffering or "acting out," speaks for the whole family. Through a complex and unconscious process, the whole family may collude to keep this person "sick" and thereby keep themselves "well." If that person got well, the family system would be thrown off-balance, and the whole family would risk losing its identity. Being identified as the family of that alcoholic woman or that delinquent child may not seem particularly desirable, but it is a way for the rest of the family to avoid examining their own responsibilities and roles in the family.

In fact, it was the observation that schizophrenic children seemed to recover slightly in therapy, only to be "sick" again when they returned home, that led to the development of family therapy. This, in turn, led to our own belief that individual personality develops within a context—a family context of immense importance. The pioneers in family therapy—Murray Bowen at Georgetown University, Nathan Ackerman in New York, Don Jackson and Jay Haley in Palo Alto—realized that schizophrenic children had mothers and fathers and sisters and brothers. And when the whole family came into the consulting room, it became clear that family structure had a critical and pervasive effect on individual personality. That realization about "sick" families was soon found to apply equally to "well" families. In short, we are all influenced and formed by those closest to us.

The Hidden Forces

In every family system at every stage of family life there are psychological forces that affect each individual as well as the family group as a whole. Most families are totally unaware of these dynamic, shifting, and conflicting forces, but, in fact, they are the motivational foundation for family systems—and family indelibility. Each family has a history of managing the conflicts of everyday life in very particular and (for them) traditional ways. The founding members of the new family carry these methods from their families of origin, and other methods develop from the experience of the new family group itself. Most families do not consciously seek old solutions to new problems, but they sometimes overlook their own potential for more creative problem solving partly because they do not know how to look at themselves. Many family systems, for example, do not encourage self-examination. But even an awareness of this fact is usually not enough. Because the family system regulates these hidden forces, it is vital to know what they are and how they manifest themselves in order to create any real change in the system.

The five hidden forces that we will examine—power, dependency, autonomy, love, and separation—will be referred to over and over in this book, for they are omnipresent in family life and particularly pressing and in need of management at the transition points in the family life cycle outlined above. Each new stage is like a window that opens on the family system and all the hidden forces that sustain it. But, once the family has found some kind of equilibrium in the new stage, the window closes, and the equilibrium, whether appropriate or not, disguises or obscures the real issues that the forces have raised.

Conflict itself is normal in family life. The family is a group of individuals at different ages and stages with different needs. Conflict is inevitable—and desirable. It is impossible for us to grow, to discover our capabilities as individuals and as a family group if we are never challenged, never pitted against another, never forced to resolve different goals. The family has to learn to negotiate its differences, strengthen its management of the hidden forces, and appreciate the importance of conflict. Most people regard conflict as a sign that they are not getting along, and they try to suppress it. However, when we understand the nature of conflict, we can avoid repeating the old patterns that have kept us from creating the kind of family we want.

Power

Power is manifested through the decision-making process. Who makes decisions and how they are made reveal a lot about the distribution of power in the family. Although some family members naturally will have more responsibility than others, every member must feel responsible to the family if the group is to be a real family. Decision making develops a sense of responsibility, and each member's degree of participation in that process determines her or his degree of responsibility within the family group. If one person always makes all the decisions for everyone else, there probably will be some very dependent and powerless people in the family. When people feel powerless they have no sense of responsibility, and they tend to blame others for their problems or mistakes. Such behavior is very characteristic of families with power problems. Furthermore, the decisions they do make are negative rather than positive. Because they can't settle on any one alternative, they decide to do nothing, as when, for example, they decide not to go to a movie because they can't agree on any one particular film.

In healthy families dominance is related to competence. The division of labor within a family does not depend on each individual's sex or age; rather, tasks are allocated on the basis of skill and ability. Thus, power is distributed fairly since each member has some power in his or her area of expertise. However, when families cling to more traditional ideas about roles and responsibilities, ideas that bear no relation to each member's skills and talents, they may face serious power problems. For example, if a woman cooks because she feels it is her "duty" as a wife even though her husband is actually the better cook, both of them will feel powerless. She knows that she is incompetent and he feels thwarted. Neither of them can take the responsibility to change this pattern because cultural notions about gender and traditional role-playing expectations interfere with actual competence. The recent changes in our society may bring an end to sexual stereotyping of this sort, but it is a very prevalent problem. In such families, decisions are made on the basis of what competence *should be* rather than on *what it is*.

Another common type of role stereotyping occurs between parent and child. The teenager who knows everything about cars is not allowed to fix the family car because the father feels that it is his "duty" as the male head of the family. Although he knows his son is more competent at that particular job, he denies his son any power and ends up feeling powerless himself because he really does not know what to do with the car. And if the family mechanic turns out to be a girl, the father may have an even more difficult time.

Families really have to know themselves in order to make fair and just decisions. They have to recognize and respect each other's abilities and avoid distributing power on the basis of social or family stereotypes.

Dependency

The emotional experience of needing other people has many facets in family life. Our need to depend on others is matched only by our need to be depended on. Children need to feel that they are as important to their parents as their parents are to them. All family members must feel that they belong to each other, that they are important to each other, that they can help each other. A sense of trust forms the basis for these vital family connections. We need and want to trust others, to be trustworthy ourselves. That includes trusting each other to make decisions, to be competent—one way in which power is related to dependence.

Of course, some people in the family are physically, financially, or psychologically better equipped to care for others, at least for a time. But caretaking can be a dependent role and may be used to fulfill the caretaker's own strong dependency needs. The woman who becomes pregnant as soon as her youngest becomes a toddler is a classic example of this. Her trustworthiness is only realized when someone is totally dependent on her. As each baby begins to move away from her, her own dependency needs overwhelm her, so she has another baby to fill the void. Some of these babies will probably turn out to be super caretakers, too, not just because they have their mother for a model but because they lost her to a more dependent creature just when they were developing a sense of trust.

Autonomy

Independence, the ability to stand alone and function as an individual, is an especially critical factor in personality development.

One goal of childrearing is to raise children who can stand on their own, who believe in themselves and their abilities. However, individual autonomy cannot develop if the family itself has no autonomy. Some families have very vague boundaries and very little sense of themselves as a unique family group. Generally, this occurs when one of the parents has not fully separated from his or her family of origin. The two families do everything together; one generation fades into another; the feelings and needs of one family become part of the other family. Needless to say, family members lose any sense of their own individuality; they cannot tell whether they want something or someone else wants it. They cannot act on their own, be sure of their own feelings, or deal with outsiders. There is genuine fear of the outside world in such families. Their lack of autonomy generates this fear, and they keep themselves together by concentrating on the danger they perceive beyond their boundaries. In healthy families, the family acts as a bridge to the rest of the world. In families who have no autonomy, the family gathers everyone in and locks the door to the outside world.

Staying close to home does not raise one's sense of competence in the world. Lack of autonomy is closely related to lack of power and lack of trust. Staying close to home does not necessarily mean that family members literally live at home. Rather, people who are not autonomous will be more likely than most of us to re-create their families of origin when they marry and have children. The new family may look different, may even seem completely dissimilar in values or in life-style, but the dynamics will be strikingly familiar.

Love

There is a prevailing tone about most families that reveals the way in which affection is distributed around the family circle. Some families bicker or shout at each other without any expression of care or affection. Others manage to be just as angry and still convey a sense of mutual regard and respect. Through a family's nonverbal love patterns we can really see how effectively they manage and express intimacy. How family members look at each other, touch each other, stand or sit around each other tells us much more about how well the family communicates with and feels about each other than mere words.

There are many different kinds of affectionate bonds in families: adults form both sexual and nonsexual bonds; parents and children form a special bond; siblings form bonds of their own; and grandparents and grandchildren form yet another type of bond. A couple who have a loveless marriage but share great affection for their children will develop a very different family system than will a couple who shut their children out of their loving and exclusive bond.

The expression of love is often tied to the expression of hate or used to fulfill some other need, as when we withhold love to punish our loved ones or overwhelm them with love to bind them to us more closely. We may mistake love for loyalty and repay it with guilt. Still, in a loving family, there is an easy give-and-take of affection most of the time, which allows all members to be powerful, dependent, autonomous, and separate within the family group. Love, in its infinite variety, is the hidden psychological force that connects the other forces.

Separation

Life is a series of separations, beginning with the baby's separation from the mother. The theme of loss is a powerful one in individual life as well as family life. It is often an underlying current when we least expect it. Although loss is an expected feeling when children leave home or someone dies, there is also a sense of loss when children are born or someone new enters the family. That is the loss of the status quo, of life as it was, and it is not a sensation to be taken lightly. A person who is promoted to a new job loses his or her old job. The new job is better, more prestigious, and offers more money, but the old job, whatever it was like, is gone. Each loss in our lives, even an insignificant one, raises memories of every other loss. And this echo from the past may generate a feeling of loneliness, or even despair, that is out of proportion to the present loss.

Families have to balance their sense of loss with an awareness of regeneration. Family members do not realize that the loss of roles and the consequent addition of new roles are a natural part of the family life cycle. We mourn the losses but we go on. Separations are not treated like normal events in our culture. Indeed, this force is particularly powerful simply because it is so infrequently acknowledged or recognized. Power, dependency, autonomy, and love are all underscored by separation.

As we examine each stage in the family life cycle we will refer to these five forces often. Every family has to deal with them on some level; every family system is developed to regulate them in its own unique way.

The Family Forest

Because our society is so preoccupied with individual psychology, we tend to focus on the trees, not the forest. Yet nothing happens to us out of context. The goal of family—to nurture and support all members throughout the family life cycle—has been obscured by a widespread belief that the changing family is the dying family, by an ignorance of normal and predictable stress in the family life cycle, and by an insistence on examining the individual out of context.

This is a book about that context. Families develop their own special personalities that affect every family member. That is why *any* member of the family can change the family system by simple, slight alterations in behavior. Any small change will upset the equilibrium and give the family a chance to reorganize itself. By refusing to play into the established family system, anyone can bring about change. But first, it is necessary to know what the system is, why it exists, and where it comes from. Such knowledge gives each of us the chance to make changes that we and our families have longed for, perhaps without conscious awareness. When you finish this book, you'll know more about how to look at your family, how to anticipate what is going to happen in it, and how to understand and evaluate what has already happened. Then you can put that knowledge to work altering the systems that do not work for you and your family and bolstering the ones that do.

It Runs in the Family

Most of us know that we "inherit" our sense of humor and our various talents along with our eye color and body build. We are aware, especially as we get older, that we are repeating certain behaviors that we learned in our families of origin. We can hear echoes of our parents—or even their parents—in our own voices. Our family points out that we are getting absentminded just like our mother or stingy just like our dad. We tend to assume that these similarities are just coincidental. We don't realize that they add up to anything significant because we don't add them up. We don't realize that we are repeating more than one characteristic or behavior.

Actually, we inherit a whole complex of behaviors and interactions from our families of origin. First, there is the family personality, that which identifies us with a particular and special group of people. Second, there is the family system, that which identifies us with a particular and unique way of working within the family. These two legacies from the past carry the individual family forward and account for the indelibility of the family as an institution.

Who Are We? The Family Personality

All families feel special—no matter what kind of family they are or how severe their problems. Each family group separates itself from all other family groups by the ways in which it defines itself. Families are eager to find proclivities, predilections, and peculiarities that "run in the family." This special identity gives family members and the family group itself a place in the larger social context. Every individual family member identifies with the family personality and thereby becomes a member of something special. This mutual identification creates a cohesive family unit.

Oddly enough, the family identity does not have to be positive to be cohesive. Many families derive that special feeling from their problems. Families that have no special identity are not cohesive and will probably break up. But most families form a bond by reaching for whatever gives them an identity of their own:

"We aren't close. I never see my parents and neither does my brother. We talk on the phone, but we don't enjoy being together."
    (We are special. We are not close.)
"I have a very loving family. We do everything together."
    (We are special. We are close.)
"I come from a long line of scientists."
    (We are special. We're scientists.)
"My family fights all the time. We can't get along."
    (We are special. We fight.)

This most unifying, yet commonly overlooked, family drive to define itself in a special way is a clue to how families repeat themselves. A sense of belonging, of being part of something that is passed on, gives each family member an investment in the group and its survival.

A family reinforces and supports its identity in many ways. For example, there are family sayings. One woman, who grew up in a neighborhood where her family were the only Catholics, remembered a little phrase her brothers and sisters used to chant in the playground,

"E–I–E–I cuss,
Nobody is like us!"

Although the phrase was an attempt to create solidarity and build the family's sense of strength and uniqueness, this woman heard it differently. Her own perception, "corrected" years later by her siblings, was,

"E–I–E–I cuss,
Nobody likes us!"

The message she got was that her family felt excluded on the playground.

Every family has stories about events that happened in the past, such as "Remember when Sally first went off to school carrying. . . ." or "I'll never forget when Dad was out of work and we had to. . . ." Everyone knows the stories but they are repeated anyway, not because they are so gripping (after all, everyone has heard them before), but because they confirm the family identity. That is especially important at family gatherings, where such stories are often told. Holidays, funerals, weddings, birthdays, and anniversaries sometimes may be the only occasions when families can assemble as a group. The stories tell them that they *are* a family, that they belong together, and that they are related to others who are no longer with them but who are nonetheless part of the family mythology. Even the descriptions of family gatherings invoke family identity:

"We never celebrate holidays."
"We give presents for any occasion."
"We eat."
"Everybody gets drunk."
"It's expected that. . . ."

Many families have certain rituals they follow (such as Sunday breakfasts together) that reinforce their identity indelibly. These events often demonstrate the degree and character of their cohesiveness. In one family of four, for instance, the father always made waffles after the family came home from church. He didn't do much cooking at any other time, so it was always a special occasion even though he always made the same thing. The mother would read the papers, and the two daughters would help their father with the preparations. When they ate the waffles everyone would say that these were the best waffles they had ever eaten.

As the family changed over the years, there were changes in this ritual. At one stage, there was a lot of arguing about how these could be the best waffles week after week since they always tasted the same. There were times when the father didn't feel like making waffles and times when the daughters would refuse to eat them, especially when they were adolescents.

The waffle breakfast was a very small part of this family's experience, and yet it was something of a gauge to their feelings about themselves and the degree of their identification with their family personality. Years later one of the daughters was amazed to find herself fixing waffles for her children and asking them if these were the best waffles they'd ever had. What had been a family ritual for her became one all over again in her new family.

Families also have codes that reveal their sense of themselves. The special names families use when they are alone and the way they refer to themselves collectively when they are with others indicate how they see each other and how they feel about themselves. We hear such identifications being made all the time: "That's just not the Raley way," or "We Romans always. . . ."

One remarkable example of indelibility in coding came up in the Camrose family. There was an uncle in the family who assigned special names to all the family members, such as Our Leader, the Joker, Moneybags, the Brow, and Little Dumpling. These names were really only used when everyone gathered together for a special occasion. After the uncle died, the names seemed to die as well —for about five years. Then, quietly and without much surprise on the part of the family, this uncle's son began assigning the same names to different people. The faces had changed but the roles were the same. The family accepted, even expected, that he would do this. The roles that belonged to the family personality had been preserved.

Another example of cohesive identity turned up in the Grant family—a blended family of a woman with two children who had married a man with one child. Because the father only had his daughter on alternate weekends and the other girls lived with their mother and stepfather, his daughter never seemed to be a real part of that family. Her two stepsisters would entice her to join them in some forbidden activity and then let her take the blame. Their behavior expressed their cohesiveness and her status as an outsider. And because she wanted to become a full-fledged member of the family, she took the blame. It wasn't until the father arranged for joint custody that she really became identified with the family. As she spent more time with them, she developed the confidence to refuse to take the blame, and her stepsisters had less need for her to do so. They all began to see themselves as a special blend.

Expectations and Myths

All families have certain expectations for themselves as a group that influence their family identity and self-image. If they feel they live up to their expectations, they have self-esteem. For example, a family of winners who describe themselves as "a family of winners" will have a positive self-image based partially on an accurate description of themselves. On the other hand, if a family feels that they don't live up to their expectations, they may have a low self-image and little self-esteem. They may feel like failures because their expectations are not met.

Some families create myths to counter unrealized expectations and their own sense of failure. They will affirm their identity as winners even though they really know that they aren't and never have been. However, reliance on a false image undermines confidence even further. All families have certain expectations that won't be realized, and it is important to separate those expectations from the family identity in order to avoid creating harmful myths. We are who we are, not who we think we should be.

A change in external circumstances can generate unrealistic expectations. A classic example is the aristocratic family who continues to live in the castle even though they can no longer afford to heat it. It is natural to try to hold onto greatness, or whatever it is that separates us from the masses. Families are certainly buoyed by distinction on the family tree. But when a group actually lives in the past or attempts to cling to unrealistic expectations, they will have trouble dealing with the normal stress of the family life cycle and changes in the internal and external life of the family.

Furthermore, families who cannot live up to their own expectations may blame one member for their failure as a group. They may try to disown or hide an alcoholic, handicapped, or misfit member because that person is seen as a threat to their perfection. However, such behavior only intensifies the problem because hiding that person lowers group esteem anyway. Alternatively, some families may exalt one member and let that person carry the burden of their perfection. That saint, that one bright hope, becomes the focus of their personality, again undermining group esteem because they don't all share in that mythical perfection.

Although myths and unrealistic expectations can be harmless and even a positive source of identification for the family personality, more often they are a clue to the nature of a family's real identity and a route to a more honest self-appraisal. If, for instance, we've always thought of ourselves as a family of losers because of a couple of bad apples, perhaps it's time to look at the winners we've produced and ask ourselves why we persist in identifying ourselves negatively. That kind of evaluation can open the door to the family system—revealing how we get things done and how we work to keep our family personality (and our family itself) intact.

How Do We Work? The Family System

Family systems can be uncovered simply by watching a family together. A toddler falls down and begins to cry. Mother leans toward him but Father is faster. He scoops the little one up and rocks him back and forth. Older Brother howls with laughter and runs to sit on Mother's lap. This scene or a variation of it is played over and over again. The Baby has fallen asleep in Mother's arms. Older Brother takes him from Mother and carries him over to Father who, in turn, carries him to his crib. Father and Mother sit at a table going over their accounts. Older Brother watches television, and the Baby crawls on the floor. As long as the Baby stays within five or six feet of Older Brother or Father, nothing changes. But as soon as Baby moves within five feet of Mother, Older Brother or Father reach for him. They either play with him, leading him further away from Mother, or pick him up and carry him away from her. They do it without fanfare, without conscious awareness. And Mother doesn't notice what's going on either.

The essence of family systems is that we don't notice them. They function automatically, and it is difficult for family members themselves to recognize what is happening. As outsiders, we can see that the family described above has a strong keep-the-Baby-away-from-Mother family system. Older Brother and Father act almost in unison to put themselves between Baby and Mother or to move Baby out of Mother's range, or even her arms. However, even though we can see this system in several different forms, it is impossible for us, as outsiders, to judge whether it is a permanent system or just a temporary one. That depends on the motivations for the system, something only an insider could really know.

Family systems are the arena in which the hidden psychological forces of power, dependence, autonomy, love, and separation are played out. For example, in the above case we can speculate that Father and Older Brother were afraid that Mother wouldn't love them anymore if she loved Baby, so they acted as a barrier to keep her away from this possibly threatening love object. Unconsciously, they might also have felt that they would lose her if she paid too much attention to the Baby. She would not take care of them; she couldn't be depended upon if she had to take care of the Baby. So they took care of the Baby.

On the other hand, maybe Mother needed care, and Father and Older Brother were actually protecting her. Maybe she'd been sick and they were helping out. In this case we might be looking at a temporary system that would change when Mother felt better. Perhaps Mother hated the Baby, and Father and Older Brother were protecting the Baby from her. Perhaps Mother hated Father, and Older Brother and Baby were protecting them from each other.

There are innumerable psychological explanations for the dynamics of any system, but it is impossible to recognize these motivations until we can learn to see systems in the first place. And it is true that different behavior on the part of any member of the system will bring about different behavior in other parts, regardless of the underlying forces. A change that creates a more balanced and rewarding family system usually brings about a correspondingly new and better alignment of psychological forces.

Although each family has its own unique way of getting along, all family systems develop in response to similar needs and tasks. Every family has to meet the changes and challenges that surface throughout the family life cycle. Every family has to juggle the problems and demands that arise when a group of people of different ages and needs live under one roof. Every family has to deal with loss, whether it be the loss of their children to the outside world through school or marriage, or the actual loss of a member through death. Every family has to confront the identity crises of its individual members. And every family has its own way of responding to each task, from expressing feelings to washing dishes.

If we take an example like food shopping, we can see how families do the same things differently. In Family No. 1, the mother makes a shopping list, and the father shops on his way home from work. When he forgets something, he always sends his younger daughter back to the store, never his older daughter. In Family No. 2, the list is posted, and everyone adds to it as the need arises. The mother nags the father to do the shopping, but she always ends up doing it herself. In Family No. 3, the father makes the list and does the shopping.

Each of these systems reveals a different family dynamic. In Family No. 1 the father appears to have some resistance to doing the shopping or, at any rate, all the shopping. His younger daughter may be his ally in the family, the person he can trust and turn to for help. On the other hand, she may be his whipping boy or girl, to whom he passes on what he regards as dirty work. In Family No. 2 the mother seems to be convincing herself that she is the only one who can really satisfy everyone's needs. She might be quite undone if the father actually did the shopping. In Family No. 3 there are several possibilities—the father may have all the decision-making power in the family; no one else may want to take responsibility for this task; he may be the single parent of young children; or his wife may be ill.

We can also examine the way various families express feelings and notice the same kinds of differences. In Family A no one ever cries. When children or adults are hurt, they are praised for their grit and expected to bear both physical and emotional injury stoically. Anyone who does cry is ridiculed, and quickly learns to curb the impulse. In Family B tears flow easily and often. It is not unusual for the whole family to leave a movie in tears. In Family C there is one crybaby—the last-born child. He is the only one who cries, although some of the others occasionally cry in private. However, in public and even at home, the baby cries alone. Each of these families has its own special way of managing the tension that brings tears. In Family A the tension is held in by each family member. In Family B it is let out by each family member. And in Family C one family member publicly expresses what the others feel in private.

None of the systems described above are better or worse than any other. Indeed, it is completely irrelevant to judge systems on that basis; systems just are. Like the family personality, the family system does not have to be positive to be workable, cohesive, or significant. How well a system works for the family is all that matters. It may sound enviable to hear about a family that cries together, but what if they do nothing else together? They may have difficulty with other tasks even though they are held together by a vale of tears. Family A may seem inhumanly stoical, but they may have a system that carries them gracefully from crisis to crisis. It is impossible for anyone but the family itself to know how well its systems work and, before they know that, they have to recognize that each individual in their group is part of a larger whole.

This larger whole, though special to each family, is descended from families that have gone before. It is not unlikely that one of the parents of the crybaby in Family C was also a crybaby or came from a family in which there was a crybaby. It is not unlikely that the father in Family No. 2, who is nagged about the shopping but doesn't have to do it, heard the same routine when he was growing up. His mother might have nagged his father or vice versa. Or, one of his parents might have nagged him. We take from our families of origin familiar ways of doing things as well as a common identity or personality. We don't necessarily set out to replicate them in any way, but when we don't know exactly what to do, especially in a new situation, we will unconsciously follow the patterns we learned when we were young. Even when our families seem very different from the family we grew up in, we find ourselves repeating certain patterns. In some ways, it is all very simple: all families, whatever their form, shape, state, or style, have to manage tension and do the shopping.

But it is also all very complex. Systems are made up of hundreds of interactions, many going on at the same time. What we've outlined here is only an introduction to the mechanics of systems. In the next two chapters we'll discuss some components of systems, specifically the rules and roles through which systems operate. Rules really determine the framework for the family system. They help stabilize family interactions and maintain family equilibrium. Each family's rules outline what has to be done, how it will be done, when and where it will be done. And these rules are enacted through a family's roles. Without roles, rules would be meaningless. We have to work out *who* is going to do what, how, when, and where. And that is inevitably going to depend, to some degree, on indelibility and the history of the family's founding members.

The Rules of the Game

Family rules govern the structural quality and clarity of the family. Rules about our family's activities and behavior—what we do, how we do it, where we do it, and when we do it—become standard expectations for our own family and for other families as well. In other words, we tend to assume that others follow the same rules that we do. Furthermore, we believe that they should. Our rules delineate our family system, and we cannot always understand how other families survive, given all their peculiar habits— they eat dinner at six instead of eight; someone is always on the phone; they never listen to each other; they all run around in the nude. And few of us are aware that such ruminations reflect our own family's rules. Indeed, our own rules become very clear when we notice the differences in another family's rules.

Our rules are also revealed in the way we treat outsiders. These rules define the boundaries between us and the rest of the world. The Rinconias, for example, never considered entertaining beyond the family circle. They simply had no friends who weren't family. Although they complained about their familial obligations and grumbled, sometimes not at all subtly, about one side of the family or the other, it did not occur to them to socialize with neighbors, other parents, or colleagues from work. In fact, they had a rule against such activities, although they weren't consciously aware of it. They would not have said that they retained their family cohesion by excluding all outsiders, but when their only son married a woman who was very social, they were very threatened. Their son and daughter-in-law always had parties and houseguests and a full social calendar. Although the family was often included, they did not feel right about it. They thought there was something wrong with "that" woman. Their rules about family boundaries suddenly became very clear.

Rules also delineate the boundaries between family members, particularly between the generations. Children are expected to behave in certain ways. Adults are expected to be responsible in other ways. Sometimes, children are expected to take on adult responsibilities, which may blur family boundaries. In such a case, the rule might be that one or more adults can act like children if a child takes on the role of an adult. Again, these rules are not generally conscious. They form a hidden structure that determines how family members will interact with each other.

If a family rule forbids the expression of anger and someone gets angry at the dinner table, that person will have to leave the table. If the person won't do it of his or her own accord, someone in the family will suggest it. A family that has such a rule will not be able to tolerate the expression of anger and will unite to annul it. Rules like this have a lasting effect. No member of that family will feel comfortable if anger is expressed either inside or outside their intimate family group. We internalize the rules we learn in our families of origin, and they, in turn, affect our behavior and actions long after we've left that family. It is no accident that our expectations, disappointments, and standards often clash with our present situation. We have developed an often unconscious identification with a group of people we may no longer live with, but who live with us, figuratively anyway, all our lives.

Rules can be seen in the way families communicate with each other. In one family the father never said a word, but he always sat in the biggest and most prominent chair in a room. He had a habit of turning to various individuals during conversations, and those were inevitably the people who spoke next. In some nonverbal and probably subconscious way he was always directing his family's actions, although none of them was aware that they had a rule about responding only after he had made that ever-so-slight move in their direction.

In another family, there was a rule that the parents would only talk to each other or to other adults, and the children would only talk among themselves—unless one generation asked the other a question. There appeared to be plenty of talk, but when adult-adult and child-child conversations were screened out, what remained were questions: "What did you do in school today?" "Can I have some ice cream?" "When are you going to clean up your room?" "Will you play with me?"

To uncover all the family rules, both verbal and nonverbal communication must be examined. Every action and reaction is a clue, from tone of voice to what is said, to who sits where, to who talks to whom. A child who sees her parents sit up in a certain way, almost as if they are squaring off for a fight, begins to bang her head on the wall. The parents, who were squaring off, might go on with their confrontation for a little while, but they will eventually be stopped by the growing intensity of the head-banging. They may not be aware that the child's behavior is related to their own. They may think that the child is too young to be upset by them, that she doesn't know what is going on (they hardly know themselves), that she is just a bad child. But this child has already learned a rule. In order to keep the family stable, to avoid a dangerous confrontation, the parents must not fight. She will always distract them.

When there is tension in the family, some rules become more obvious, but most families still remain unaware of them because the tension itself is a binding factor. For example, when a family faces a major problem or experiences some internal conflict, one member may get sick. Although the whole family may realize that this person often gets sick, especially when the family has a problem, they are too concerned with the sickness itself or with the problem to see the sickness as a symptom of the group's distress. Similarly, a family member may "act out" in some way whenever conflict arises, distracting the rest of the family from the source of the conflict. Acting out can take many forms—sickness, tantrums, misbehavior, weeping, withdrawing—any action that pulls the person out of the family circle, forcing the rest of the family to concentrate on getting that person back again. That's what happened to the Wilcox family.

The Wilcoxes came into therapy because of the poor school performance of one of their three daughters. They sat in a semicircle facing the therapist, and all eyes were downcast. When they did talk it was always to the therapist and never to each other. They were, however, physically affectionate with each other, which the therapist first noticed as they were taking their seats. They touched each other often, giving each other little pats or squeezes and sometimes even holding hands, especially when asked direct questions. The child who was doing poorly in school was somewhat out of this support system but not far from it.

The therapist sensed that this family's nonverbal closeness was a powerful positive force for them despite their rules against dealing with problems verbally. She suggested that they form a circle, hold hands, and describe their family in unison. Hesitantly, shyly, they began. As they went on they looked up at each other, started to speak up, began shouting, laughing. They liked the exercise and were then able, unselfconsciously, to speak individually to each other about the way in which the exercise related to their family. Of course, one small breakthrough won't change a long-standing rule about verbalizing problems, but it gave the Wilcoxes a feeling for the added dimensions of verbal communication. And at the same time, it made them all aware of a previously unconscious family rule.

It is easy to see that rules would be important to royal families or to the Kennedys or the Carnegies. After all, they have a family destiny to be concerned about. But so do the Romans, the Raleys, and the people next door. Families have expectations for everything they do, and they expect each other to act in accordance with the rules that will confirm their destinies in the future. It is all too common to overlook the existence of these rules until we come into conflict with a person or a family whose rules, values, and behavior differ from ours.

The Forces of Rules

Rules form the basis for the family system's regulation of the five hidden psychological forces. If the system is one in which one child always creates a disturbance when there is conflict between two other children, the rule is "Children don't fight." If one or more of the children try distraction, such as demanding attention when parents are in conflict, the rule is "Parents don't fight." If nobody does anything or if everybody takes sides, the rule could be "Fight." Some families do communicate by fighting; others may communicate by talking, by not talking, or by saying one thing verbally and quite another nonverbally. For instance, when some people talk, nobody listens, or everybody else talks at the same time. Or side conversations begin. Or people roll their eyes. In such messages we begin to see how power, dependency, love, autonomy, and separation are expressed in the family.

Rules About Power

Rules about power are revealed in a family's pattern of communication and decision making—who talks to whom and who makes the decisions. Some family members may communicate only when one tells the other what to do. Basically, they have no other relationship. One person has all the power; the other, none. But there are myriad other rules about what types of things can be said at what time to which other family member. In one family the only child, a girl, could say anything to her mother, and she often did. She called her mother Piggy, swore steadily, and contradicted just about everything the mother said to her. She rarely or never spoke to her father that way. Actually, she didn't speak that way to her mother unless her father was around and, indeed, her father would scold her for her behavior. The little girl had almost total power over her mother, but power to attract her father's attention only through her mother.

Rules About Dependency

Rules about dependency reflect a family's ability to trust and depend on one another. Certain members are considered trustworthy; others are not. This may have to do with the age, competency, or inclination of various family members. Or, it may have been based on those reasons in the past and have no relevancy to a family's current situation. In either case, dependency can be seen in who turns to whom in times of need. The "turning" may literally be a nonverbal leaning toward another family member, as when a child runs to a parent, or adults turn to each other and shrug or cling to each other. But it can also be a verbal request for advice or comfort.

In one two-person family, dependency was frowned upon. The couple, who had decided to remain childfree because they did not want to take care of others, really wanted to be dependent on each other. However, they didn't recognize the strength of their mutual need for support and care because they invested all their energy in acting independent, in "standing alone." Not needing each other or, rather, not acknowledging it, was the basis for their special identity. The only clue to how they felt, other than a growing restlessness with each other that brought them into therapy, was the way they slept—completely entwined. Verbally they stood alone, nonverbally they didn't.

Rules About Love

Rules about the expression of love in families are fairly obvious. Parents should love children; children should love their parents.

Parents should love all their children equally; children should love both their parents equally. However, in all families there are alliances of greater or lesser intensity that belie these sentiments. Rigid adherence to rules that do not accurately reflect the distribution of love tends to lower a family's self-esteem.

The expression of affection toward those outside the family circle will be governed by family rules, too. One mother was horrified that a friend's teenaged son and his girl friend sat in the living room kissing every day from the moment school was out until the girl friend had to go home to dinner. The woman told her friend that she'd never let her kids do that "right in front of everybody." Her friend just laughed and said that it was better this way. "If they weren't in front of me, I'd go crazy wondering what they were up to. This way I'm not a victim of my own imagination."

But that wasn't all there was to it. One woman was in a family that could face a display of affection toward an outsider as long as it was open. The other woman's family was not even able to admit that such things went on. Certainly, these were rules for this particular situation. They may not have applied to other family members in other situations, but they are the stuff of family patterns. Their cumulative effect is important.

Rules About Autonomy

We've already discussed the importance of rules in relation to family boundaries. The amount of autonomy and independence a family can allow its members is also revealed in their rules about time. Family members are expected to be home at certain times, whether it's from a date, from work, or from school. We expect to spend a certain amount of time with the family, and we expect the family to know and honor those obligations. Curfews and restrictions on our time are ways of communicating how much autonomy we want for ourselves and from each other. If one person is always late for family functions or responsibilities, that "says" something to the rest of the family. The family's response to this member's action "says" something, too. If a child is always late getting home from school, she or he might be telling the others, "I'm not sure I really want to be with you" or "I'm not sure I really belong with you" or "Do you really want me to be with you?"

There are many possible reactions to this type of behavior. The family or any one representative—even the baby-sitter—may be angry, rejected, hurt, or even completely unaware. There might be a rule to accept tardiness in one or all members. Rules permitting the family to ignore or break other rules are certainly not uncommon. However, they tend to threaten a family's self-esteem because the family does not live up to the standards they've created for themselves.

Rules About Separation

Rules about separation are most often revealed when a family faces a real separation, such as a death, a divorce, a child going off to school, or even a vacation or business trip. Any event that changes the family structure, even temporarily, offers a clue to rules about the less obvious facets of separation in family life.

We respond to separation and loss in many ways, but one of the most obvious is grieving. Families communicate rules about grief in very specific ways. Some people are allowed to grieve and others are not. In families that repress emotion, members may show no obvious signs of sadness. In families that express emotion, it could be de rigueur to be depressed even if the family members don't really feel sad. Grieving more or less than we expect to at any time may "say" more than we realize about the power of separation and the rules concerning it.

House Rules

To become aware of some of the rules that govern our families, it is only necessary to take a little walk through our homes. Every nook and cranny we inhabit exudes rules about how we behave and what we expect. The home as a whole reflects a family image and communicates our identity both to outsiders and to ourselves. Our feelings about our homes are a result of the standards and expectations we have for ourselves. Pride, shame, or indifference often have more to do with these expectations than with the reality of the situation. When visitors come, we may say, "Oh, everything's always such a mess around here," if we feel that our home should be a model of neatness. On the other hand, if we feel it's too orderly, we may say, "The cleaning woman was just here."

In fact, having strangers in our homes, especially as houseguests, unveils many house rules. We find that we are shutting a lot of doors that we would normally leave open. Or, we find our guests shutting doors that we usually leave open. They expect breakfast and we never eat breakfast. They go to bed early and we are night people. We find ourselves eating in the dining room instead of the kitchen, monitoring our children's television viewing more carefully, and feeling mildly uncomfortable that a guest is sitting in our chair.

When breaking bread with others, we may become aware of manners—ours and theirs. We are careful not to talk with our mouths full or leave our elbows on the table, and we are surprised that they butter their bread before breaking it and read at the table. We also find ourselves relaxing certain rules, such as letting our children have dessert without finishing dinner, because we don't want a confrontation when there are observers. Other people in our family suddenly act differently. The spouse who never does the dishes begins clearing the table and organizing a kitchen crew. The child who is normally so well behaved starts acting up. All these observations and reactions reveal the way in which we protect and test our identity as a family. Such behavior reflects our expectations for ourselves and others as well as the extent and power of our own rules.

Every room in our home can be scrutinized for rules, rules that reveal a great deal about a family's behavior, attitudes, and interactions. For example, a children's room that is totally designed and maintained by parents tells us many things, depending on the age of the child or children. It tells us whether or not the child is trusted or given responsibility and privacy. It tells us if the child is being preserved or protected by the family because they need someone to care for. And the children's attitude toward such a room will tell us how they see themselves in the family.

Often, families set aside one room for company. The room is always immaculate, and the children are not allowed to play there. It is a room designed for the outside world—the front parlor that our company sees while we go on living, fighting, and interacting in the back parlor. Thus, the family reveals its double standard— different rules and a different image of the family for outsiders.

House rules change as relationships within the family change. One young couple had a rule about seating arrangements at the table. The husband sat at the head of their little dining room table, and the wife sat across from him. Her seat was closer to the kitchen and, in the beginning of their marriage, she did all the cooking even though they both worked. His seat was more comfortable, having arms, and he could look out the window while eating. Neither of them thought much about it until she decided that they really could share the cooking. She began sitting in his chair on the days that he prepared meals. He didn't like that. She said that it was more reasonable for him to sit close to the kitchen. He said that he didn't feel comfortable in her chair, and that reason had nothing to do with it. She said he should sit there because she liked his chair. They argued endlessly, but eventually they did evolve a new rule. He sat in the chair for breakfast; she had it during dinner. If they were both home for lunch, he got the chair since breakfast was less important than dinner, and if either of them ate alone, that person naturally sat in the best spot. And, of course, this new rule reflected a change in the distribution of power in their relationship.

The smallest room in most homes, the bathroom, tells us the most about the family's inner life. First of all, it may not be the "bathroom"—it could be the john, washroom, can, lavatory, little girls' or boys' room. If everyone in the family uses different names, that may indicate other communication problems. Then, there are rules governing the use of the bathroom—who can use the bathroom first; how much time each family member is allowed. Certain proclivities, such as "being so slow," "kissing herself in the mirror," "reading on the throne," "forgetting to wash his face," or "being a whirlwind" will be duly noted by the whole family; however, the relationship between time spent in the bathroom and hidden psychological forces probably will not be noticed or commented upon. Yet the person who spends the most time in a bathroom with the least amount of comment or teasing from others could very well be the person in the family with the most power—the person for whom there is a special rule. There also may be rules about who cleans the bathrooms, who repairs the plumbing, and whether bathroom doors are open or closed. And the same rules may apply similarly or to the same people in other bathrooms and in other situations.

Obviously, many house rules originate in the past. We have a loyalty to our families of origin that perseveres both consciously and unconsciously. We have a sense of what *should* be done where and by whom that we bring into any household of which we're a part. It is possible, in touring our homes and uncovering the rules revealed in every room, to compare our findings with the rules we learned in our childhood homes. Some of the rules will be exactly the same; others will originate from our mate's family of origin; and some will be special to our current family. Clues about families of origin will even be evident in the way we furnish our homes and the rules we have about moving furniture around or jumping up and down on it. Antiques, for example, may express some desire to hold onto the past, especially if they are heirlooms. One family furnished their home totally in castoffs from both sides even though they had more than enough money to buy their own furniture. In their case, holding onto the past was their problem. Neither husband nor wife was able to separate from the past and form an autonomous new family. For other people, however, such preservation simply shows a healthy respect for their families of origin.

Any home is a nest of rules. Rules are tied to family destiny, family identity, family roles, and family expectations. They are not right or wrong except in the context of that particular family, but that is precisely why it is so important for every family to know its own rules. Some rules may prevent a family from functioning as well as it can. A rule to suppress anger, for instance, does not do away with the anger; it only assures that no one will talk about it. Rules that were once appropriate, such as those regarding curfews, may no longer be necessary, yet the family may insist on sticking to them. Becoming aware of our rules gives us a chance to modify and update them.

From Central Casting

F amilies cast their members in roles that they never forget. Although we may be separated, literally or figuratively, from our families of origin, these major roles are indelibly engraved on our memories. We replay these roles over and over again, not just in families we form but often in other groups as well. We are attracted to people who play, and let us play, the roles we know. Sometimes, we do not want the role we played as a child and choose another role. But that role will also be familiar to us—a role someone else played in our family of origin.

Through roles we enact the family rules. If our family has a rule about expressing affection whenever it is felt, someone has to take the lead and show the others how to express it. This may seem very simple and instinctual, but all families have leaders, even for such a natural act. We don't know what to do with feelings except in context, and it is through roles that we learn what the context is.

Many of us don't realize that the context is generally broader than just our immediate family. The parents and siblings of our parents, as well as friends and relatives who live with or near our family, can also serve as role models and may be part of the interworkings of the family in intimate ways. One woman was quite sure that she had modeled her life after that of her father's mistress. The mistress, her mother's best friend and longtime business partner, lived in the household in her own separate apartment. Although it was never openly acknowledged that she and the father had a special relationship, all the children considered her an important part of their history, and each was later found living in a family with one or more extra adult members.

The roles that we and others played in our families of origin follow us for the rest of our lives. We don't remember just the roles we played or those that our parents played, but also those grandparents, crazy cousins, and others played. And we can often play any of them ourselves. Although we tend to play the same role we played in our family of origin in our future families, and even in less intimate groups, we know the other roles and may play them in situations where they seem necessary to maintain the family system.

Most important of all, we do not have to play the role someone of our own sex played. Although we do model ourselves after our same sex parent in making a sexual identification, roles are not necessarily transmitted along sex lines. Firstborn children, for example, may have more in common over generations than same sex children. A family's expectations for a firstborn girl will be more like those for her firstborn father, or even uncle, than those for her secondborn mother. This doesn't mean that she will be unfeminine or even unlike her mother; rather, her role within the family will be more like that of her father's in his family of origin. One male middle child, who grew up in a family where his firstborn father paid no attention to the children, identified with and supported his mother, a younger child, and the nurturing parent. Later, when this man became a father himself, he was the nurturing parent. Although this was, in part, a reaction to his own father's indifference, he learned the role he wanted to play from his mother.

White Tie and Tails

The formal roles in family systems are those developed chronologically—from baby to daughter, to wife, to mother, to grandparent, to retired person, to old person. These roles are affected by the age and the structure of the family. When we add a member, we add a role. When our family changes—when a mother becomes a grandmother, for example—we add a role. When we lose someone —when a wife becomes a divorcee or a widow—we add a role.

Within the family structure there are prescribed duties for certain family roles. A mother or father has specific tasks, although the nature of these tasks varies from family to family, especially as sexual stereotyping becomes less prevalent. The "script" for these formal roles is written in society and is significantly modified and affected by similar roles in families of origin. We get our ideas about what fathers do and children do both from the outside world and from the fathers and children with whom we grew up. However, even though we know these roles, they are not always easy to take on. A woman knows her mother, knows that she can be a mother, knows other mothers, but until she is a mother herself she can't really play the role or feel confident that she'll succeed at it.

When we become fathers or mothers, we look to our predecessors for guidelines. We are often not consciously aware that we model ourselves after our forerunners. It is the difference between saying "I'm doing it that way because my mother always did it that way" and saying "Good grief, there I go, acting just like my mother!" On one hand, the mother is consciously used as a role model. On the other hand, she is the role model without the speaker's conscious consent. Role modeling preserves and solidifies the family identity, and it is yet another indication of the family's need for continuity and its powerful drive for indelibility.

Come as You Are

A family's informal roles serve to regulate tension. These are the roles that we need in order to maintain our equilibrium and stay together. They reveal the family's emotional climate. Conflict is common and necessary to families, but it has to be regulated. Too much means chaos and destruction; too little means stultification. The roles that provide this regulation are at the center of the family's dynamics. Together with the family's rules they determine how well the family will get along, how well it will be able to support and sustain its members, how well it will learn to solve its problems. The most important factor about these roles is that they are created by the whole family for itself. Every member of the family is invested in every role.

Examples of informal roles are mediator, manipulator, jester, saint, scapegoat, leader, crybaby, and follower. The mediator, obviously, is the person everyone turns to when differences have to be resolved. The mediator is usually seen by the rest of the family as the one who will treat others fairly. In most families parents are the mediators. They are usually the family's leaders, and the ones who are expected to make judicious decisions. But it doesn't always work that way.

In the Holly family, young Amelia did the mediating, especially between her mother and younger brother. Amelia's mother constantly picked on Casey, who reminded her of herself at his age. It's not unusual for parents to be in constant conflict with a child who reminds them unconsciously of struggles they've never settled.

Casey lied a lot, which infuriated his mother because she had done exactly the same thing as a child. The mother would turn to Amelia for the truth, and Casey would turn to her for protection. Amelia became very skillful in her role as mediator—she always managed to reveal some of the truth without hurting Casey. Although this did not create an open, trusting family system, it did create a stable one.

Not every family has a mediator. Sometimes a jester or a crybaby will serve to reduce the tension. If, for instance, Amelia started clowning around or crying when her mother and her brother turned to her, the effect would be similar. The conflict between the two antagonists would be defused or diverted. The antagonists could come together by laughing with Amelia or by trying to comfort her.

Similarly, Amelia could have been the scapegoat for her mother and her brother. Instead of letting Amelia amuse or divert them or find a middle ground for them, Casey and the mother could blame Amelia for their conflict. They could turn on her and decide that she was responsible for their inability to get along. Casey, knowing that he had indeed lied, could accuse Amelia of tattling on him, whether or not she had and whether or not he knew she had. The mother, convinced that Amelia knew the truth of the matter whether she did or not, could blame her for not tattling, for not being loyal to her mother. Scapegoating behavior in particular keeps families from really confronting their differences. In mediation or diversion there is some awareness of conflict. But when families find a scapegoat they are avoiding any acknowledgment or responsibility for themselves and their problems.

Casey and the mother are also taking roles in the interaction described above. Casey is somewhat manipulative in getting the attention he wants. He knows what will stir his mother up and make her think about him. It isn't a very pleasant sort of attention, but his mother may not give him any other, more positive kind. In a way, Casey is a victimizer, making his mother pay for her inability to give him positive attention. She is a natural victim for this ploy because she feels guilty about being unavailable to him in a loving, supportive way. Furthermore, he is able to punish her because her conflict dates back to her childhood, where she felt guilty about demanding attention herself in an indirect, negative way. This is the way indelibility works. Unresolved conflicts are carried along with us. When the situation is similar and stress develops, these conflicts reassert themselves without our conscious consent or, often, awareness.

If family members are just bit-players and no one person is trapped in a role all the time, the family may be flexible and resilient enough to roll with the punches. But when behaviors are crystallized through repetition, roles become fixed. Then one person always plays the scapegoat or the saint, and only the jester's jokes will relieve the tension. Parents, as leaders of the family, have the responsibility to see that this doesn't happen. That means knowing what is going on.

Know Your Roles

Most of us know our formal roles, but we do not know our informal ones, and we don't always realize that the two can be in conflict. A formal role can be undermined by an informal one, depending on our definitions. A father, for example, who believes that a father should be the leader of the family, may feel somewhat disenfranchised if his wife is the real leader. Although she may be a very effective leader, his preconceptions about family structure and roles clash with the family's actual structure, weakening both his wife's authority and a previously workable family system.

It is possible to "see" the informal roles in our families by looking at interactions like the one between Amelia, Casey, and their mother. Mealtimes, for example, can reveal a great deal about roles —as well as rules. Seating arrangements, meal preparation and service, the nature of conversations, and fights all reflect family structure, family rules, and family roles.

Rob and Marylou Glendon, who both worked, ate dinner together with their two children at their large kitchen table every evening between six thirty and seven o'clock. Rob, who usually prepared the dinner, sat at the end of the rectangular table that was near the kitchen sink. Marylou sat at the other end, near the door and the hall telephone. Terry, aged nine, and Annie, six and a half, sat across from each other.

Terry always started first, piling food on his plate and beginning to eat, often before the others had even sat down. He would be reprimanded by his father and tsk-tsked by his mother, while passing various dishes in response to everyone's requests. Marylou talked steadily, telling them about her day at work and gossiping about friends and co-workers. Annie served herself, taking one thing at a time, and played with her food before eating it slowly. Rod said little, but many remarks about the food were directed at him. Each dish was analyzed or criticized, and he joined in to justify his choice. If the telephone rang, Marylou answered it and brought the phone to the table, talking to the caller and the family all at the same time. When Terry finished eating (and he was always first), he passed his dishes to his father and got up and left the table, again to a chorus of mild objections. Marylou passed her dishes to Rob, who then stacked hers, Terry's, and his own together and turned to Annie expectantly. Annie was invariably still playing with her food. Both parents tried to hurry her along, but unless Terry came back in the room to invite her to play, she generally sat alone at the table while her parents moved toward the sink to clean up. All this action was obscured by Marylou's continual chatter.

Marylou was the entertainer in the family. She kept center stage even when the others were not particularly interested in her conversation. Her chatter filled in the spaces around them. She was also their link to the outside world through the telephone, and not just during dinner. She determined their social life, what kind of entertainment they would participate in and when. Little Annie's role was to try to hold everyone together. By dawdling over dinner she kept the others bound a little longer. She was slow in everything she did and often served to pull the family together as they fussed over her and waited for her. Rob seemed to be the one everyone dumped on. He prepared and served the meal, and he took the criticism for it. Indeed, he seemed to encourage it by joining in their nightly critiques. Moreover, he received and accepted all the garbage when they sent their dirty dishes down the table to him. Terry was the family's leader; he initiated everything. Although scolded for doing everything first, he was consistently followed by the others in all family activities.

Nicknames and pet names provide another clue to a family's informal roles. An adult who still responds to a baby name in his or her family of origin may continue to play that role for them when they are all together, even though it is not a name his friends or current family use. The names siblings use for each other often express their rivalry as well as the family's expectations of the role the new child will play in their constellation. A little girl who is referred to as "Our Princess" may become a princess. Pet names like "Carrot Top" or "Bones" may tell us who is going to be teased or scapegoated in the family.

The history of the family itself often sheds light on informal roles. The Beverly family had a boy who wouldn't go to school. He became a problem the moment he turned thirteen. His parents simply did not know what had happened or what to do next. Mrs. Beverly had given up her job to stay home with Jimmy and help him get back to school. Mr. Beverly had begun to drink more, which seemed to increase the always-present animosity between him and Jimmy. These two fought bitterly about school. Mr. and Mrs. Beverly also fought about that and, more fiercely, about their declining income now that Mrs. Beverly was staying home. In addition, the Beverlys had doubts about each other. Mrs. Beverly began to feel that she and her husband should have separated years ago. Mr. Beverly, who was fifty-eight and very conscious of his age, resented the time he had given to a marriage in which there was no sex and very little communication on any other level. When Jimmy's school recommended family therapy, the Beverlys wearily agreed to try it.

In a way, Jimmy was holding his parents together. Their concern about him kept them in the family and distracted them from their mutual dissatisfactions. But in exchange, Jimmy had to be a "problem." Had the Beverlys been aware of their own conflicts and disappointments, Jimmy might have been free to take on another, less painful role in the family system.

However, the family system was actually much more complex, as the therapists discovered when they looked at the family's history. Four years earlier, Tommy, the Beverlys' firstborn son, had been killed by a hit-and-run driver. He had been thirteen at the time. Neither the parents nor Jimmy had been able to come to grips with their past because they had an unconscious family rule prohibiting any mention of Tommy. And because the family could not talk about or resolve the experience or their sense of loss, they were reliving it through Jimmy.

When Jimmy turned thirteen, his parents began treating him as if he were Tommy. Their unresolved guilt and anxiety surfaced to protect Jimmy as they had failed to protect Tommy. Mrs. Beverly quit her job in order to be home when Jimmy came home from school. She had been at work when Tommy was killed, and she had always felt, unconsciously, that his death was her punishment for deserting her role as a full-time mother. She believed that a good mother "should" stay at home with her children, as her own mother had done. Indeed, in rejecting her mother as a role model when she took her first job, she had already begun to feel guilty—long before Tommy's death.

Mr. Beverly was guilty, too, but not about being a father—about being a man. He had been impotent for several years. He knew that his drinking made sex impossible, but he didn't seem to care. When Tommy reached puberty, Mr. Beverly became extremely jealous of Tommy's future sexual prowess, as well as Tommy's place in his mother's affections as the firstborn, favorite son. When Tommy died, Mr. Beverly felt that he'd killed him with his jealousy. And when Jimmy turned thirteen, his suppressed guilt resurfaced. He was terrified that his jealousy would kill Jimmy, too.

Jimmy himself was torn. He wanted to grow up, establish his own identity, become a man, but he recognized and internalized his parents' fears. He was equally afraid to grow up, to pass his brother, because he was afraid he would be killed in the attempt. His fear was not rational, but, after all, his adored, seemingly perfect, older brother had not made it. No wonder Jimmy could not go to school; he was afraid to cross the street.

Both Jimmy and the ghost of Tommy were holding this very troubled family together. Breaking their rule about discussing Tommy was the family's first step toward breaking up their unhealthy system. Mrs. Beverly was also encouraged to return to work. Her fears about Jimmy's safety when he was out of her sight were fueling his own fears. Left alone, his normal curiosity about his friends and school resurfaced, and he returned to school eagerly. Finally, the therapists encouraged Mr. and Mrs. Beverly to spend some time alone with each other. They had to find out if they could have a relationship independent of Jimmy and Tommy's ghost. Only then could they see one another as man and woman with sexual and individual identities separate from their roles as mother and father, husband and wife.

Changing Roles

Both formal and informal roles change as the family changes and grows. Similarly, when a family becomes aware of their tendency to cast members in various roles, they may choose to give up that practice and allow members more flexibility. Some of these changes are reflected in the new names we use for family members. The teenaged girl, who had always called her mother by her first name, begins to call her mommy, even when introducing her to friends. The girl is about to leave home and wants to be sure that her mother will always be with her. Many teenagers also insist on using their given names, putting old family nicknames aside. If the given name isn't separation enough, some may choose a new name or a new nickname that is not associated with the family.

We also have ceremonies to announce our role changes to the world. Bar mitzvahs, graduations, weddings, even christenings and funerals serve this purpose. These rituals are public statements that our baby is our adult, our boy is a husband, our girl is independent and on her own, our marriage is over, our life has changed. If we persist in believing privately that nothing has changed despite our public avowal to the contrary, we may really be expressing our fear about taking on a new role. And because a change in a formal role brings about a corresponding change in an informal role, we have reason to feel uneasy. Our family will have to make accommodations and our systems will have to change to deal with the loss and addition of these informal roles.

Who Gets the Part

A family's expectations have a great deal of influence on role designations. These expectations develop from the past experience of each family member as well as from the current needs of the group as a whole. Certain behaviors and characteristics are encouraged and others ignored as the family searches for the roles it needs and with which it feels comfortable. But a family cannot arbitrarily assign roles, especially in the early stages of family life when roles are quite fluid. There is no specific "script" for each family member, nor is there a predestined finale to the drama of family life. The family, after all, does not precisely replicate itself.

Family roles are collections of random behaviors, influenced by the interactions of family life. A shy, physically passive child, for example, probably won't become the family provocateur. But a physical resemblance to another family member, being named for someone else, or being expected to fill a certain role will influence which random behaviors the family notices and supports. Certain characteristics in a child can set off reverberations in other family members that cause them to reinforce, just by their attention, some behaviors and not others. And the nature of these reverberations—whether they are happy memories, old rivalries, or deep fears—will have a tremendous impact on the formation of the family system.

Most children have been told at one time or another that they are just like Auntie Sue, their father, sister, or another relative. The comparison could refer to a physical resemblance, a personality likeness, or may be made on the basis of brains, talent, or even birth order. This kind of identification can be positive or negative, depending on the family's needs and their feelings toward the person that the child resembles. On the other hand, families may find a saint or a black sheep because they are used to having one or because they need one, even if the child in question does not actually resemble previous holders of those titles. And if the family has lost someone recently, a newborn baby might be assigned as an unconscious replacement.

When a child is named after someone in the family, it is hard to avoid comparisons, even if that person is no longer living. Since children usually aren't named after unpopular family members, the family, or at least some of its members, probably are hoping for a repeat performance. This may create jealousy or resentment in other branches of the family because the name, and thus the person who had it, is no longer available to them.

However, every given name, and even the naming process itself, reveals something about the family's attitude toward the new member. Parents who haven't chosen a boy's name for what turns out to be a boy child may not feel that they have a place in the family for a boy. Parents who cannot choose a name, even after the child is born, may wonder what role this newcomer will play in their lives. Special or peculiar names may indicate that the child is to have a special, even scapegoated, role in the family. The parents of Amelia, the child mediator mentioned earlier, could have had her ameliorating or mending role in mind when they chose her name. There may even have been a precedent for the name and the role, another helpful Amelia on the family tree. When families fight about whose forebears or whose side of the family the child will be named after, they're also arguing about the role they need or want this child to play.

In clinical work with families, it has been observed that a person who loses a parent of the same sex when very young grows up to resemble that parent in uncanny ways. Many sons of World War II widows, for instance, not only remind their mothers of their long-dead fathers but shock friends and relatives of their fathers with their similarity in gestures and style as well as looks. This happens because children identify with loss even before they really understand what the loss means. And this identification is especially powerful if the parent is of the same sex. The child recognizes his loss because he doesn't see someone around who is about his mother's size but who resembles him sexually. And in order to become whole he must incorporate that part back into himself.

Furthermore, he has a more conscious awareness of his loss because his mother, his relatives, and the family's friends tell him about his dead father, and he identifies with their recollections and descriptions. There is a less pronounced identification if he has a stepfather, but it will nevertheless occur to some degree. The mother and others who knew his father will unconsciously reinforce and encourage behaviors and characteristics that remind them of his father. They do this partly to help themselves get over their own sense of loss. Through the son they have a replacement, someone in whom they can invest similar hopes and dreams. By making the son into the father, their own sense of separation from the father is blurred a little, and they can keep the father, or, at least, his memory, alive. "Like father, like son" takes on an added dimension.

The family may also reinforce certain characteristics in the son because they want him to take over his father's role in the family. In general, when a family member dies, the role or roles that he or she played may die with him or her, may be taken on by another, or may be shared by the survivors. Each family's response to a role loss through death depends on the type of role lost, the strength of the family system, and the adaptability of the surviving members. When the family leader dies—the one who kept everything together—the family may already have a replacement; they may flounder about for a time as they seek another member to play the role; or they may decide to do without that role. However, many families find it difficult to do without that kind of central figure, and a child who resembles the dead leader will often become the family's choice for that role. And when a family member dies young or unexpectedly, the family is even more likely to search for a replacement rather than attempt to give up the role. Whenever there is a change in the membership of the family, all roles are affected because they are all interrelated.

Sometimes, we don't recognize that we have resources for new roles and new behavior in our history. Even if we weren't the leader, the martyr, or the saint in our family of origin, we know the role, and we can play the part if necessary. One account executive whose father had been a minister found himself thinking a lot about his father's work, ministering to the family as well as to his parishioners. Although the executive had never played such a role in his family of origin or in his present family, he felt that he could minister to his young son who was having terrible problems with schoolwork in his new school. He began, for the first time, to spend time with the boy that wasn't just play time. As the boy became more confident, so did the father. Always a passive player in the family drama, he was able to take on a more active role when his son and his family really needed him.

He/She Did It

A pivotal and predictable role in troubled families is that of the scapegoat. The family scapegoat bears all the blame and suffers for the rest of the family. Although the scapegoat could be the family dog, who is kicked or mistreated when family members are angry at each other or themselves, pets are not capable of the interaction implicit in family roles. Generally, a scapegoat actively participates in the family system. He or she knows when to take the blame and may even create a situation in which she or he can be blamed in order to reduce anxiety in the family. Having a role, even a painful role, means belonging to the family. It is better to be the scapegoat than to be alone.

Families scapegoat members when they are insecure about themselves, their beliefs, their authority. Parents who feel inadequate in the family (or even outside the family) will scream at a child and tell each other that everything would be fine if that child would only behave properly. By placing blame elsewhere, families can suppress their own feelings of inferiority or incompetency.

Sometimes in family therapy we see a child act out or misbehave as a conflict between parents or other family members escalates. Then it is possible to stop the action and ask the parents, "Why are you letting this child get ready to be blamed for your fight?" The warring parties are surprised by the question and can often see themselves about to turn on the child. It is then possible to examine the fears that their fights raise and speculate on the possible outcome if the fight wasn't stopped.

Similarly, the therapist can ask the person about to be scapegoated, "Why are you doing this for your family?" He or she can then begin to examine how the role fits into the family system. In general, families who scapegoat members do so in a desperate attempt to hold the family together and maintain the status quo. When families see the process in action, they begin to realize that the scapegoat's behavior is always a response to some other element in family life—fighting between other family members, drinking, or illness on the part of someone else. The scapegoat role allows the family to incorporate these other negative roles into their family system. Furthermore, these behaviors may create so much anxiety that the family has to blame someone for their own failure to solve their problems. If they didn't have someone to blame, they would be forced to confront their problems and face the possibility of change or the breakup of the family. So the role, although painful, is an integral part of the family system. And as we've seen, there are compensations for the scapegoat. He or she is part of the family—an important part—and works with the family to keep things stable.

Scapegoating behavior can take two forms: general or specific. In the former, the entire family shares the blame; the family as a group feels that they can't do anything right. In the latter, the role may shift from member to member, depending on the situation, but usually, one individual becomes the designated scapegoat simply because he or she is in the wrong place too many times. The role becomes crystallized in one specific person who is appointed to take all the blame. That person may be chosen randomly, or she or he may have a predisposition for the role. Predispositions range from being too aggressive or too retiring to being named for, or otherwise resembling, some past scapegoat.

Scapegoating can be predicted to some degree. If scapegoating occurred in the family of origin, it is likely to be carried into succeeding families simply because the family has not learned any other way to resolve conflicts. It is also possible to predict who the scapegoat will be. If there are two people in the family, and one of them was the scapegoat in his or her family of origin, it is very likely that the pattern will be repeated. If there are two parents and a child in the family, the child is most likely to be scapegoated because he or she has fewer resources than the adults and, therefore, fewer alternatives in terms of roles.

The Weyburns, a couple in their late thirties who had decided not to have children, changed their minds during a period when career conflicts between them peaked. They viewed the pregnancy as an accident but nonetheless decided to go through with it. Perhaps not surprisingly, they began to blame the child for their continuing vocational crises even before he was born. In later years, he was always a part of their arguments over whose work had priority. He was, in effect, born into the situation, and there was no possibility that he could refuse the role.

If there are two parents and two or more children in the family, the scapegoat may be determined by the birth order of the parents. A firstborn parent is likely to protect his or her own firstborn. A secondborn parent will protect the secondborn, and so on. Two secondborn parents, for instance, who had been scapegoats in their families of origin, made their own firstborn the scapegoat. However, birth order isn't the only determinant. If conception has been difficult or if the pregnancy or birth has been arduous, the child of these labors will be treasured, and another child or another person in the family will become the scapegoat if one is needed.

A marked child, one who threatens the self-esteem or image of the family, may be treated with such ambivalence that his or her role is always a little uncertain. If the child is handicapped, the family may feel ashamed. If the child is asthmatic or autistic or has some handicap for which the parents feel responsible, they will feel guilty. In any of these situations, parents may respond by overprotecting the child or martyring themselves to the child. Although the family won't blame the child in the same way that they might blame a healthy child, their feelings are very mixed, and the child's role in the family is similar to that of the scapegoat. In both cases, the child becomes responsible in a way for the state of the family.

Well Siblings

Whenever there is a scapegoat in a family, there also may be someone who is overcompensating, trying desperately to keep things in balance by being "good." It is not uncommon for families to handle their own mixed feelings by designating one child as the repository for their positive feelings and another as the repository for their negative feelings. In other words, one child becomes the "good" child, and another, the "bad" child. This is called the "well-sibling" syndrome. The sibling who is not scapegoated or bad is under tremendous pressure to cling to the family's good feelings about itself. But of course this is not realistic, and sometimes the good child breaks down because he or she never has a chance to be free of the family system. Furthermore, the good child never has the chance to learn that he or she can be bad and still be loved, nor does he or she have a chance to develop as an individual within a more flexible family system. The child is locked into a pattern of good behavior because only that pattern assures his or her place within the family.

Old and New Business

Flexibility in role designations and in the development of workable rules is vital to the evolution of effective family systems. We tend to overlook the power of the past in the choices we make and to underestimate the ease with which we fall into old patterns of behavior based on the rules and roles we learned as children. It is normal to confuse feelings about people in the present with feelings about people in the past. The survival and the indelibility of the family depend on some unconscious repetition. But it is not desirable to be bound to the past in destructive ways. In examining the family context that we have inherited from our families of origin, we can attempt to separate the aspects of our past that can be put aside as old business from the useful aspects that can become new business in our current families. Old business and new business can clash mightily during the process of mate selection. In the next chapter we will examine how rules, roles, systems, forces, and family trees can be upended over this experience in family life.

You Can Go Home Again

They're right, the ones who say "It's bigger than both of us."
The love that makes the world go round is the creation of an
entity that is bigger than, and separate from, the individuals involved. Mate selection is the birth of the "special we," the development of an idea of the couple we will become, what kind of family
we will form, and what we can accomplish as a twosome. This
quality of specialness is what binds a couple and leads to a truly
unique commitment. In psychoanalytic jargon, it is narcissistic
identification with the idealized psychological group of two. In
other words, our identity as a twosome reflects positively on our
individual identities, raises our self-esteem, and gives us a powerful
and rhapsodic new identification. When this happens, when two
souls have but a single thought and two hearts beat as one, we may
not recognize how very transparent our choice is and how much it
reflects family patterns.

Although mate selection may seem serendipitous to us, it is not
entirely random. Sociologists used to say that we tend to marry
people who live within five blocks of us. Today, greater mobility
and better educational opportunities have expanded our range of
choices, yet many of us marry people who *could* live within that
five-block radius. People who grew up in similar surroundings and
neighborhoods tend to have parents with similar interests and values. People with backgrounds in common have at least a few interests in common. Even if the class, religion, or history of the families differ, the structure, style, or perceptions of the families could
be markedly similar. Because we are "rapt up" in the "special we,"
we do not always recognize that we fall in love with those we
meet. And we tend to meet people like us. Rarefied and remarkable
as our meeting may seem to us, an outsider might think that we
were meant for each other.

We met in Tokyo. I was there as a student and he was a tourist. I moved in with him when my Japanese family politely pointed out that the term was over—and I've been with him ever since. Neither of us expected this. We still can't believe our luck.

Luck? Well, yes. But this couple had attended the same American college, one that specialized in foreign study programs and liberal arts. Both liked to travel, and each had majored in literature. Although they hadn't known each other at the university, they met in Japan because they had friends in common. And if they hadn't been introduced, they might have met anyway because they lived in the same neighborhood in Tokyo, an area frequented by students from their university. Although one had grown up in the city and the other in the country, they both came from families with similar values and expectations. They had a lot in common.

I had never given Mark a second thought. He was my best friend's younger brother, and I just considered him a tag-along until I came back from living abroad for a few years and met him again. By then we'd both been married and divorced. I found him very attractive and he felt the same way. Who would have guessed we would find each other after all those years?

Anyone might guess that best friends' relatives would have much in common, including neighborhoods and parental values. We don't always need Freud or Oedipus to explain attraction—sometimes the rationale is in our own backyard or right next door. Part of the specialness of this particular "we" was in not recognizing their attraction years before. Exactly the reverse is true for childhood sweethearts who do recognize what they have found in each other. Like Romeo and Juliet, their specialness comes from knowing that they were "right" for each other, regardless of their youth or their families' feelings.

She worked with me and I couldn't take my eyes off her. I was always dropping something when she was around, and I so wanted to impress her with how good I was at my job. I was a married man, too, and didn't realize where my feelings were going to lead. They led to divorce from a woman I should never have married in the first place and marriage to the woman I wished I'd met earlier. It was a miracle to me that I ever found her at all—or that she found me.

Well, maybe not all miracle. After all, they shared an interest in their work, and they were equals in a profession (banking) with few women. They had similar training and, although their family backgrounds were quite different, that in itself was a reason to be together (a phenomenon to be discussed later in this chapter). He was a little older and had married and raised small children while she worked her way up. When they met, she was ready to settle down, having achieved her career goal, and he was ready for a relationship in which he shared the same interests with his partner. Because of the differences in their backgrounds and their marital situations, they regarded their attraction, which was in some ways destined, as unique.

Our romantic hopes for meeting someone across a crowded room notwithstanding, who is likely to be in that crowded room but people we know or might be likely to know? Even romantic encounters on desert isles, on long train rides, or in dangerous situations can be demystified a little. Who, after all, is likely to be on a desert isle but someone from our sinking ship or another trans-Pacific sailboat racer? Who is likely to be riding that train at that time of day or year in that compartment or car to that destination? And who but another spy, firefighter, or adventurer would be on that dangerous assignment? Although danger, isolation, or excitement may make it difficult to distinguish between fear or loneliness and passion, we must acknowledge that some of these people, sharing a love of boats, trains, and adventures, might meet anyway.

Keeping the Home Fires Burning

However, accidents of birth are not solely responsible for the mates we choose. We do much of it ourselves. We arrange to join a good club. It isn't just a matter of finding someone from a similar background or neighborhood. We also want someone with slightly higher status, better looks, more connections. We like to think that we are bettering ourselves in some way, that we are making a good match.

To make that good match, we search for someone who fills our blank spaces, who complements us and makes us feel whole, full, and invincible. This is that part of the "special we" that is personal and interpersonal, which cannot be explained by our family background or surroundings. This is the province of poets, philosophers, songwriters, and, of course, psychotherapists, who have been describing the vagaries of mate selection since the beginning of time. Consider Plato's description in *The Symposium:*

Aristophanes says that in the old days man was a round creature with four arms and four legs who rolled around the world, raising havoc wherever he went. Zeus, the king of the gods, was getting impatient with man's destructive antics. Man was too much trouble, always fighting and carrying on. So Zeus decided to slice man in two. That would cut man down to size and give Zeus twice as many men to do his bidding. That's how man became a two-legged, two-armed creature. That's also how man became interested in finding a mate. Man spent his life looking for his other half, the missing half, the better half.

Although many theories of mate selection focus on the idea of finding the perfect complement, it is our belief that we are looking for the perfect "special we"—a relationship that ensures that we will never have to leave home. To achieve that goal we seek a partner who will let us play roles or combinations of roles that we always played or wanted to play in our families of origin. Furthermore, that person will agree to play the parts that we want or need her or him to play. Through this exchange we'll create something bigger than both of us, a relationship that allows us to keep our home fires burning so that we can relive the passions of our childhood. The "right" mate can help us re-create the part we're missing—the part that makes us feel at home. As with other aspects of the "special we," we tend to overlook the obvious.

Family Narcissism, or Like Attracts Like

In psychoanalytic theory much is made of wanting to marry a girl (or boy) just like the girl (or boy) who married dear old dad (or mom). A child is assumed to be jealous of his or her parents' relationship and prone to fantasizing that he or she will replace the same sex parent and marry the opposite sex parent. Through an unconscious process, these incestuous wishes then form the basis for later attractions.

However, we can be attracted to any member of our family and may seek a mate who reminds us in some way of that member, or even of our entire family. Being attracted to people who look like members of our families is like being attracted to ourselves. Some couples really do look alike. They resemble each other in gait, speech, or style, if not actually in looks. Popular mythology holds that the power of love creates such similarity, but many of these couples were originally attracted because they recognized something familiar in each other. They may not realize that their beloved resembles their mother, father, aunt, or brother, but they are drawn to each other as to their own reflections. It isn't just the familiarity and the comfort of predictability that is so reassuring. It is the sense of belonging. A person who reminds us of ourselves or our family of origin buoys our identity, our sense of self, and makes us feel universal. And we attribute our positive feelings to that person rather than to the family he or she reminds us of.

The visual impulse that propels us toward another is not easy to isolate, but we are even less aware of the connection between attraction and scent. Female dogs excrete a vaginal pheromone during ovulation that signals their fertility to males. Babies find the mother's nipple by a smell secreted around the surface of the breast. Perhaps we are subliminally (or not so subliminally) seduced by a person's natural scent. This scent might remind us of an odor we sniffed around the house, or it might remind us of the house itself as well as the people in it. At times, we are all aware that someone's home smells different from ours. Such conscious awareness of unfamiliar odors of food or smoke may be an indication that there are less obvious odors that don't penetrate our consciousness. "Chemistry" between two people can contain a dash of déjà vu, a reminder of a special identity associated with our family of origin.

But marrying into our families of origin is most apparent when we consider birth order and the history of birth order in mate selection. Our own position in our family of origin as an only, elder, middle, or younger child has a major impact on the kind of future families we form. Siblings spend much more time with each other than with either parent, and this is becoming even more prevalent as two-paycheck and dual-career marriages become more common. People who marry those in sibling positions complementary to their own seem to have a greater range of responses to the demands of the family life cycle than those who marry people in the same sibling positions. If a woman with a younger brother marries someone who has an older sister, their relationship is likely to be more successful in many ways than if the woman married another older child or the man married another younger child. There are many variations of complementarity, of course, depending on the numbers and sexes of siblings. A younger sister of several brothers may get along quite well with the older brother of just one sister or even one brother.

Couples in noncomplementary sibling positions may encounter

more problems as a family because they have so much to learn. For example, when two younger children marry, no matter how many siblings each has, neither may be able to play a leadership role or take responsibility. Prepared to be more dependent in family life, they often have difficulty getting things done. On the other hand, two older children may have trouble solving problems because they are competing for positions of leadership and responsibility. Neither has learned to play second fiddle or accept support from the other. Of course, noncomplementary siblings—those in the same or similar sibling positions—have a lot in common and may be better able to empathize and identify with each other. This is reassuring, but it can create a static relationship.

Only children are more likely to select a parent figure for a mate because they are most comfortable relating to adults and haven't had much experience living with peers. An only child who marries a person with a sibling of the opposite sex will have an advantage over the only child who marries another only child. At least one of them will have had some experience living with a peer. And it is always an advantage to have grown up with people of the opposite sex. A man with several younger sisters and brothers who marries an only child will draw on his experience with his sisters to make the new relationship work. When only children do marry each other, their parents' sibling positions may help them. They may have picked up some sense of identity from hearing about their parents' siblings that will affect their relationship to each other and to their children. Sibling identity is a family dynamic that is passed down through the generations.

Sara Kingsley's story illustrates the importance of family love relationships in mate selection. Sara was crazy about Harry when she was a teenager, but he never returned her interest. It wasn't until she met Paul that she was thrown into a really mutual relationship. She and Paul were married as soon as she graduated from college, a few months after they had met. He was a professor, and she felt he was wiser than she. He was extremely dominant, funny, and attractive, but their relationship soured almost immediately after their marriage. They separated after two years.

Sara's next serious love affair was also with a dominant and charming older man. Jim was in politics and he knew everyone. Sara had drifted into politics herself, the politics of health care, and she was appreciative of the connections she made through Jim. However, she was becoming increasingly ambitious, and neither she nor Jim was willing to defer to the other. They spent five tempestuous years together and eventually went their separate ways. Then, after a series of short-term affairs, Sara met Andy. He was a shy, unassuming, but determined, medical student who adored her and shared her interest in medicine, family, and good works. He was younger than she, and in some ways they seemed an unlikely pair. She was outgoing, dynamic, attractive, and serious. He was retiring, methodical, tenacious, and droll. They lived happily ever after. Why?

Part of the answer lies in Sara's history, in her family of origin, and in Andy's, too. Sara's husband, Paul, and her lover, Jim, were very similar in personality and temperament to her flashy, ambitious father. She had been quite devoted to her father, although there was occasional antagonism between them. Andy, however, was more like her adored younger brother. He even made the same kind of silly jokes that her brother did, and their physical resemblance was startling. Furthermore, Andy had an affectionate and dominant older sister.

Although Sara was initially attracted to men like her father, those relationships were unsuccessful. Never close to her mother, who seemed to be something of a cipher, she may have originally and oedipally wanted to be the woman in her father's life who was worth something. But when it came to selecting a permanent mate, she chose to be her father rather than to live with him. But, just as important, both Paul and Jim were also older children. She competed with them in a way that wasn't necessary with Andy. He was easily able to give her warmth and affection and certain leadership roles in exchange for her love and protection.

The ideal mate can also be a transference object, someone who resembles—and thus represents—a parent, sibling, or another figure from the past with whom we can replay old issues. This is a motive in all selection processes to some degree, but it becomes a problem when the old issues are continually replayed without resolution or accommodation. People who have the same complaints about everyone they fall in love with exemplify this dynamic. They choose partners who are very similar to people they could not get along with in the past; not surprisingly, they still cannot get along with these people in the present. Their preoccupations are often revealed by frequent or inappropriate references to family members or others from their pasts. Because they don't recognize that they are repeating old patterns, they are likely to see themselves or "women today" or "men I meet" as worthless. Still, an unresolved familiar situation is sometimes preferable to the risks in an unfamiliar situation. And that's what Todd Gower opted for. He did not recognize how he was transferring his childhood experience into the present.

Todd was an only child whose mother was very close to her sister; in fact, they lived next door to each other. The sisters were very different. Todd's aunt was warm, open, and magnanimous and he adored her. His mother was less affectionate and expressive, but she gave him marvelous, expensive presents. Todd spent most of his childhood at his aunt's, playing with his cousins under her watchful eye. His parents ran a business together and were rarely home. When his mother was home she was generally tired and distant.

Todd eventually married an extremely wealthy woman and did very well with her money. His wife was capable, cold, and loyal. But Todd always had a mistress who was warm, expansive, and, according to objective witnesses, resembled his aunt. However, Todd did not see the connection until it was pointed out.

When his children were grown, Todd began to wonder how he would spend the rest of his life. He decided to divorce his wife and marry his current mistress. In the past, when his wife discovered his affairs he had always left his mistress, but this relationship seemed different. However, his wife didn't want to give him up. Despite his philandering and her coolness, she wanted to save the marriage. Her insistence melted his resolve, although he may not have been able to go through with the divorce even if she hadn't objected. He did not feel able to leave his wife. So he gave up this mistress, too, and a few months later he found another warm, magnanimous woman to help him maintain his childhood situation.

This is really the story of a man who could not, or would not, move out of his past. He had found a mate who was distant but still very much a part of his life and who allowed him to have a succession of mistresses who resembled his warm and responsive aunt. He had transferred his feelings about his mother to his wife, reacting to her as he had reacted to his mother. He also transferred his feelings about his aunt onto his mistress, thereby duplicating his childhood. Handling his wealthy wife's money was a way of continuing to receive the expensive presents his mother had given him to compensate for her unavailability. His mother had also entrusted something of value to him—the proceeds from her real estate business. She had also entrusted him to her beloved sister. Similarly, his wife entrusted him to his mistresses. She didn't like this arrangement, but she must have sensed that it was the only relationship possible with a man who had loved his aunt but could not leave his mother.

Opposites Attract

Not everybody tries to set up a new family that replicates their family of origin. Many people do just the opposite. In fact, they would be shocked to learn that they are doing anything at all like their family of origin. They marry to escape their families, to belong to other families, or to build different kinds of families.

This desire for change and improvement has led to the development of new family groupings. Because the older, more traditional family forms are no longer meeting people's needs, blended families, childfree families, and families extended by friendship networks are springing up. And because these new families may indeed be quite different in form, we don't always recognize potential problems. In other words, the changes in the outward family structure may blind us to the fact that interpersonal relationships, family systems, and the roles people play are no different at all.

People sometimes try to change their family by choosing a mate who is quite different from themselves or their relatives, someone outside their class, race, or neighborhood. Psychoanalysts interpret such choices as a protective device against incestuous feelings. An outsider does not remind us that our heart still belongs to daddy because the outsider does not look, talk, or act in any way like daddy or anyone else in our family. Exogamous, or outsider mates tend to run in families. In the Los Feliz family, for example, the three sons each married a non-Catholic, non-Hispanic woman. When queried about this, the youngest son would wink and say, "Ah, mama. She was too much for us." To have chosen a mate too much like mama would have reminded these men of "unnatural" longings.

Ironically, someone unlike mama may turn out to be more like mama than we expect. The mate who is different is often regarded as a tabooed figure by the rest of the family, and even by us. Someone who is black, white, rich, poor, foreign, Protestant, gay, Jewish, or whatever may be considered off limits to our class or family, someone some of us do not quite approve of. It is not so different from being in love with a family member because we are having a sexual relationship with someone who is off limits. We are living out our earlier fantasies. We are, in a way, repeating ourselves.

But we do not bind ourselves to our families of origin just by fantasizing about incest. By choosing someone who is not like our mother or father, or brother or sister, we can remain true to our original family, especially if our mate is of lower social status or inept or clumsy in some way. But it is true even if the person merely has different habits, standards, or rules. It's a way of letting our family know that no one can compete with them, that they still come first. This new person either doesn't amount to much or is plain strange. Complaining to our family of origin binds us closer to them. We need them to complain to, and we get emotional support from them rather than from our partners. Thus, we can never pull away from our old families to form a truly autonomous new one.

People who marry into their mate's family, like those who marry outsiders, may not be able to survive the differences. For example, an only child might be drawn to a person from a large, close family only to find the necessary sharing and lack of constant individual attention very upsetting and disorienting. Who am I if I'm not the center of attention? Who are we if so many of us are peers and so few of them are parents (adults, elders)? The big, happy family swallows up the lonely only. Belonging to a large group means losing that special intimacy with mom and pop. That had its problems, but so does the new relationship.

Although many exogamous relationships are based on differences in family size, values, class, race, religion, or nationality, the most common attraction in this category involves personality differences. For example, the shy, taciturn person may seek an open, garrulous mate. But, as in other exogamous relationships, complementary couples often face greater difficulties with the ways that they are the same than the ways in which they are different. We see the partner as the solution to an old problem, and then we discover that we still have the problem. We choose someone who complements us perfectly, whose background, personality, and interests match our own hopes or desires. Our expectations for being a dynamic duo go sky-high. We get carried away, only to face later the kind of problems that Arthur and Zoe Van Ness had.

Arthur is an actor—outgoing, gregarious, constantly "on," and very charming, if a bit hysterical at times. Zoe is reserved, steady, gracious, and somewhat obsessionally controlled. Arthur is the center of attention at parties—lively, expressive, and lots of fun. Zoe remains in the background, circulating, greeting guests, refilling drinks. When the guests leave, Arthur becomes very affectionate, and Zoe wants him to help clean up. They often begin bickering. Arthur complains that she's more interested in the dishes than in him. Zoe responds by observing that he's had more than enough attention for one night. Arthur says that she just wants him to be a maitre d'hôtel. Zoe says that he wants her to be a busboy. As they speak, Arthur's voice becomes loud and shrill, and he waves his arms around. Zoe becomes increasingly quiet.

What's happening to this "perfect" couple? The same personality traits that drew them together are now keeping them apart. They got more than they bargained for, or, rather, they could not cope with what they wanted. She was attracted to him because he was from a large, boisterous family. He was always the center of attention, the star of any gathering. She envied him because she felt mousey and unnoticed, too reserved and conservative to get the attention she craved. As his wife, she felt she could have some of that glamour. And she was genuinely entertained by him. Still, she wasn't the star of the show herself. Important as the association was, she hadn't changed. She was still basically mousey—and capable. She recognized that they were perfect, for he needed her as much as she needed him, but her expectations that together they could conquer the world were not realized.

For Arthur, Zoe was the rock he needed—the stability, control, and class he lacked. He zeroed in on her immediately as someone who would not compete with him for the spotlight. She appreciated his talents, was from a more refined and responsible family, and was a managerial type, capable of running anything from a kitchen to a theater. He felt that she could help him achieve success as an actor. Although he had talent and drive, he knew that he needed someone with a level head to handle him. But he, too, was disappointed because he wasn't becoming much of a success outside the living room. Although he loved her and depended on her, his career expectations were not being met. The stability he so envied in her did not make him more stable or directed than he was before.

When these two sought family therapy, the therapist took them back a few steps. How did their family histories create such high expectations for their match? Why were their differences so important to their relationship? It turned out that Arthur, the youngest and favorite child in a large family, never felt he got enough care as a child. Although he was often the center of attention, he felt obligated to perform. He was actually a very dependent child who learned to subvert his dependency and get another kind of attention. But being a star didn't really satisfy him. As an adult he was still dependent and still seeking a similar form of attention that didn't meet his needs.

Zoe, on the other hand, was the only child of parents who expected her to behave as they wished. To win their approval she was good, polite, reasonable, and controlled, but her own desires and interests were thwarted. She was never allowed to make any decisions, even those that concerned her. When she grew up she was still trying to do the right thing, even when it wasn't what she actually wanted. In Arthur she found someone she wanted, with a personality she wanted, and an imagined life-style she wanted. It was her chance to make a decision for herself and to have some power in the new family they would form. She knew that he admired her control. Now she could put it to good use.

But actually she used that control to keep him away, just as he used his dependency to keep her away. With the therapist's help, they were able to discuss their fear of an intimate relationship that would require them to reveal their secret needs and desires. Intimacy had been in short supply in both their families, and neither of them was aware that they were unconsciously re-creating some of the unhappy patterns of their childhoods when they selected each other as mates. Although superficially these two complemented each other and were drawn together by their obvious differences, on a deeper level they had much in common. Each expected the other to supply the missing ingredients in their lives.

They had to find out just what was missing by sharing their pasts, their childhood feelings and fantasies about their futures, their roles in their families of origin, and the unmet needs and unresolved conflicts that surfaced as a result of their union. Tracing their histories to see what they had in common and, more importantly, what they did not have in common, helped this couple begin breaking down their defenses against intimacy. Although they both had to face the fact that their original expectations weren't being met, they were able to build something better, something more realistic, by starting over. The therapist helped them find ways in which they could capitalize on what they had in common and what they had that was complementary. The attraction was actually on both levels, but they had been unconsciously competing with each other. They had to rebuild their self-esteem, their "special we," by accepting themselves realistically rather than living out the fantasies they had for themselves and for each other. That took some time and some thorough examination, a review and adjustment that's necessary for most couples, whether they choose to emulate or escape their families of origin.

Sometimes we don't recognize that our choice of mate fits into our family because we are only looking at the current generation. It is not uncommon for certain roles to skip a generation. For example, the celebrated father has a no-account son who has a successful daughter. The alcoholic's daughter won't touch alcohol, but her son will and does and becomes alcoholic, too. The no-account son and the teetotalling daughter reject their parents in such a way that their own children reject them and come up full circle, repeating their grandparents' roles. The character of this rejection is such that no real change occurs. A pattern is repeated, partly because no one recognizes that it is a pattern and partly because the family as a whole has an investment in maintaining equilibrium and holding onto their special identity.

All Things Being Equal and Mate Selection

Whenever there is a change or a prospective change in the family constellation, the family system is laid bare. In such periods of transition, doubt, opposition, joy, anxiety, or excitement are expressed more openly by all family members. Parents who have always maintained that they only want their child's happiness suddenly reveal other ambitions for their child's marriage. Their child's happiness is not the only thing on their minds and probably never was. We all have ideas about whom our children will marry, even if we do not want to or mean to impose those ideas. Feelings that we kept to ourselves are now, given the threat of change, harder to contain.

Children are often so wrapped up in their love affair that they cannot imagine what is going on with the rest of their family. We believe that our parents want our happiness, and we cannot accept anything less than their total approval. We feel that our marriage or mate affects only us, so why would anyone else be upset or involved? Our desire for autonomy is underscored by a need for our family's unquestioning affection. We don't want them to be involved in any other way, yet we find that they are involved and that we are not as free as we thought. The usually invisible inter-active elements of family life become more visible. The forces of power, dependency, love, autonomy, and separation are all thrown off-balance. The old equilibrium is disturbed, and we can see how the forces are usually regulated.

Power

When Jaimie Bronson first brought Sarah home from college for a visit, his parents and older sister Judy were in turmoil. It wasn't that they didn't like Sarah; actually, they hardly noticed her. They were stunned because they hadn't known about Sarah or about Jaimie's serious involvement with her. They knew about Hazel, his childhood sweetheart. They had always assumed that Jaimie and Hazel would eventually marry, and they thought that Hazel shared this assumption. Now, they were confronted with a woman they had neither chosen nor known about. They felt betrayed and left out, as indeed they were. Actually, Jaimie had not thought about Hazel for some time. They were still friends, but neither had ex-pectations of being together and hadn't for years. He could not understand why his parents didn't greet Sarah with open arms.

The real reason they didn't had little to do with either Sarah or Hazel. It had to do with power in the family system, particularly the power to make decisions for others. The Bronsons had always made decisions for their children—about schools, friendships, social activities, even their prospective mates. Judy had accepted all their decisions docilely. Now here was Jaimie, in the middle of medical school (as he was supposed to be), coming home with the wrong woman. Power in the family system was about to be challenged. Jaimie was claiming some power for himself, the power to make his own choices.

Dependency

After Jaimie's defection, Judy became the dependable one, the family member who could be relied on, who did the right thing. Both Jaimie and the Bronsons realized that they needed her. Jaimie immediately tried to solicit her support by confiding his feelings about Sarah and his hopes that she and Sarah would be friends. The Bronsons, in turn, asked Judy to talk to her brother about his re-sponsibilities. Although they implied that this meant his responsi-bilities to his studies, they really meant his responsibilities to the old family structure in which they made all decisions.

This was a new role for Judy, one she came to relish. She had always been the dutiful daughter, the follower; someone had always taken care of her. Now she was a mediator, the person everyone needed. Although there were risks in relinquishing that dependent status, the shifting family system created a new role for her that assured her of an important place in the family. The importance of her new role more than compensated for the change involved.

Autonomy

When families with indistinct boundaries (no sense of where one member ends and another begins) go through mate selection, there may be no distinction between the new family and the old one. The Bronsons all had a sense of their own individuality, but until Sarah's arrival neither of the children had really been on their own. Jaimie's assertion of his own interests put Judy in a more independent position. She could no longer be just the obedient daughter because she recognized her brother's sincerity and admired his rebelliousness. She did not want to rebel herself because she still appreciated her parents' concern for his future. She found a place for herself between them, a place that was more clearly defined than any she'd previously had.

The children's growing autonomy forced Mr. and Mrs. Bronson to see themselves as a family with grown and independent children. That led to some reflections on their marriage, which had been centered on the children for a very long time. Although they had always functioned as a unit, they began to realize that they were not one and the same person. Of course, this was a slow process. Jaimie's action did not change everybody overnight. But it did create a potential for change and the outlines of a new family system.

Love

During such a period of transition, the expression of love is usually tied up in other forces, as when those who want their way withhold their love and those who trust us shower us with affection. The Bronsons were able to live with their conflicts and disappointments, able to trust each other in new roles eventually, precisely because their love and respect for one another was stronger than their desire to maintain an old, unworkable family system. It was not an easy transition, especially for the parents, because their love for Jaimie and Judy had always been expressed by deciding what was best for the children. Now the children were making these decisions themselves, and it was harder for the Bronsons to love them in the same way. But that was the key. Love, like the other psychodynamic forces upset by mate selection, would be in a new juxtaposition in the future family system.

Separation

Separation and loss are persistent themes in family life, and they are especially evident as a family prepares for the literal or figurative separation of a member from the group. Jaimie Bronson's love for Sarah did not mean that he was ready to start a new family with her, but it was a potential threat felt by the whole family. And the threat went beyond the loss of Jaimie. It was the loss of a family identity. When the family of origin splinters into several separate and new families, a part of each individual's identity is lost. We no longer belong to the same group. We are still a part of our family, but the structure and dynamics of that original group have changed, and they will exist in our memories only. The sadness or drunkenness that frequently characterizes weddings often reflects this. We are not responding just to the loss of the bride or groom but to a whole of which we were a part.

Couple Equilibrium

There are many reasons to hold on to a mate that have nothing to do with our feeling for that person. In fact, we might realize our mistake and refuse to admit it, especially if there was opposition to the union. If we have idealized the mate and the couple we will become, it can be very hard to give up that fantasy. We keep hoping it will become real and justify whatever pain we have already suffered. If we've given up our family of origin, other possible mates, our freedom, and other more tangible assets in order to have a different kind of family and a better life, we may be unable to admit that it did not turn out the way we predicted, and we are afraid to give it up because we burned our bridges. We stay together to maintain the illusion that we did not make a mistake.

Some couples respond to change within their relationships by exchanging roles, thereby maintaining a "we," even if it seems somewhat less than "special." For example, a homosexual man tyrannized his partner with infidelities. The partner was always unhappy, distressed, and threatening to leave. For some reason, the unfaithful one decided to settle down, put his energies into his primary relationship, and stop running around. Then, the partner started having affairs and treated the other in exactly the same way.

We see this syndrome over and over again—the recovered alcoholic whose partner becomes alcoholic, the hypochondriac whose partner gets sick. This static type of coupling usually illustrates the couples' inability to be really close to each other. Their problems distract them from any kind of intimacy, and their fear of intimacy is tied to their original families. The hidden forces of family life were never, even unconsciously, dealt with in the family of origin. These people learned how to keep everything in balance, albeit somewhat bizarrely, but they did not learn that there were any benefits in facing conflicts or change.

Although the idea of hidden forces in mate selection is only a metaphor for the vast, complex motivations that lie beneath the surface of our awareness, it is a way of examining whom we choose, why, and how we keep everything balanced. It is also a way to look at those who do not choose mates. Those hidden forces keep some of us in our families of origin forever, perhaps because we secretly fear a loss of some kind—love, identity, power or position in the family, nurturing. Indeed, some people do not choose partners until a parent or some other relative they are in some way unable to separate from, dies. Still others marry late— late enough to be past childbearing. Although single people may say that they never found the right person, that the right person never found them, or that they just didn't have the opportunity, a look at their family of origin will often reveal other motivations. And these motivations are influenced by more than their relationships to mother or father. When we dig deeply enough, we discover the complex network of group needs and family equilibrium that affects so many of our decisions and actions.

Mate Selection and Falling in Love

We've written a whole chapter on mate selection, and we haven't even mentioned falling in love. In truth, we don't know any more about falling in love than anyone else does. We do, however, know that there is more to mate selection than falling in love. We do know that mate selection is not a totally random process, that we marry whom we meet and we meet people like us, that we choose those who fit into or out of our families in fairly specific ways, and that our choices cause us joy and grief in ways connected to our relations and our family history. We can trace the reasons for a particular selection at a particular time, in a particular place. We can see how this selection fits into previous family patterns. But we cannot, with hindsight or foresight, by divination, interpretation, or intuition, tell you what falling in love is.

PART II

✿◈✿◈✿

THE
FAMILY
LIFE
CYCLE

Stage One:
Conjugal Blitz

A marriage is a contract between two people, a contract that is both legal and psychological. As is often the case with contracts, some of us don't bother to read the fine print, or we don't believe that the stated contingencies could ever apply to us. Most of us are simply unaware of the unwritten, unspoken, and unconscious expectations we have for marriage. Furthermore, we are ignorant of the contracts already out on us—those held by our parents and other relatives. Marriages, beginning with the wedding itself, involve other people, too.

All families have systems or patterns of behavior that stabilize them in times of change, but we do not always realize that marriage is one of those times. An event as predictable, happy, normal, and commonplace as a wedding is not supposed to cause much upheaval. And yet, it is a major change in the original family's identity and the beginning of a new family identity for the couple. We are no longer a family of parents and children; we have become parents with married children. We are no longer just sons and daughters; we are husbands and wives. The changes in personal and family identity create change in the family system. We are adding more roles, collectively, to the family than at any other stage of family development. The family system must change to accommodate the new designations, including all the permutations of in-laws. We even take on new roles in relation to friends.

We change so profoundly because we expect, and are expected, to do most things together from now on. Married people sign the same Christmas card, have children, and stay together. Despite the prevalence of divorce and remarriage, we still believe that marriage is forever. We don't realize that forever takes some getting used to, that the psychological forces of family life will continue to affect us, that the new roles that seemed so natural and easy require time and practice. We think we know what society, our mate, our family, and we ourselves expect our marriage to be, but we cannot be fully cognizant of the particular fantasies, hopes, and obligations that will shape and define our evolving new couple identity.

The Contract and the Forces

Because marriage unleashes the hidden forces of family life, the first few weeks, months, and even years are a time of testing, a time to confront our hidden contracts. And we may discover that even such a seemingly positive force as love has its underside.

Love

Although our modern society assumes that love is an integral part of marriage, we do not always seem to know just what kind of love that is. Our particular definition of love, especially married love, determines both our expectations and our satisfaction or disappointment in the relationship. In the excitement and confusion of getting married we rarely explore what love means to our partner or to ourselves. Our ideas about love and the expression of affection may not match our mate's. Devotion, support, loyalty, attraction, respect, and admiration are all possible ways to prove our commitment—and disprove it.

One young woman complained that her husband never held her hand in public. She believed that married people should show their intimacy in rather specific ways—kissing each other hello and good-bye, touching and being demonstrative around others. To her new husband, however, such exhibitions seemed inappropriate. He felt uncomfortable in the presence of people who "only had eyes—and hands—for each other." He felt such behavior was rude and exclusive, and he did not want his friends to experience that discomfort. His wife had noticed this before the wedding, but she interpreted it as shyness and believed that marriage would legitimize and relax her lover. She had her own set of expectations about their relationship.

Her husband felt this was a minor point. His own family had been extremely reserved, both inside and outside the family. He loved his wife very much and showed it when they were alone. In fact, he had been attracted to her because she was demonstrative, and he felt he'd come a long way in being so free with her. It was something he'd missed in his family, something she could give him.

She was teaching him how to show his love—in the privacy of their home. But not in the street. He could not understand why she wanted more.

She did not realize that she did want more until after they were married. She wanted someone to love her and, in return, she would be open and loving. That was her contract. He did love her and she was loving, but something was wrong. His inability to show his love in public violated her expectations of their contract. Neither one of them had realized that a difference in style could cause such conflict. It wasn't reasonable. It wasn't fair. But it was the case.

The real conflict here is one of family identity. His family of origin was completely undemonstrative. He had already made great strides simply because he was able to hold and caress his bride when they were not having sex. But her family expressed love and care with touches and kisses, and his inability to meet her expectations made her feel that the marriage was not working, that he had misrepresented himself, or that she was somehow at fault. Their earlier identifications with very different styles of loving generated a loss of confidence in the love they did have for each other. They had to reassure each other of that love by discussing the reasons for their different expectations. She needed to explore what she really wanted and why she was disappointed, and he had to understand that his perception of their contract was not shared. Crossing the chasm from the old family to the new one is often difficult in unexpected ways.

Much of this is tied to our early expectations of married love. Some of us expect to be loved as our parents loved each other. Some of us expect to be loved as our parents loved us. We want to feel cared for, protected, and receive love automatically because we are married. We may model our concept of love on grandparental love, sibling love, the love an aunt and uncle seemed to have for each other, or the love we saw in the movies when we were growing up. Perhaps we want anything but those family or childhood models. Like the husband mentioned above, we seek what was missing in our family of origin. A person who felt stifled by the heavy obligation of a loving family might seek a more liberated, unfortified marriage. If we think we want to emulate our parents' marriage and then discover that we are different people, we are disappointed. If we do not want to emulate our parents in any way and then find that we do, we are disappointed. Most of us do not realize the number or strength of our expectations, nor the loss of self-esteem we may suffer if the relationship doesn't meet those expectations.

These expectations and the difficulties we encounter in making new identifications are intricately connected to unconscious forces other than love, even though they are labelled love. Power struggles, for example, might be expressed as "If you loved me, you'd do it my way." "You wouldn't leave me alone if you really loved me" masks feelings about independence and autonomy. "We'd have sex all the time if you loved me as I love you" reveals doubts about being taken care of, having trust. Love is a vital ingredient in marriage, whatever it means to us. Actually, because we do not always know what it means, we expect it to solve all problems magically. Thus, it's natural that differences and conflicts in marriage would appear to be a failure of love, rather than a normal consequence of clashes in style, history, and romantic fantasies.

Separation

Marriage is a major separation—from both our families of origin and our past and future lovers. We have to separate ourselves from past alliances of all kinds in order to form a new family. Although we will continue to see our parents or visit our ex-in-laws, the things we have in common will change, as will our obligations and expectations for one another. Very few, if any, of us can carry on an affair with an old flame while marrying someone else. The commitment of marriage implies some degree of fidelity or loyalty. Choices are necessary, and one of the most important ones is separation from past affiliations. Indeed, it may be a choice that we bring up again and again throughout our marriage; as in "I could have had anyone I wanted and I chose you," "I'm giving you the best years of my life," "I should have married Harvey," and "I wish you had married Harvey."

Some marriages are haunted by the ghosts of other lovers. A woman who had been married for fifteen years, seemingly happily, still thought about her first and most intense love affair. When she met the wife of this man through a mutual friend, she introduced herself as "Tom's girl friend." Both the wife and the friend raised their eyebrows until she rather halfheartedly corrected herself with "Tom's old girl friend, that is." To her, however, Tom really still was her boy friend, even though she had a husband and two children. Tom had ended their affair against her wishes. She could not bear to lose him or her idea of him so she incorporated him into her life on an unconscious level and carried him along with her in fantasy.

When we marry we must also separate ourselves from future alliances that compete with the family we are becoming. We do not begin a marriage thinking about the time we are going to spend with the boys, the affairs we're going to have, the time we'll have with our relatives, or the opportunity we'll have to get away from each other. Most people think about being together. Although married people need to retain their individuality and a certain amount of freedom, overly competitive relationships may indicate that the couple is having trouble forging an exclusive coalition.

The most likely source of competition (and the one least likely to be taken seriously) is the family of origin. Separation is not felt just by the people getting married. The family itself must adjust to the loss of one member in its most intimate systems. And they must incorporate an additional member in both new and old systems. Their identity is threatened by the loss of a member because the family structure changes. They lose more than a physical presence; they also lose a role. They may be in turmoil because they are trying to find a new scapegoat or someone else to play the saint.

Rather than give up the role, most families seek a new player within their ranks. However, if the role is not pivotal, or the family is particularly healthy and ready to let go, they may not need a replacement. The Griffiths were more typical. When their sixteen-year-old scapegoat, Sandy, ran off to follow a charismatic guru, they continued to point to her whenever domestic conflict arose. But it became increasingly difficult to blame an absent member, so they turned to her young sister, Catherine. Catherine was only four at the time, too young to really take the role, but by age six she was as "bad" as Sandy had been. No one in the family seemed to recognize that they were repeating their own history.

If the family regards their child's mate as a rival, the son or daughter may try to conceal the separation by complaining to the family about the mate. Comments like "Well, Mary isn't much of a cook, mom," suggest that this man has to come home for good nurturing. "John doesn't really make enough money for us to go out, daddy" could be an invitation to dad to provide what John cannot, thereby keeping dad in the family and closing John out. Children, picking up on separation fears in their parents, might spend more time with their family than their spouse, thereby not leaving home. Or, the newly married person could insist that they both spend more time with the family than alone, thereby denying the separation from their family of origin and their commitment to the new family.

All separations involve lost roles, and this can affect any member of the family. A young boy whose mother was marrying a man with three children was very excited about becoming part of a large family. The other children, all older, were very pleased about having a younger brother. They had all played together for a couple of years, and the older children were quite protective of the only child. They taught him to swim, took him to movies, and included him in their daily activities.

However, after the wedding, when they were all living together, they hardly spoke. The three older children ran off to play without consulting the boy, and he often went out on his own. During family activities the boy stuck close to his mother, whispering to her, having little accidents that required her ministrations, refusing to join the others. The father tried unsuccessfully to initiate group games, but his children, who were bigger and more skilled than the boy, quickly carried the games their way, pulling the father along with them.

This blended family made a contract to be a big, happy, active group. There was no misunderstanding or disagreement about that. There was no hidden contract. But meeting the terms of that contract was harder than they had expected. Once again a question of identity is apparent. Neither side was quite ready to give up or separate from their identities as single-parent families. When the boy sought his mother's special attention and the three children pulled their father, rather than their stepbrother, into their games, it was a clear sign of their uncertainty about their new identity. They were not yet ready to give up the old one. Everyone had gotten along so famously during the courtship period because there was no real threat to family identity; each family went home intact. Becoming a blended family was not as easy as they had expected.

When they discussed the problem, they recognized that jealousy cropped up whenever there was any conversation between blood relatives. So they made a rule permitting conversations only between blood relatives for one week. There was to be no conversation between nonblood relatives, including the parents, but sign language or notes were permissible. They knew the rule was an arbitrary and difficult one, which meant it might be broken, but they all agreed to try.

By the end of the second day they were all going crazy. The older children bombarded the mother with notes—from "Where's my green T-shirt?" to "Want to take us to the ball game?" The father and young boy turned their notes into paper airplanes, which they tossed throughout dinner. And the mother and father tried to pass notes under the table to the great amusement of all the children, who began intercepting them and passing them around. Oddly enough, there was very little verbal conversation at all.

The family did not last the whole week. By the end of the fourth day they had begun to form new alliances and see themselves as one family. The notes made them realize how much they could, and wanted to, depend on each other and how interconnected they already were. They were becoming more confident about leaving their old families and becoming a new one. Of course, there was backsliding. Four days does not a new family make. But they made a new rule. Whenever anyone felt left out or jealous, she or he would say the word "kinematics," and everyone would halt his or her own activities and try to figure out if they were reverting to the old bloodlines. Their vigilance, diligence, and basic care paid off—they were able to build a new family that worked.

Dependency

Expectations about caretaking roles are a classic example of contractual blitz in marriage. Who takes care of whom in what ways? Again, there may be a clash between fantasy and reality. Because our expectations are often based on our fantasized needs, our real needs may not be met because we choose a partner to fulfill the fantasy. Furthermore, needs and expectations change over a marriage. This has been a particularly serious problem in the past decade as economic recession and the women's movement have combined to make both women and men question their roles in marriage. The old, traditional division of labor no longer applies. Too many women have to work or want to have careers, and too many men have begun to question the limitations of the bread-winner role. Our confusion about where we are needed and what we need in the society at large is mirrored in the expression of dependency in the smaller world of the family.

Before their marriage, the Roses decided that Barbara would be the main breadwinner. They were both in law school when she and

George met, but George had already decided that he wanted to write about law, not practice it. They concentrated on building Barbara's practice so George could work at home and be available for childrearing. Barbara did devote herself to her work and George handled the homefront, including (when they came along) the major care of the two little Roses. They were quite proud of themselves for managing to make the most of their real talents. They were held up as models by other couples, and eventually even their families praised their success.

But problems began to occur, primarily related to their role reversal. No matter how hard we try to change our family, we are always carrying around our history. Both Barbara and George had come from families that were very straight and conventional. Their fathers worked and their mothers stayed home. It is not easy to make a complete reversal without having some residual doubts about our masculinity or femininity if we are not emulating our role models.

In addition, the Roses expected the reversal to be totally fulfilling. This happens in any marriage. They fantasized that the marriage would change them in some significant way. For Barbara that meant not "needing" to be the mother that her mother was. For George, it meant not "needing" to be like his father. But that did not erase their own need to be needed, to be cared about and cared for, both by each other and by their children.

Their case was further complicated by an obvious contractual misunderstanding. Both believed that if they fulfilled their side of the bargain—if she were the steady breadwinner and he the steady at-home parent—their own needs would be magically realized. This unconscious contractual assumption translates into "If I give you what you tell me you want, if I am the person you say you want me to be, I will be happy because you will give me what I tell you I want." Most of us do not realize that our attempts to fulfill a partner's needs are based, in part, on the assumption that our own needs will thereby be met. This unconscious reciprocity component is usually obscured because we can't or won't admit that the contract we established together and seem to be adhering to, isn't really satisfying. Because the arrangement is not as fulfilling as we expected, our sense of self-worth as individuals and as a couple is threatened. We tend to assume that there's something wrong with us, that we are deficient or at fault in some way.

George and Barbara were lucky enough to recognize the problem and discuss possible causes. They realized that they both felt locked into the roles they had established with a now outdated contract. Barbara felt that George did not care about her work or her as long as she brought home money and an occasional story about an especially interesting case. She felt isolated from the children and uncomfortable when she was with them and George. George felt trapped in the house and uncertain about the real-world base his occasional articles seemed to need. He was proud of the children, but he felt that Barbara didn't share his love for them, or care about him any more than she would about any baby-sitter.

Once they'd finally laid their cards on the table, which is often the hardest part of making a change, the next step seemed obvious. They had to alter their life-style in a way that would increase their self-esteem, their sense of competence, and their love for one another. They decided that Barbara would assume sole care for the children two mornings a week. This would build her sense of competence as a mother since she always felt inept with her children in George's presence. George would go to her office on those days to prepare briefs or do research on pending cases. That would give him a chance to see the law in action in a way that he couldn't at home. It was a simple change, but it worked to help them help each other. Intimacy and trust in marriage do not develop automatically, even when we do live up to our contracts. Dependency can be felt on many levels. It is important to reassess our actual expectations and needs on a regular basis to determine if they are still accurate and how they can be realistically achieved.

Power

There are countless kinds of power struggles in marriage, most involving decision making and taking responsibility. Often, the issue itself is symbolic of other, less conscious issues teeming below the surface. Fighting about money, the dishes, the children, sex, in-laws, or the garbage may have more to do with power and decision making than the actual issue at hand.

Mike and Lois came into therapy because Lois refused to initiate sex and Mike felt like an animal because he was always the aggressor. Before their marriage, Lois was an eager and active sexual partner, but once married she became nervous and unhappy about

sex and never suggested it or seemed to enjoy it. She told the therapist that she just didn't seem to want sex any more and could not
understand why.

A review of their sex history revealed an interesting pattern in
their use of birth control. When they first started sleeping together he used a condom and did so until she started on the pill a
couple of months later. They both described those early months
as sexual perfection. He guided her and she became confident and
sexually assertive. They had sex often, and Lois initiated it at least
as often as Mike. But then she began to have problems with the oral
contraceptives. She gained weight and seemed edgy much of the
time. Her doctor had recommended the diaphragm and had fitted
her for one shortly before their wedding. The honeymoon was a
disaster, with Lois taking as long as an hour to insert the diaphragm. Afterward, she spent hours worrying about its effectiveness. Neither Lois nor Mike wanted children right away; she
wasn't sure she wanted them at all. She didn't want to experiment
sexually because she fervently believed that the diaphragm would
be dislodged. She withdrew more and more from sex after the
honeymoon. Oddly enough, neither of them connected their sexual
problem to their birth control problem. Perhaps that was because
there were other issues involved that they could not discuss.

Lois was very guilty about sex. Her mother had become pregnant before marriage and constantly warned Lois about the dire
consequences of sex. Since Lois was the result of that pregnancy,
her mother's words had a special effect. As the child of illicit sex,
she felt guilty. And she was guilty because her mother's unhappy
marriage was her fault—her fault for being. Although birth control eliminated the more obvious consequences of sex, it did not do
away with the evil she associated with sex. She did not want to be
responsible for sex in any way.

Part of Mike's great appeal was his willingness to assume responsibility for both contraception and sex itself. Later, the pill
had the same effect—she was not responsible. First, Mike took care
of her, then the pill took care of her. But the use of the diaphragm
required a degree of responsibility that raised fears about being
responsible for wanting sex, as well as for preventing conception.
Unconsciously, Lois felt that she could only be sexual if someone
else or something else was responsible. In this, she was repeating
her mother's pattern. Her mother blamed Lois, her unwanted child,
for her own lack of sexual drive. Lois blamed her diaphragm.

Many people complain about diaphragms, foam, or even condoms because these devices interrupt lovemaking. People dislike such necessary interruptions because they lose their sexual desire. They are really afraid of sex or guilty about it, and when they pause, even briefly, these inhibitory forces take control. To enjoy sex, many people have to be out of control, beyond responsibility in a way. Anything that shatters the mood, from certain birth control methods to unrealistic fears of being interrupted, illnesses, or noises next door, can hopelessly break the sense of unreality they need to enjoy sex. In fact, many people get drunk or stoned to create that sense of unreality and help maintain it by making the participants oblivious to interruption.

Lois seemed to abdicate any sexual responsibility by giving Mike all the power over their sex life. But on the other hand she did take responsibility by avoiding sex, a negative power play in their marriage. Mike did not have enough power in the relationship to override hers. Although she seemed to give the power away, he actually had no power. That's why he felt so uncomfortable. It was not because he felt like an animal, but because he did not feel like a person. And neither did she.

In some relationships, one partner will happily take all the power, become dominant, possibly with the complicity of his or her mate. But in this relationship nobody had any kind of positive power—until they started talking about their sexual feelings. They decided to alternate taking responsibility for birth control to see if that kind of shared competency would strengthen their sex life. It did.

Autonomy

When we marry we must mark off the boundaries between ourselves and our families of origin or other families we have been part of. It is also important to define boundaries between ourselves and our spouses. Marital styles differ: some couples do everything together; others do everything with their families; some maintain their separate interests and friendships.

These boundaries may be less obvious than we or our spouse or our families expected. We may look forward to marrying into our spouse's family only to learn that they are not prepared to let us in. We may anticipate independence from our family only to discover that they expect to see more of us now than ever before. Our mate may expect us to spend a lot of time with his or her grown children, which we may find very uncomfortable. Setting up a new family often turns out to be a very different experience.

People who run away from home to marry, only to return because they cannot afford to live on their own, give up some independence and autonomy. So do welfare families. Being supported by Uncle Sam is just as hard as being supported by any other relative. A family that has to give up some autonomy also loses some self-respect, but only the family itself can decide how much autonomy is necessary for its survival. One of the main tasks for newly married couples is to find those boundaries. And that may mean running into preexisting contracts in which other boundaries applied, as we see in the case to follow.

Something Old, Something New. Cathy and Karl Cienega, married for one and a half years, sought therapy because they fought all the time. During the two years they had lived together before marriage they never fought seriously. Cathy, aged thirty, had been married before, and she was determined to make this marriage work. They began therapy at her instigation. Karl was thirty-six, and this was his first marriage. After waiting so long to find the right woman, he was extremely depressed by their inability to solve their problems.

As a preliminary step, the therapist suggested that they describe their wedding to her, since they both agreed that their relationship had been better before the wedding. Karl began by saying that his parents had been very opposed to the match. Cathy was a divorced woman of a different religion, and he was the baby of his large and loving family. Before their marriage, his mother did not even acknowledge Cathy's existence, refusing to invite her to family celebrations and treating her as the receptionist when she called to talk to Karl. Cathy had only met the family once when Karl's favorite sister invited her to a family shindig.

When Karl announced their marriage plans to his family he expected the worst. However, his family was just wonderful. His parents offered to pay for the wedding. His sister suggested that they use her house for the reception. His oldest brother gave them the key to his condominium on Bimini for their honeymoon. Cathy and Karl could not believe their good fortune. This family that had ostracized them was truly generous and well meaning after all.

Cathy, whose own family was small and aloof, was very pleased. Although Karl's family had not been particularly warm toward her, their warm, loving style was one of the reasons for her initial attraction to Karl. She wanted to belong to that kind of family. Karl was relieved. He had been attracted to Cathy in part because she seemed to be so free, so unfettered by her family. But he was very glad that his sometimes overbearing family was coming through on this one. It made things much easier. They decided that his family had been embarrassed by their previous living arrangements. Legitimizing their relationship made it possible for Karl's family to be supportive and involved.

Since Cathy and Karl both had well-paying jobs, Cathy felt that they should pay for the wedding, and Karl agreed. Her family had already paid for one wedding, and she preferred to pay their way to this wedding since they lived across the country and it would be much too difficult to take Karl's large family out west for the event. She thought they might have the wedding and reception in a public place, but neither she nor Karl wanted to hurt his sister by refusing her generous offer to hold the wedding in her home. So it was settled. They invited Cathy's family, a couple of Karl's business associates, a few close friends, and scores of Cienegas.

Karl's sister recommended her caterer, and Cathy and Karl made all the arrangements for food and liquor. One of Karl's brothers secured the services of a judge. Cathy and Karl chose the photographer and decor and attended to a hundred details. Karl's father arranged for the transportation and parking for guests.

The wedding took place on a soft autumn afternoon. It was beautiful and everything worked out perfectly. To Karl it was a golden memory, a very happy and warm blur. Cathy noticed a few more details. Her mother seemed to share her own sense of good fortune in marrying into such a family. She basked in her own family's approval and felt proud of Karl and his family. All the Cienegas were very open and friendly, and she tried to remember all their names.

Cathy also noticed that there were two photographers at the wedding although she had only hired one. She asked Karl about the second one, assuming she was a family member. Karl asked his mother, who triumphantly announced that that was her photographer. She'd decided to give the newlyweds a wedding album because they had said they were only going to have a few prints made up for framing. She felt they'd regret that decision so she was taking action to prevent that. Cathy and Karl were amused by this rather quaint meddling.

Karl's sister had also done a little meddling, for which they were more grateful. She had asked the caterer to add a few special treats that she thought they would like. In all the excitement and confusion, Cathy and Karl weren't even aware of the "extras" until one of his sister's children pointed to an elaborate caviar-terraced ice sculpture and said, "My mom did that." Cathy turned to the sister in amazement and was assured that the caterer had done it, but that she, the sister, had ordered it and arranged to be billed for that and a few other little things. Cathy and Karl were very impressed.

They did go to Bimini for their honeymoon, but not right away. First, they had to move the contents of their two apartments to their new apartment. Although they had been living together at Cathy's place, Karl had kept his own apartment. They had their first serious fight during that week. Cathy had exquisite, rather spare, Nordic taste. Karl had some comfortable chairs, but the rest of his furniture was not particularly tasteful. They had agreed to sell most of his things, put some in storage, keep most of her things, and buy a few new pieces.

But one of the things that he wanted to keep was his trophy collection. Cathy could not believe it when he began unpacking those horrible old antlers and stuffed animal heads in their new living room. She had thought they would be put into storage. Karl could not believe that she was serious. After all, he was a hunter and these were his trophies. Why would he put them in a vault somewhere? Cathy did not feel they matched her taste, and she didn't believe in killing animals. It was a barbaric reminder of one of the few things they did not have in common. In the end they left the animals on the floor and went off for two glorious weeks in Bimini.

When the therapist asked what their current fights were about, they both said, "The trophy collection." They never figured out where to keep it and had moved it from the dining room to the bedroom when Cathy refused to eat another meal under those glassy eyes. It was currently in a hallway, but Karl was unhappy with that because it didn't show up very well, and a couple of guests had been caught on the antlers.

But they also fought about money. Despite his age and financial success, Karl still took money from his family. Or, more precisely, he didn't refuse it. He said that his family had lots of money and if they wanted to give it to their children that was all right. Cathy pointed out that all parents did not give money to their children.

Furthermore, she could not understand why Karl did not have credit cards in his own name, especially gasoline credit cards. His father still paid for all Karl's gas as well as his auto insurance. He had done so ever since Karl first started to drive twenty years ago. Karl said he'd just never gotten around to putting the credit cards in his own name.

Cathy also complained about their social life. Before their marriage they spent time alone or with friends. Now, all their leisure time was spent with his family. Although Karl's family had been very sweet to her, Cathy could not bear the thought of celebrating one more religious holiday with them. She had tried to counter by celebrating national holidays, but that was just too much. Karl did not seem to notice or care whom they spent their time with. He thought his family was fun. He was not bothered by his mother's daily phone calls, his sister's weekly dinner invitations, or the regular weekend family gatherings. He told the therapist that this was the first time he'd heard Cathy complain about his family.

Something Borrowed, Something Blue. The therapist felt that Cathy and Mike were attracted to each other for the same reasons they were in trouble now. She liked his large, interdependent family and he liked her independent life-style. She wanted to be part of something bigger—not necessarily his family, but another one of her own making. He wanted to be part of something smaller, but he could not seem to get away from his family. She was not able to live with his family, and he wasn't able to live without them. They were living up to their contract, but it turned out to be the wrong contract. It was more complex and layered than they had expected. Hidden clauses and forces were making it hard for them. Before their marriage, they were not committed to the shared destiny that brought out other issues—particularly the preexisting contract Karl had with his family regarding his autonomy, or lack of it, and the relationship between that autonomy and other forces.

Karl seemed to have most of the power in the marriage. Cathy was the one who complained about their lack of independence from his family. Karl was not upset by the amount of time they spent with his relatives—he made all the decisions about their life in that regard. But his decisions were not clear-cut because he refused to take responsibility for Cathy's discontent. Actually, they ended up with his family by default. Their constant bickering indicated that he wasn't really happy with the situation either. Although he told Cathy that he could not do anything about it, he married her because he wanted her to help him leave his family—to stand between him and them. But he was also happy and relieved that they liked her and that she appeared to like, or get along with, them. It is a familiar dilemma: maintain stability, security, and equilibrium, or seek change by taking responsibility for new decisions, regardless of where the chips may fall. Karl had made a decision and created change by marrying. However, the responsibility was hard to accept. The chips seemed to be falling on his head.

Cathy had made a decision to be taken care of, not just by Karl but by her idea of family. Her own cool, rigid upbringing made her long for the kind of nurturing that Karl received and gave. But she did not really want to live with his family; she wanted the family that she and Karl would become.

At the wedding, Karl's family showed Cathy what she could expect from them and in what ways the issue of dependency would surface. When Karl's sister arranged and paid for the extra food, she was expressing the difficulty this nurturing family had in entrusting their favorite son to someone whose nurturing abilities they evidently did not trust. And perhaps Cathy had some doubts, too, because she allowed them to take advantage of her. Knowing how protective they were and how little experience she had in protecting or being protected, she let them do what she had hoped she could do herself. And Karl did the same thing. He also had some unconscious doubts about the nurturing he would receive in his new family. His old family had always provided so completely for him. His previous affairs had always been with older, often married, women—women who were not able to be completely devoted to him because they had previous obligations. His family had given him the kind of caretaking that these women gave their husbands or children. Now he was going it alone and he was scared.

Another sign of the family's incursion and separation anxiety was the extra wedding photographer. In fact, that gave Cathy an early indication of the problems to come. When she received the wedding album from Karl's mother about six weeks after the wedding, she realized that Mrs. Cienega must have chosen the dozen prints. Although Cathy could not put her finger on it at the time, in the therapist's office a year later, she realized that every shot of her was bad. Either she had her eyes closed or she was looking off in a different direction from everyone else or she was slightly out of focus. She simply did not seem to be with, or part of, the rest of the family. And, of course, to the Cienegas she wasn't. Hiring their own photographer (and thereby assuring their version for posterity) was the first hint that the album would be a gift to themselves, not to the newlyweds. The choice of proofs cinched it. Needless to say, every one of the Cienegas looked terrific.

The trophy collection was another indication that autonomy and its relationship to other forces were at the root of Cathy and Karl's fights. For Karl, these relics represented his family; he couldn't put them into cold storage. So he kept trying to put them into another room, someplace where they wouldn't be too obtrusive but would still be present. Cathy didn't object to the trophies or even his hunting, as long as she didn't have to live with the trophies or go hunting herself. Her complaints about their social life and the money that the Cienegas gave them were related to living with Karl's family. Karl had never heard her complain about his family, but that's what all their fights were really about. They seemed to be fighting about stuffed animals and auto insurance, but they were really fighting about who they were going to be as a couple and as their own family.

It was Cathy who recognized most clearly that they had to separate themselves from past affiliations, but, ironically, she was acting as distant and cold as her own family in reaction to the cloying presence of the Cienegas. Karl sensed that he had to please Cathy in order to please and free himself, but he did not know how to deal with the problem in a way that would please them both. They had to work out a contract that dealt realistically with their expectations and needs, based on their genuine desire to stay together.

When people live together, as Cathy and Karl did, they often imagine that marriage will only be an extension of the relationship, and they are startled to find out there is a difference. When we live together we do have a certain degree of commitment and certain types of contracts. But we are not expected, nor even encouraged, to be a couple in the way married people are. We may fantasize that our covivant—our live-in partner—will be there for richer or poorer, in sickness and in health, but our fantasy expectations are not backed up by social, family, or historical expectations. We may share a bed, a mind, a loaf of bread, but we do not share a destiny. Although we know and count on each other's biological and sexual rhythms, opinions, and families, we each function as a separate person. As the Cienegas found out, there's more to marriage than living together.

Dearly Beloved

China and silver aren't the only patterns we choose when we get married. We make literally hundreds of decisions about the kind of family we will be, who will dominate in what areas, how our families will be involved, which past experiences will color our future. Weddings themselves are richly symbolic of the issues and answers that will surface in the marriage to come. They also reveal the kind of contract a couple has and the hidden clauses they may not have realized. Naturally, class, religion, values, and financial situation determine much about the nature of a wedding. Time, season, location, and circumstances further delineate its form. But some of the most traditional aspects can be surprisingly indicative of the broader issues at stake.

First of all, it makes a difference whether we marry in a judge's chambers or a chamber by the sea. If we have a religious background or family, a civil ceremony may be a slap in their face or a way of rebelling against our past. A seaside ceremony could be de rigueur for our set or a statement of another kind. If our future spouse or some other family member makes the decisions about details of time and place, that person is very likely to make or be involved in other decisions in the marriage. If the bride decides on a small, private wedding that suits her family to a tee and the groom and his side are not consulted, that may say something about similar decisions in the future. What it says depends on the couple's contract, what they each want. Perhaps the couple has agreed that she and her family will handle certain social events and that the groom, perhaps with his kin, will make other decisions. But it may be a sign of encroachment by the family of origin, as we saw in the Cienega case, or separation anxiety in the bride. Many people dismiss these considerations by explaining that their wedding was for their families. But if keeping the family happy was important to them then, it probably continues to be.

Deciding on the guest list can tear families and couples apart. Once the question of size has been settled, conflicts may arise over which "side," bride's or groom's, will have more guests. In fact, the traditional church wedding with guests lined up on each side of the aisle is a good example of the psychological alignment that may develop. In some marriages, the bride and groom have to walk a fine line down the aisle that separates not just their families and guests but also the beliefs and identifications these people represent. And these people had better represent us properly. One of the reasons for guest list conflicts is that both sides want to look their best. They don't want Aunt Hattie arriving drunk as usual. They don't think it's appropriate to include the groom's brother's ex-wife. The family identity must be protected and promoted.

As we discussed in the Cienega example, food can be very symbolic, too. The amount, type, arrangement, and quality of the food tells the world at large, even at a small wedding, that this couple will provide for each other in specific ways. There is a distinct difference between a potluck wedding reception and a reception in which the groom's mother cooks all the food. Again, money and circumstances certainly affect the choice of food, but we can read a lot into what's left after those considerations are made. Even the tradition of the bride's dowry, the idea that her family pays for the reception, is open to interpretation. How this is done and with whom it is discussed say something about how the bride, the family, and the groom regard each other.

Wedding photographs may all seem to look alike, but not to someone as observant as Cathy Cienega was. This is another one of those traditional exercises that tells us more than we might expect. But we can examine the expressions of the participants to learn something of the joy, relief, doubt, or nervousness they felt. Naturally, everyone in the wedding party lines up in order around the bride and groom. But are people touching each other, smiling, frowning, wishing they were elsewhere? What does this tell us? If there are so-called "candid" shots, do people look happy, drunk, sad?

Looking back at our own weddings, in albums or in memory, we may recall observations or feelings that flitted through our consciousness but were not really confirmed until months or years later. One couple, who took three and a half years to decide to marry at all, spent five months preparing for the wedding and finally set the date only one month before the actual event. They didn't go on a honeymoon for three months because they could not decide where to go, and they were married for eight years before they decided to have a child. Drawn-out decision making was definitely a pattern for them. It seemed pretty inefficient and frustrating to those who knew them, but they themselves seemed to prefer a perpetual state of suspended animation. Although they enjoyed making the final decision, they found the process itself spellbinding.

Any wedding can be scrutinized for patterns of what is to come and what major conflicts are likely to arise. This is not a foolproof method of predicting the future, but it may offer some clues. One couple who had five children between them wrote their own wedding ceremony with a part for each of the children to play. The wedding was wonderful. One year later his children had returned to their mother, one of her children was in boarding school, and the other had run away from home. Somehow that idyllic picture of the family in which each person had a role was false. The wedding was an attempt on the part of the parents to create that vision, but evidently the children, and perhaps unconsciously the parents, too, were not up to it. The parents knew it was not going to be easy. Their elaborate ceremony was an attempt to cover up what they knew were major conflicts not just over their remarriage but between each of them and each of their own children. The new family could not possibly obliterate the old ones. This wedding ceremony itself showed unrealistically high and false hopes.

We have only looked at a few of the symbols surrounding weddings. Almost any aspect of a wedding will provide a wealth of details about the couple, their families, their future problems, and some of the features of their developing family system. Consider rings, for example. First of all, a decision must be made about a single- or double-ring ceremony. A double-ring ceremony may indicate equality between both partners—unless one partner decided on two rings over the objections of the other partner. A ringless ceremony might symbolize an open marriage. Old-fashioned rings might mean an old-fashioned marriage. Using family rings could indicate the couple's hopes for a marriage like their parents or grandparents. If family members are involved in the decisions about rings, they may be involved in some or even all decisions this couple will make. If there is difficulty making this decision, that could be an incipient pattern for similar, future decisions. If a ring is dropped or lost during the ceremony, that could illustrate some trepidations about the commitment the ring symbolizes. Any aspect of a wedding, from the guest list to the honeymoon, can be examined for clues to the decision-making process, the issues that will arise, the family members who will be involved, and the roles that everyone will play.

Standing on Ceremony

A backward look, especially during or prior to a wedding, will tell us a great deal about the present. In other words, a look at our parents' weddings, or their parents' weddings, may reveal ongoing patterns. Wearing mother's wedding gown may indicate that we, or mother, expect us to have her marriage. Some of us are very determined to have marriages that are not at all like those of our parents. Or we are determined that our children's marriages will be very different than ours. These are powerful influences on our choices and actions. A parent whose closest sibling ran off and got married and who has always identified us with that sibling, might react to our marriage, particularly if it is an elopement, in ways to offset the pain of that early experience. For example, that parent might suggest a church wedding or even an annulment.

This does not mean that children are doomed to react against their parents or relive their parent's lives. Attention to history, however, makes it possible to understand why one generation might expect or need a new generation to be like them. It gives them a second chance, and if they feel they have made mistakes, they will try to prevent their children from making the same mistakes. Events surrounding other family marriages may show us what we are being protected from and why certain issues that do not seem important to us are important to our families.

These earlier marriages also give us the chance to see how the wedding predicted the marriage to follow. Knowing that we will invariably repeat some family patterns gives us a special interest and advantage in investigating the past. Our power struggles, concerns about love and trust, separation and autonomy may all be echoed in the experience of people we know fairly well and may be destined to "inherit from," whether we want to or not. A little attention to their experience may be very helpful in seeing the hidden clauses in our own marriage contract.

Bringing the Point Home

In the last chapter we spoke of the "special we" that every couple fantasizes they will become. The decision to marry is the beginning of the collaboration to make this fantasy a reality. It is the first time we make decisions and plans as a couple. It is the first time we begin to internalize each other's personalities in order to form an entity that is almost a third party, the marriage. It is the first time that we really have to determine where our boundaries are.

Most of us expect something good to happen to us through marriage. Being ready to settle down means being ready to grow in a new way, a way that will make us feel competent and responsible. Marriage itself will not change us, but it will give us a place in which to change, a time in which to grow, and an identity in which to find love and security.

Because some couples have to face poverty, pregnancy, or other overwhelming and consuming issues immediately, it may seem that their experience of marriage will differ from a couple who has more control of their destiny. Actually, although adversity may compress the period of adjustment and give the couple less time to work things out, the same issues will have to be dealt with. All couples have to meet their responsibilities, handle their families, and support each other to feel strong both individually and as a couple.

That's also true of second and third marriages. It may seem that all these issues involving separation, autonomy, families, and children would be less important the second time. They certainly may be less intense, but they are not necessarily less important. In a second marriage many people have to separate from their first marriage, as well as separating all over again from their family of origin. Second marriages do tend to be less formal than first marriages, and some aspects of the wedding may be different. But we can't eliminate symbolism in life or weddings any more than we can eliminate hidden contracts. Regardless of our experience and caution, life presents constant challenges.

It can take from one week to several years simply to understand all the dimensions and aspects of our marriage contract. Implementing or changing it is even more difficult. No wonder most of us are nervous at our weddings. We may not know why we feel so emotional, but on some level we must recognize that we have work to do.

Stage Two:
The Dynastic Imperative

The dynastic imperative is the drive to reproduce not just ourselves but our family of origin—the whole configuration of familiar roles, rules, patterns, and values. Although we may consciously wish to create a family that is different from the one we grew up in, few of us have the necessary models for such a change. We may be able to stake out our own territory in certain ways, but underneath there is a powerful drive to repeat that first family. Our situation may seem unique until we learn that we had a precedent on the family tree—a childless aunt, a grandparent who had children early, another relative who was a single parent. Or we may discover echoes of our own parents' experience with us in the decisions or processes of pregnancy. We find out that we are the same age our parents were when we were born, that they, too, had a first pregnancy aborted, that "accidents" often happen in our family. Unwittingly we reinforce, and allow others to reinforce, behavior that is reminiscent of patterns we don't know we know. Even couples who do not have children find that they repeat certain family-like interactions. We tend to associate "having a family" with having children, but everybody has a family. And a family's indelibility is often most clearly visible when decisions about pregnancy are made.

Until relatively recently, such decisions were not even a stage in the family life cycle for most people. We went directly from marriage to firstborn children without any sense of making a choice or of a decision-making pause in between. But now that we can control the when and if of pregnancy and are paying more attention to the changes it brings to family structure, it has become another period in family life that illuminates the patterns and systems of the families involved. As a result of better birth control, the women's movement, and concerns about overpopulation, many people are having fewer children later, some are remaining child-free, and others are opting for single parenthood. The element of choice in family size and structure has changed the family and separated sexual drive from reproductive drive to some extent.

Most people assume that there are two kinds of pregnancies—planned and unplanned. There are also, then, planned and unplanned nonpregnancies. But within each of these categories there is an element of its opposite—a little of the planned in the unplanned, a little of the irrational in the rational. In looking at the context in which pregnancies do or do not occur, we often find clues to the dynamics of the dynastic imperative. And we get further examples by following the context of pregnancy itself.

Planned Pregnancy

We don't need a reason to decide to have children. Most people just do it. But there are decisions involved, ranging from when to how many, to how they will be spaced. Some people claim that they made no decisions about these questions, that it all just happened. Our biological imperative certainly substantiates these claims. Still, most people are aware of wanting to have more or less children than their friends or parents, of hoping for girls rather than boys, of wanting to finish school before having children. Of course, these desires and hopes do not mean that a conscious decision has been made to fulfill them, especially since it takes two people to have a baby. But if we expect to have a child within the first three years of marriage, any pregnancy during that time will not really be unplanned.

Other conscious decisions regarding pregnancy may be made in the context in which a couple finds itself. If friends are having children, if family is pressing a couple, or if they are older and do not have too much time, the decision may seem quite easy. And there are less noble, conscious reasons for planning a pregnancy. We may hope a child will keep the marriage together or give life meaning, which puts quite a burden on the child. But the strongest conscious reason is the sense of being ready, of feeling it is right, of wanting to have a child.

The strongest unconscious factor in planned pregnancy is subtly connected to our identification with our parents as role models. In order to feel truly grown-up, truly a man or a woman, truly complete, we have to become a parent because our parents and their parents were parents. This may seem like a very simple and obvious observation, but it raises doubts in the best of families. The planning of a pregnancy is also the planning of a parent. In order to insure that we will become the parent we want to be, we may plan a pregnancy with a kind of magical precision we are not even aware of. Thus, we find people who have children at exactly the same age their parents did, whose children are spaced exactly the way they and their siblings were, whose circumstances or life situation are remarkably similar to those of their parents when they were conceived. Of course, we all live in the same country, have somewhat similar cultural experiences, see the same TV and films and, in families especially, have similar personal expectations. But there appears to be more than coincidence operating for the woman whose three children were each fourteen months apart, just like her sisters; or the man who decided at age thirty-five, after ten years in a child-free marriage, that he wanted children, never thinking about his birth, when his father, in a second marriage, was thirty-five.

Often, we do not remember the stories about these events, and we may not realize the impact they had upon us as children, but they are an important part of our personal and family identity. The circumstances of our births are important to us; they place us in the family and, as children, we want to hear about them. Most parents can refresh our memories about such incidents if we've forgotten them as we have grown. In fact, when we are planning a pregnancy, parents often will talk about being pregnant with us whether we solicit their reminiscences or not. They are preparing us and themselves for a change in the family. Hearing those stories again (however casually we may tune into them) reinforces that earlier identification and encourages us to carry out that imperative.

Unplanned Pregnancy

Accidents happen. Indeed, some people who do not actually "plan" their pregnancies are not disappointed to find themselves pregnant. Although reactions to unplanned pregnancies can range from dismay and sorrow to relief and delight, in general, unconscious factors outnumber the conscious ones. The failure of birth control—the most common explanation for unplanned pregnancies —sometimes coincides with less conscious factors. In such cases, couples may not use birth control as carefully as they normally do because they are distracted by other events or facing some kind of stress.

For example, a Jewish man who had been living with a non-Jewish woman for five years practiced coitus interruptus. That may seem surprising in a time of more effective and pleasurable birth control, but he had to be sure, and withdrawal seemed to give him that assurance. Actually, it is not a very effective method of birth control since sperm can be released prior to ejaculation, but he didn't know that.

His partner wanted to get married and have a child, but he wasn't able to defy his parents who expected, even demanded, that he marry a Jewish woman. Coitus interruptus not only gave him control of the situation, but it was also a punishment for his sexual involvement with a woman who could not bear his child. His parents disapproved of a sexual relationship that could not lead to marriage and childbearing, and he shared their disapproval on a subconscious level. Lessening his pleasure in sex was a way of dealing with that disapproval.

During the same period, he was setting up his own business in order to free himself from his family and pay them back for his schooling. Just about the time he reached this position, he became careless at home and impregnated his partner. How could that happen after nearly six years of almost perfect control on his part? Well, financial freedom from his family seemed to free him in other ways. He was not free enough to marry her, since he knew his financial independence would not influence his parents in that regard. But he was free enough to let go sexually. Unconsciously he knew his parents would not deny their grandchild married parents.

Unplanned pregnancies often allow people to do what they want to do but feel they cannot do for various reasons. People of different backgrounds, religions, or races who feel strong social or familial strictures against their union may not consciously be able to plan a pregnancy, for that would be as bad as planning a marriage. But a pregnancy that just happens because birth control fails or they fail, is more forgiveable and acceptable than the conscious rejection of their families or friends.

Young people who want to marry often have unplanned pregnancies that are usually chalked up to ignorance or inexperience. It is true that one-third of the people marrying in this country are pregnant, despite the wide availability of birth control information and methods. But some of these young people are not ignorant or inexperienced. The pregnancy serves a purpose for them, and that purpose isn't simply marriage—it's an escape from home and family. They imagine their lives will be better once they've left home, but they may be doomed to repeat their families' patterns because their youth and inexperience hasn't prepared them to see alternatives.

Accidents also happen to people who want to stay married. It is supposed to be a feminine wile to get pregnant in order to keep a husband. But there are also men who keep their wives pregnant so that they will be too busy to run around or think of leaving their husbands. Most of us are not very willing to take responsibility for such possibilities. It is easier to blame accidents on our sex drive, faulty contraception, liquor, or carelessness. And none of these are invalid explanations. However, a look at the context in which a pregnancy occurs—the relationship between a man and a woman, between the couple and their families, between the couple and the world—may reveal some strong unconscious reasons why pregnancy might seem more convenient or less painful than facing a problem or changing in some other way.

Some unplanned pregnancies have very little to do with marriage. Instead, they seem to be a reaction to another issue or aspect in family life.

Loss

Birth is one of the most common responses to loss in a family. The loss does not have to result from death, although in clinical practice we often see unwanted pregnancies in women whose families have suffered a death within the past year. In such cases, the whole family may be seeking someone who can help them replace the family member they lost or are losing. These subliminal currents may influence a fertile family member to "take chances" or to make a decision he or she had not really planned to make at that time. One unmarried woman got pregnant three times by three different men in the three years following her mother's untimely death. The first two pregnancies were aborted, but she decided to go ahead with the third after her father and older sister offered to help her.

Other kinds of loss can also encourage this behavior. When teenagers get pregnant in their senior year of high school or older people have an unexpected pregnancy near the end of their childbearing years, they are often responding to the loss of youth or family of origin. And pregnancy does not necessarily occur in the person directly affected by the loss. Loss reverberates around a family, depending on previous losses and the whole family's reactions to them.

The loss of a job or a dream can also trigger a pregnancy. When we are changing careers or life-styles or are out of work altogether, it may seem like a hell of a time to get pregnant, but an impending birth acts as a buffer against the loss. It is a distraction in the face of reactions that can range from existential woe to fear of failure to failure itself. The creation of life is positive, even though an untimely pregnancy may feel like the last straw and cause great despondency and depression. But a pregnancy can protect us from our own anger about failing—or anger toward loved ones for failing, for leaving, for dying. Consciously we know that we cannot replace that person, that dream, that life we had, but unconsciously we try.

Acting Out

Sometimes an unwanted pregnancy, particularly in a young person, is a form of acting out on the part of one family member. Acting out is a sign of family problems. One person's misbehavior indicates that the family equilibrium has been shaken by change or stress. A pregnancy may be a reaction to conflict in the parental relationship, conflict between a parent and another family member, or between other members of the family. It might also be a reaction to the kind of loss described above, to illness or to depression, or it might serve as a distraction from another problem or issue in the family.

Incest was uncovered in one family through the unwanted pregnancy of the eldest daughter who was sixteen. The family was in therapy because the youngest child, a boy of eight, was caught stealing lunch money from other children at school. The family was very resistant to therapy, often missing appointments or refusing to speak to each other when they did show up. The two middle daughters, aged eleven and thirteen, were the only ones who had any conversation with the male therapist. Although they were shy and withdrawn at first, they began talking to him, laughing, and keeping all the appointments. The other family members who came remained glum and unresponsive. After several months of this, the eldest daughter suddenly announced that she was pregnant and was going to have the baby. That woke everybody up, and it abruptly changed the relationship between the two middle girls and the therapist. For the next few weeks they simply ignored him. Everyone talked about the pregnancy and what they were going to do about it.

Although it took several sessions, the therapist eventually was able to see that the family had a secret. They had been very animated ever since the pregnancy. He recalled that they had acted similarly when they were first interviewed for therapy and very much caught up in the problem of the son's thefts. But once therapy started, they had been extremely sullen, especially after the two girls began having a real relationship with him. The therapist began to suspect that the pregnancy was a distraction from some family secret, which he was getting close to through his relationship with the two girls. He also surmised the son's problem had developed in response to an earlier threat of disclosure. He speculated that because he was a man his relationship with the girls was more threatening than it might have been with a woman therapist. And these thoughts made him realize that the two daughters were extremely flirtatious, especially in contrast to their older sister.

At the next session, the therapist told the family that he'd noticed they seemed unhappy when he was flirting with the sisters and much happier when something else was going on. Nobody responded to his observation. But when he went on to speculate that they had a family secret, possibly concerning these two children, which they did not want him to discover, they became very, very quiet. No one talked; no one moved. And no one came to the next session.

So the therapist called the father and gently suggested that they had something to talk about. The father agreed, sounding relieved. The next day the father confirmed the therapist's hunch. He was indeed having sex with both those daughters. He had also had sex with his eldest daughter, but he now left her alone because she had threatened to disclose the relationship. She was pregnant by a boy friend. He and his wife had not had sex for years. The man was ashamed, morose, desperate—and very ready for help. The therapist suggested that the two of them work together initially, then include the wife, and eventually bring all the children back in an attempt to face the problem openly and rebuild the family to-

gether. The therapist also offered to counsel the eldest daughter individually to deal with her feelings about the pregnancy. The
father agreed.

This case is a good example of a family maintaining a desperately
sick pattern despite the pain it causes. Most of us do not have such
a bizarre situation to hold on to, but it is not unusual to try to pre-
serve the status quo, whatever it is. Change versus status quo is a
constant dynamic in family life and there are positive aspects to
both reactions. Change offers growth, and it is a necessary and
normal feature in family development. It is also upsetting. Per-
petuating the status quo gives us the strength of continuity and the
security of knowing who and where we are. It can also be stagnat-
ing. We need both. An unplanned pregnancy that brings no change
is a sad event.

Sexual Identification

People who feel insecure about their masculinity or femininity
may try to compensate by becoming pregnant. This has become a
particularly poignant issue as both men and women defer childbearing. It is a more critical issue for women who cannot bear
children after a certain age, but it is also an issue for men who may
not want to have children after a certain age. In order to "test"
their ability to have a child—their continuing fertility—they may
conceive. However, frequently they have no intention or desire of
carrying out the pregnancy. Such behavior may seem astonishing
or even irrational, but it is probably not a completely, or perhaps
even partially, conscious act, although on some level these people
are certainly aware of the availability of abortion. Ironically,
women who have had an abortion, especially an illegal, late, or
otherwise difficult abortion, are often most likely to do this kind
of testing. They are afraid that they may not be able to conceive
because of that past experience.

Of course, most people do carry through with a pregnancy
(whether planned or unplanned) that confirms their sexual identity
on some subliminal level. This is particularly true for people raised
in strict or religious homes where sex was permissible only to conceive. Maleness and femaleness may be affirmed by the number of
children a couple have, or even just by one child. A man who feels
powerless at work or in his family may be able to regain some sense
of potency by "making his wife pregnant." A woman with a shaky

sexual identity may feel more womanly by having children. This reaction is equally possible for a woman in a traditionally male career field and a woman addicted to pregnancy. Of course, these reasons also motivate planned pregnancies, but they are more serious in unplanned pregnancies because the pregnancy itself raises other problems, and it is unlikely to solve the problems that led to it.

Someone to Love

An increasingly common kind of unplanned pregnancy involves very young adolescents who want someone to love. Many teenagers who get pregnant did not have strong love relationships in their family of origin. They feel unloved, and they want a baby to fill that gap in their lives. Unfortunately, they are often totally unaware that a baby is a demanding creature unable to give the love they so desperately seek. Although this syndrome is more common in women, it is possible that men, or boys, share this need too.

The same motivation for pregnancy can affect older people as well. Many older women, dubious about the future of relationships between men and women, consciously decide to become single parents. Unconsciously, they may believe that their relationship with a baby will substitute for a relationship with a peer. This can lead to a very unhealthy family system if the parent becomes so dependent on the child that he or she cannot establish a separate identity.

Unplanned Nonpregnancy

If we always planned to have children and find that we can't, we become very aware of the many unconscious factors that influence unplanned pregnancies. Even those who had no doubts about sexual identity in the past are bound to feel inadequate, to feel that their masculinity or femininity is threatened. Couples who believe that children are a natural extension of their feelings for each other cannot help wondering if a childless marriage can work.

Reactions to infertility may range from sexual acting out to engaging in an affair or affairs to confirm desirability and regain some feeling of competency. Other people respond by blaming each other, not necessarily for their infertility, but in other, less obvious ways, such as blaming their partners for an inability to make enough money or keep the house clean. In many cases, both people blame the infertile partner, so he or she feels twice as despondent. Although these reactions may not be entirely conscious, most people in the situation have enough self-awareness to recognize them easily.

All these reactions, including the fact of infertility itself, are connected by the theme of loss—loss of the role of parent, loss of the idea of the person we would become, the family we would become, the partner we would become. Thus, in unplanned *non*pregnancies we see all the same issues that crop up in unplanned pregnancies except that they are raised *after* the fact rather than before.

It seems cruel to suggest that there may be unconscious motivations for unplanned nonpregnancies given the pain that infertility causes. Besides, it is a biological matter, not a psychological one. Still, we all know of cases of infertility that have been reversed after adoption. Although this is a very unlikely occurrence and certainly not something to count on, it provides a clue to some of the unconscious factors that seem to influence psychologically based cases of infertility.

Inability to Be a Parent

The most obvious unconscious feeling that operates in such cases is a couple's doubts about their ability to be parents. When they adopt and see that they can indeed take care of a baby, they can then "allow" themselves to conceive. But what is the basis for their unconscious doubts, especially when they have a strong conscious desire for children?

People who had unhappy childhoods, or who felt that their parents made disastrous mistakes raising them, generally take one of two courses. Either they want to improve on their parents' performance and be the parents they wish they'd had or they do not want to have children at all, fearing that they will be the parents their parents were. Other people are torn between these two reactions. Outwardly they want to be parents, to be wonderful parents. But on a deeper level they fear that they won't be, so they never conceive, although they seem to be doing everything possible to assure conception. But are they really?

Pregnancy cannot occur if a woman does not ovulate or if a man has a very low sperm count. But what about women who ovulate, or ovulate occasionally, but never seem to have sex at that time? What about the couple who knows that a low sperm count has to be combined with abstinence prior to ovulation, sex at the time of ovulation, and the female in the prone position for at least a half hour in order for there to be a chance of pregnancy, and yet somehow it never happens that way? We may not be conscious of ovulation but we may be *un*conscious of it. Most women know or could figure out about when it happens for them even if they are not aware of a change in cervical mucus, a pain in the ovulating ovary, an increase in sexual drive—signs of which some women are quite aware. And, although men do not have these signs themselves, they may pick them up from women partners who tell them what they feel or act differently at that time.

Unrelenting Guilt

Guilt can also produce the same kind of behavior. People who feel guilty about sex may not believe they deserve to be parents. Sexual guilt often stems from the oedipal stage of development in which children view parents as potential but unacceptable sexual partners. When we conceive, our spouse becomes a parent, and we may associate them with our own parents and feel an irrational but very strong sense of guilt about our sexual relationship. If our partner is identified with any other taboo figure, such as a sibling or someone of a different race or caste, the same sense of sin may develop.

We might also feel guilty about some act in the past, particularly if it involved children. One couple entered therapy because their doctor had been unable to find a physical cause for their infertility. During therapy, the husband revealed his guilt about an incident that had happened long before he met his wife. When he was just twenty he had run over a four-year-old child. Although it was not his fault, the child had died, and he could not free himself of that guilt unconsciously, even though he had forgiven himself consciously at the time.

Couples who have had a deformed child are often unable to conceive a second time, although they may express a desire for another child. However, many people unconsciously believe that the deformed child was punishment for some sin yet to be expiated, so they are afraid of bearing another deformed child. Of course, unconscious guilt is not the only factor in such a case. Infertility could be directly linked to a conscious fear of deformity, whether it has actually happened before, runs in the family, or for other reasons.

Not Sure of Partner, Not Sure of Self

Couples who really are not committed to each other often cannot conceive although they may profess a commitment and anticipate a pregnancy. One man who had been married twice to women who eventually left him, ran around a lot and impregnated three other women. However, neither of his wives became pregnant, although both wanted to and both went on to have children by second husbands. Time was not a factor because he had been married for five years the first time and ten years the second time. Nor was he infertile. However, his marriages were, and his affairs indicated his lack of commitment. He wasn't sure of himself or his partners, and his partners certainly were not sure of him.

When we become parents, we give up a part of our previous identity as a childless couple as well as a certain amount of freedom. People who are very unsure of their identity or autonomy may fear, deep down, that they will lose themselves completely if they have a child. This is especially true for people who are very fused to their families of origin. They fear that a child would separate them from their families and, at the same time, they are jealous and afraid that a child would usurp their role or place in the family. So they would lose either themselves or their families if they reproduced.

Planned Nonpregnancies

All these *un*conscious reasons for not getting pregnant may also be conscious reasons for not wanting to get pregnant. In both situations, the choices are influenced by our pasts and our families in subtle ways.

People who choose to remain childfree simply may not like children. This isn't easy to admit because society in general, and our family and friends in particular, may feel there's something monstrous in such a decision. But people who feel that way probably should not have children, and modern medicine has made that choice a real option. The difficult part comes when we confront our parents with that choice. They may interpret it as a form of rejection—that we did not like being children or do not believe that they liked us when we were children. And that could be the case.

On the other hand, many couples consciously decide to change the family structure by refusing to perpetuate it. This may not be a negative decision at all, nor a rejection of the family of origin. The couple may view their decision as a challenge, an experiment that will open them up to different and more exciting experiences than their parents had. Many young couples see their parents as people unable to seize opportunities simply because they were tied down with children.

Although older parents may envy their offspring for having choices their generation lacked, they are more likely to feel that it is deviant and in need of justification. They may assume and even tell their peers that the young couple is sterile. Or they may do as one mother did throughout the long, childfree marriage of her son: suggest adoption. She started with Korean War orphans, went on to American Indians, then to Biafrans, Vietnamese, Cambodians, and so on. In between, she turned to worldwide natural disasters such as floods, famines, and earthquakes, suggesting that the survivors needed homes. The decision to have no children affects the family of origin as much as the decision to have them.

Many childless couples like children but derive even greater enjoyment from their careers, friends, or the freedom of their childfree life-style. They may not consciously decide to remain childfree, but they may defer pregnancy until it is really too late. For other couples, this decision has a political, cultural, or economic basis. They may feel strongly about overpopulation, the use or misuse of natural resources, or pessimistic about the world situation or even their friends' relationships with their children. One woman said she did not want children because she did not know one person who liked his or her parents or one parent who liked his or her kids. But this woman, who liked other people's children, was a career woman who found her work very rewarding and probably did not want anything to compete with that.

Some people find that they can be children in their adult lives to an extent that was not possible when they were children. This is particularly true of "parentified" children, those who had to act as parents to their own parents. When parents are excessively dependent, sickly, depressed, or unable to care for themselves or the family, their children have to take over the parent role. However, children are not equipped to meet the dependency needs of adults, and if they face such premature and excessive demands, they may not wish to become parents themselves, except possibly to a spouse who will baby them in return. The delight of finding oneself a child if one did not experience that as a real child can be a very strong motive for remaining childless.

On the other hand, people who have always been treated as a child in their families may be unwilling to give up that role. That may be reason enough not to change the situation by adding a child to the family. Protected, perhaps spoiled, by their families, they may marry, but show no interest in anyone who would compete with them for that role. In some cases, this may even serve the family's interests as well.

In times past, there was often one member of the family who never married, who was always available to take care of others' children, to help out around the house or houses, to support and care for their elderly parents. It was almost as if families chose and "saved" particular individuals for that caretaking role. Other family members would express surprise about that person's single state since he or she was so attractive, personable, or smart. But if that person was earmarked to care for others, there may have been benchmarks in his or her life that would reveal the family's resistance to other alliances on the part of that member. Perhaps there was a serious illness in the family when that person was about to marry, leave home, change jobs. Perhaps someone in the family got into financial difficulties when this special person was planning to leave home to go to college or to marry, forcing him or her to get a job instead. A series of such incidents might add up to a family member who is being saved to care for others. Today, these people can marry and defer childbearing. A spouse will not interfere with their caretaking mission, but a child would.

Then there are those who do not marry in order to avoid parenting, or who marry too late to have children. Some deep-seated fear of being a parent, or being infertile, or of being swallowed up by a child may motivate such decisions. Although this fear may represent the flip side of being "saved" by the family, it may also be an independent and unconscious factor for those people whose personal survival is a more overwhelming concern than the survival of either the family or the race.

The Haves and the Have Nots

The conscious and unconscious reasons for choosing or avoiding pregnancy underscore the link between this experience and others in our family life cycle. A couple is connected to other people in varying ways. The decision-making process involved in pregnancy, the reactions of other people, and the repercussions that arise all reveal patterns of interaction between the couple and within their families that are consistent with patterns seen during other periods of change. In the last chapter we saw a couple who took a long time to decide to marry, a long time to decide where to honeymoon—so long that they took their honeymoon three months after the wedding—and an even longer time to decide that they would have children. Although they drove their friends crazy with their indecision, it was a stabilizing and reassuring pattern for them. And as long as it works for them, they will continue to draw out the decision-making process.

In pregnancies, how a couple makes the decision—whether together or pulling in opposite directions—is very revealing and rooted in their family histories. One person may seem to decide that it is time to conceive, but in fact the pregnancy is actually and unconsciously sparked by a problem or need in the other person's life. For example, one woman became pregnant during her husband's last year in graduate school. They had planned to wait until he was set up in his field before having children, but they were delighted anyway. However, he couldn't finish school that year because he needed extra money to compensate for his wife's loss of salary. The following year he finished his course work and began his dissertation, but before he could really get started there was another child on the way. Once again, he couldn't actually get set up in his field. Worried about money, he took a job out of his field that became quite consuming, and he decided to forget the dissertation. He said that he and his wife wanted to have the children close together.

These two incidents don't add up to a pattern, but exactly the same thing happened when this couple got married. They were seniors in college, and he had been accepted into medical school. But after the wedding he decided to study microbiology instead; it was a shorter course. His very ambitious family was disappointed when he married and disappointed each time he lowered his career goals. They blamed his wife. When he was with them he blamed her too. But never to her face. He was doing what he wanted and what she wanted. They just were not very straight about it.

In reviewing or anticipating pregnancies it is important to consider all the aspects of the decision-making process as well as the conscious and unconscious motivations that may be involved. It is also revealing to compare that decision to a couple's other decisions, as well as the decisions made by their families of origins.

We can try to recall and analyze what our lives were like when our children were conceived and how we felt about each pregnancy. In other words, what was the context in which the pregnancy occurred—how were we getting along as a couple and what were our circumstances and those of our families? What was our reaction to the pregnancy, individually and as a couple, and what did we do about it? Were our circumstances or reactions in any way similar to our parents' when we were conceived? This will require some research but it is fascinating to discover similar patterns. For example, we may learn that we first conceived at the same age as our parents, or in similar circumstances—just out of school, on a new job, or in a strange city. We are not at all aware that we are repeating a pattern, yet these discoveries are a clue to our conscious and unconscious drive for indelibility.

We can also compare our behavior and our feelings now to our behavior at our wedding or at some other stage in the family life cycle. Do we react, respond, or make decisions in the same way during other life events? Perhaps other family members react to the news about our pregnancy exactly as they did to the news of our wedding or our divorce. This is how patterns are uncovered. One woman who searched her memory in this way realized that, among other things, she had informed her mother of her wedding, her husband of her pregnancy, and her daughter of her divorce in exactly the same way—after the fact. She simply could not share an important event with those close to her until it was a fait accompli. She also recalled that she always had been startled by similar revelations from her parents when she was a child, yet it hadn't occurred to her that she was doing the same thing.

The mere thought of pregnancy raises hidden forces throughout the entire family system because it is a decision that involves our families as well as ourselves. We identify with our parents, but they also identify with us. For our parents, the birth of a grandchild represents more than immortality or continuity of the family line. It also gives them a chance to relive, or at least observe, the process of childrearing once again. Unconsciously, they feel it is a chance to improve their past performance—to correct past mistakes or relive old successes. Interestingly, however, in spite of this wish, our parents encourage us to raise our children in much the same way they raised us, even when they admit to their mistakes.

And in this process, we can really see the core of the dynastic imperative, and the way in which it links generations in an indelible pattern.

Pregnant with Meaning

Pregnancy itself, however it comes about, churns up all the hidden forces. The new issues that a couple has to deal with raise the same underlying feelings that any change does. The major issue, around which all forces figuratively swirl, is the change from being a family of two to being a family of three. The three-person family is no longer linear; there is an added dimension that shapes it into a triangle. Introduce a third party into any relationship, and suddenly there is the potential for secrets, for alliances, and coalitions between any two members that exclude the third. A baby may seem to be a rather innocent party to any such complex dynamics, but each parent will have a relationship to the baby that is special, that is separate from the couple's relationship and from the relationship between the baby and the other parent. And the baby will have a different relationship to each parent and to the parents as a couple.

When there are just two people in the family everything that happens between them is known to both of them. The line between them is not necessarily straight—it could be broken, curved, or smudged. They may not communicate or even know all their fantasies and expectations about each other. But they will know what they say and do together. They will know everything that happens to them as a family. They each will know the total history of the family.

When a new person enters the scene, the history of the family will never again be known by any one person. No one can possibly know every facet of the relationship between two other people. Even if we were to observe every interaction we could not be privy to the special nonverbal undercurrents that connect two people to each other. Although the threesome can be a strong, supportive, open group, it can easily splinter into two and one, simply because two is a more natural and intimate grouping than three. Although this triangulation is very enriching, it is the same dynamic that operates in scapegoating—when two people blame a third person for the conflicts between them rather than taking any personal responsibility.

Making psychological room for the baby is the major task of pregnancy. The couple has to start expanding their borders before the baby actually arrives. The way in which they do this is related both to patterns they have developed earlier in their relationship and to the impact that the forces of power, love, dependency, separation, and autonomy have on them during this time. For example, decision making throughout the pregnancy will be related to other, previous decisions—the decision to get pregnant, to get married, to buy a house, to take a certain job, and so on. The same partner who made all the decisions about the wedding and reception might also decide how the baby will be born—in a hospital or at home, using general anesthesia, natural childbirth, and so on. If the person who made all the decisions at the wedding now makes none of them, perhaps the relationship has changed in ways that can be noted and used. Perhaps the balance of power has shifted and is now shared or reversed in ways that are a barometer of the marriage's health. In the countless decisions made during a pregnancy there are revealing clues to communication between the couple, their relationships to their families and friends, the interactional patterns they have adopted, and the sense of power each feels in their immediate situation.

Just thinking about making physical room for the baby gives some indication of the range of decisions that have to be made. One couple was very thorough in investigating hospital services and facilities, interviewing doctors and midwives, talking to friends and associates about the best possible birth. But they had no room for the baby. They lived in a one-bedroom apartment that did *not* contain a cradle, crib, bassinet, carriage, infant seat, or snuggly. They had no baby clothes, blankets, diapers, creams, powders, pins, or any of the other items most people start collecting before the actual birth. It was as if they thought the experience would culminate in the birth, rather than start there.

Eventually, the man's mother came to the rescue—much as she had at their wedding, when they spent all their time on the guest list and the invitations and never planned the actual event. She took them shopping and told them what they needed. They ceded her that power because they could never quite deal with the *reality* of a major change.

The most difficult aspect in making room for a baby surfaces in the area of affection. The appearance of a third person necessitates the redistribution of affection and the expression of love. It doesn't mean that there will be less love, but that often is the fear prospective parents have. Most parents start to love the baby before it is born. This is especially true for women, who turn inward at some point in the pregnancy to prepare themselves for mothering. Many men feel left out at this time and become more susceptible to affairs to reassure themselves that they are still loved or desirable.

An affair at this time can also provide protection against over-identification with their wives. Some men respond to their wives' growing interest in the child and her creative abilities to actually bear the child by becoming like her. But this raises doubts about masculinity and may lead to masculine acting out—having affairs, driving too fast, drinking too much—to guard against feelings of passivity or homosexuality. Both men and women sometimes turn to their families of origin for the extra love and affection that they seem to need at this time, especially if they are having trouble getting it from each other. Seeking affection can become quite circular. A man seeks it outside the marriage because his wife doesn't seem interested in him, and then she has to seek it outside because he isn't available.

Most of us need more affection during pregnancy because the birth of a child is the birth of the child in us. Pregnancy awakens longings to be taken care of in both men and women. The desire to be loved, protected, and nurtured—feelings that we may have thought we outgrew—come rushing at us. These never-ending dependency needs are compelling now that we are preparing to take on the care of a totally dependent person. Thinking about a child also generates thoughts about being a child, and we begin to relive our own childhood. This is very important if we are to be empathetic, instinctive parents, but it is a shock to actually feel like a child. Both men and women can be overcome by the need to be babied during this time. One of the important things prospective parents can do—even the strongest, most self-sufficient of them—is to get that babying from each other, from family, from friends.

Separation becomes a real issue when the baby actually leaves its mother's womb, but a foretaste of that feeling of loss develops as parents begin to separate from their roles as nonparents. We lose a role in becoming parents and, because we tend to concentrate on the roles we gain, such as mother and father, we often pay little attention to those we lose. But the pain of loss exists on some level. Eager acceptance of the parenting role does not mean that we won't miss the childfree role. Nor does it mean that we will lose our roles as husband and wife when we become mother and father. Although we are no longer exactly the same couple we were, it is important to retain a sense of our role as spouse as well as parent.

The new demands on us, many of which we may not have realized, make us envy our own unpregnant state. This ambivalence continues through pregnancy and parenthood, generating doubts about the decision itself and what we gave up to become parents. These doubts will be especially dominant if we gave up our roles as husband and wife or are having other difficulties. When we feel especially dependent, unloved, or powerless, feelings of loss usually increase. On the other hand, loss is essential for growth.

Sometimes when we change and develop we try disastrously not to lose anything in the process. One woman who managed to do this temporarily drove herself and everyone around her to the brink. She survived, largely because her very supportive husband recognized what was happening and was able to fill in when she couldn't. She was a very ambitious woman, just having success in her field, who was surprised to find herself pregnant. She went ahead with the pregnancy because she had always meant to have a child and it seemed inevitable. But she acted as if she were not pregnant. She did not change her diet, her routine, her activities. She rushed around to meetings and conferences. She never slept. She managed to have the baby and return to her job over a weekend. She nursed the baby in her office, and her husband, a freelance writer, came in when she had to be out of the office. Sometimes they would all run off to one of her dinner or evening meetings.

Six months later, when she suffered a total physical breakdown, she finally sat down to think about rearranging her life. She wanted to be a parent, a career woman, a wife, and an individual, but she had to learn how to separate these roles, rather than piling all of them on top of each other. Fearful of losing any one role and thereby her identity, she carried them all around with her at all times.

Finally, prospective parents must make room for the baby by defining the borders of the new family. Most couples have their own borders, their individual sense of autonomy that sets them apart from other couples, from other family members. Now, couples have to decide where they will stand as a threesome in relation to others. Many people experience a new involvement with their families when they become pregnant. They want extra attention or care. They are aware that they are ensuring their parents' survival through their child. Other couples do not want family involvement but feel that the family is now demanding it.

Another common change for parents-to-be is their relationship with friends. Friendships may strengthen or weaken, often depending on whether or not our friends have children. Because pregnancy increases our need for support and empathy, we may find that friends with children are more helpful and understanding than our childless friends. But this is not necessarily the case. One couple, who were the first in their social set to have a pregnancy, brought everyone into the act. They were very concerned that both single and married friends share their pregnancy and the birth. They lived in and ran an experimental community school, and both children and adults were around day and night. Everyone was informed of the pregnancy and watched it develop. Care of the mother and the baby was the topic of classroom discussions. The birth was to be at home—in the school—and everyone was briefed on what would be needed and what to expect. Everything went as planned. The doctor came to the school in the evening and helped the father deliver a healthy, eight-pound boy. Then the new mother got up, took a shower, and the new family walked into the school's community room where the school community was waiting to toast and congratulate them. That baby was to become part of the community and was held and cared for by all the members as well as by his parents.

This case actually represents an interesting new form that the dynastic imperative has taken, both in alternative life-style families and recently in more traditional families. This couple lived far away from either parents or siblings. But they had created a family anyway. Their friends, the people in the school, and the children they taught had all become part of their extended family—the modern extended family. Some of these people even played roles similar to those from their actual extended family. And there was an older woman among their friends who reminded each of them of their older sisters both in temperament and in relation to them. Autonomy does not necessarily mean drawing a line around the new threesome. It can mean extending the circle.

Dream Work

The emotional impact of the hidden forces is often reflected in our dreams during pregnancy as well as at transition points in the family life cycle. In interpreting our dreams during these times, the psychoanalytic content is less significant than two other obvious and important aspects of dreaming itself. First of all, the manifest content of dreams—symbols, events, places, and people—often tells us what and who we are thinking about. Secondly, the fact that we are dreaming indicates that we are troubled by issues or problems on an unconscious, if not also conscious, level.

The sharing and comparing of dreams in families can be enormously important, especially when verbal communication does not reach the real issues. In some families, during times of stress, we find everyone dreaming all the time—often about the same things. Although individual interpretations for each family member differ, the common elements in their dreams may reveal an awareness of tension or change that they are not conscious of or able to express.

Maria Temple, twenty-eight and pregnant for the first time, had no ambivalence about the pregnancy. She was ready, her husband was ready, and they were very happy to be having a child. Still, there were some very natural concerns that showed up in four of Maria's dreams over the course of her pregnancy. In reviewing her dreams, we can see the kinds of anxieties she had and the way in which they manifested themselves.

Dream One: My Body, Myself. Maria dreamed that she had a room on the fourteenth floor of a New York hotel. The place reminded her of a Russian émigré apartment building, although she could not later say why she thought so. She had assumed that the fourteenth floor was the top floor and that her room would be quite swanky. She got on the elevator, which was outside the building. It had no glass. In fact, it had nothing; it was just a frame. It started up rapidly. Maria could not stop it. It zoomed to the fifty-fifth floor. When it finally stopped, it tipped onto its side and Maria was hanging from the frame. She had to pull herself up it in order to get out. She found herself in a very posh penthouse full of beautiful people. These were not her people. She found an inside elevator and woke up.

Maria had been married for a little over a year to a man with whom she had lived for a couple of years before that. They married partly because they both were ready to have children. Maria was an artist who had always wanted to be a mother and, indeed, was seen by her friends as very motherly. She was warm, open, and nurturing. She and her husband, both their families, and all their friends were very happy about the pregnancy. All was going as planned.

In the dream, Maria's size is represented by the rapidly rising elevator. She thought she was going to the fourteenth floor, but she moves quickly and uncontrollably to the fifty-fifth. The tipping elevator mirrors her own uncertain sense of balance as she grows bigger. She could fall; she has to hold onto the frame. The room she finally enters is full of beautiful people, not the émigrés with whom she could be comfortable. She has to leave.

In other words, pregnancy is not always what we expect. It can throw us off, physically and mentally. Maria's change in size and the consequent change in how she sees herself (as exemplified in the dream) are natural reactions to the changes that pregnancy brings. A pregnant woman feels different, looks different, and may not be sure where she fits in. Even the happiest and most confident woman feels a bit disoriented and unsure. Body image is self-image, at least in part. Becoming lumpy or distended affects that image, as does fatigue, morning sickness, or other symptoms of pregnancy.

Interestingly, many men also share some of these pregnancy symptoms. They become fatigued in the first trimester and may develop nausea, backaches, headaches, and upset stomachs. In fact, many expectant fathers gain weight. Although this may be a result of keeping up with their wives, eating the same food at the same time, some men actually say that they are drinking more milk or not smoking "for the baby."

One man, whose wife was six months pregnant, took to his bed complaining of fatigue. He had gastric distress throughout the pregnancy. He couldn't work, he slept all the time, and he drank only milk. By the eighth month he was talking about premature babies, and soon after that he was hospitalized with acute abdominal pain. No physical cause for his symptoms was found.

Most men do not identify with their wives to this degree nor act out their dependency needs in quite so straightforward a fashion. But there does seem to be a corollary between creation and procreation, and for many men it is manifested by more energy, harder work, greater creativity in whatever they do. A man may also begin to doubt himself as he is flooded with envy for his wife's childbearing capacity or with memories of his own childhood. Some men feel repulsed by the physical changes in their partners, possibly because these changes revive memories of their mothers when they were pregnant with unwanted siblings. Wives, in becoming mothers, and husbands, in becoming fathers, remind their partners of their own mothers or fathers, raising old oedipal fears.

Dream Two: A Whale of a Change. Maria and a friend were waiting on the shore for a boat. Then they unaccountably missed it. They tried to swim for it. The water was shallow in places, and they ran along, yelling and waving at the boat. Maria's friend got closer and closer to the boat but farther and farther from Maria. Her friend made it and turned to look back at Maria. Maria was getting nowhere. Suddenly she realized that was because she was standing on a whale. The whale was very slippery and very, very large. Much larger than she imagined possible. She woke up.

Maria's dream symbolizes not only her concern about being bigger than she thought she would be, but also her concern about the huge responsibility that she is taking on in becoming a mother. She is struggling to take on the role of parent and leave behind the role of nonparent. Maria planned to continue painting after the baby was born, but in the dream her friend, a nonparent and an artist, is getting ahead of her. Maria is afraid that the enormity of motherhood will cause her to miss the boat. Dreams like this illustrate the very real concerns of a pregnant woman, but they may also be preparatory in some way, paving the way for her acceptance of the new role.

Just thinking about motherhood seems to inspire a need to be mothered during pregnancy. Indeed, the main task for expectant fathers is to mother the expectant mother. Women want to be cared for, and they may also be unable to do certain chores that they did before. They want support and help from the father-to-be. This can be difficult for some prospective fathers because they feel that their masculinity is threatened by "women's work." As one man put it, while doing the laundry, "I can't get her to act like a woman." Furthermore, men also have a need to be cared for, which grows as the baby does. Fathers identify with both their wives and their children. Both parents identify with their own parents, and they identify their partners with their parents. All these identifications raise questions and necessitate choices about the kind of parents we want to be for the child who will probably be like us, needing what we needed and may still need.

Single mothers also need "mothering," which they may get from their own mothers, other relatives, or from friends. Young women who get pregnant while living at home may find that their family is too angry or ashamed to be very supportive. Sometimes a clinic or women's group can offer the necessary emotional support, as well as new models of mothering for a young woman whose own mother cannot help her.

Dream Three: Blessed Event. Three weeks before her baby was born, Maria dreamed that she had given birth to a canary. It was a very healthy bird. She checked it all over for any irregularities. It had beautiful feathers, well-formed wings, and funny little toes. It was normal. But it kept trying to fly away when she tried to cover it with its blanket. Then she realized that she had given birth to a canary.

Maria's fear of having a deformed child is a very common concern in the dreams of men and women in the last few weeks before birth. They want to see the child they have been living with all these months, and they do not want to see it. Mothers fear the separation of this creature from their womb. They worry about caring for this baby. Can they meet its needs? And fathers wonder if they can meet the needs of their wives. What if they have to deliver the baby? Can they do their part during labor? Both parents want to know the child's sex, who it will look like, and a hundred other things.

This obsession with the child in the last weeks may also serve to distract a couple from each other. Many people do not have, or do not want to have, sex as birth approaches. Some people, even doctors, believe that a baby can be harmed by sex, which is not true. Although physical discomfort may eliminate sexual activity, a more likely motivation is our growing concern about our new roles as parents. Few of us see our parents as sexual people. There is a cultural or psychological schism between being a parent and being sexual. Pregnancy itself, and the role changes it brings, affects our sexual identities throughout the nine months. Women who never really enjoyed sex before sometimes feel that they can relax and enjoy it now that their designated role of mother is set. Men who are envious of, or excited by, their wife's relationship to the child sometimes have an overwhelming desire to get in with the child. But, as the delivery approaches, many of us feel a certain dynastic confusion about who we are as sexual partners and parents, who our partners are, and who our parents were. If we see our partner, the father-to-be, as our own father, we don't want sex with him.

Dream Four: Mother's Milk. Maria woke up in a strange room and realized that she had had the baby. Her husband and a friend were there. The place seemed to be a sex motel with sparkling fountains. Her friend told her that they were paying $67.50 an hour for the room. There was no towel under her, and the baby was not at her breast. The placenta, which she had intended to plant, had disintegrated. Maria went to look for the baby. The sex motel turned into a big house with lots of rooms, all full of friends but no baby. She finally found the baby and he could already talk. He was not interested in the apricot juice that her breasts seemed to be producing. Maria realized that she did not have to go to her piano lesson after all so she just relaxed, sat down, nursed the now-docile baby, and fell asleep.

Maria had this dream two nights before giving birth to a healthy seven-and-a-half-pound baby boy who grew up to like milk, apricot juice, and his mother. The dream seemed to express almost every concern of the expectant mother. Maria's fears and doubts about her sexuality were expressed by finding herself in a sex motel. Her uncertainty about the delivery that cost $67.50 seems justified. Her fear of losing the child is apparent in the fact that he's not there in the beginning of the dream. Her doubts about her ability to mother the child came out in the apricot juice. A child who can already talk and will not nurse seems to symbolize both her own hostility toward the child and her fear of rejection by him. The fact that no one seems concerned reflects her sense of isolation as she nears delivery, even though her husband is actually right by her side. When she stops worrying about her piano lesson in the dream, things improve. Perhaps she doesn't really need lessons—she seems able to be a mother after all.

Something Old, Something New

Childfree families who do not go through this time of making room for another express the dynastic imperative in other ways. For example, in *Who's Afraid of Virginia Woolf?* the all-American couple, George and Martha, spend much of their long marriage talking about and to their fantasized son. A more common way of forming a triangle is to have a pet who is coddled, cared for, blamed, and who never answers back. But triangles are not always necessary. Some couples play child and parent, parent and child to each other. They may baby each other. This is not a predominant mode of behavior for childfree couples by any means, but it can be a clue to the way a family perpetuates itself. For example, the son of a single mother married a woman who did not want children so that he and his wife could be just as cozy as he and his mother had been. That way he did not have to leave home.

Couples without children sometimes put their energies into their roles as aunts and uncles. For all these people and their families, there are usually precedents for their choices and subsequent behavior. A look back at the family tree or at the social network of the family will reveal someone else who did not have children and, for some reason, served as a model for the next generation.

Events concerning pregnancy—conscious and unconscious decision making, expected and unexpected issues, and our reactions to them as a couple and as a family, the manifestations of hidden forces and their impact on family patterns—make up a stage in the family life cycle of which pregnancy itself is a part. The actual birth of a child raises new and unforeseen complexities. But that does not diminish the importance of this stage as a rehearsal for coming to grips with our own unanticipated reactions to our decisions. Learning to see and integrate hidden feelings, both old ones and new ones, is the stepping-stone to another stage. This psychological preparation for having a child or not having a child readies us for the next stage, whether we spend it with new or old family members.

8

❧◈❧

Stage Three:
And Baby Makes Three

The arrival of a baby sparks the beginning of a new family system. The way in which we communicate, solve problems, and act as a group develops out of the immediate experience of being a threesome, our history of interacting as a twosome, and our past experience in other groups, particularly our families of origin. We set up new coalitions and alliances. We behave differently. Although much of what we do in the excitement and exhaustion of early childrearing seems haphazard or merely expedient, our actions often reveal more than we realize. And many of the patterns we now adopt, for both conscious and unconscious reasons, can become fixed.

Doing Whatever Works

That's what a great many new parents find themselves doing in the rush, elation, and fatigue of having a new baby. All our fantasizing and theorizing about the kind of child we want to have and the kind of parent we want to be seems suddenly irrelevant when we are confronted with the actual experience. All of a sudden something has to be done now—a hundred times a day. To avoid being swamped by demands from the baby, from each other, and from relatives and friends, our natural and instinctual desire is to maintain equilibrium at a time when we seem most in danger of going under. The point of family systems is to keep everything steady. As groups of people living together, we find ways to live with each other's individual needs, minimize our differences, work together. When there is a new baby, we have to find new ways to accommodate the new member into the system.

What you do to meet the needs of your child is generally based on current expert opinion about childbearing. *How* you do it reflects family patterns. Whether you choose the bottle or the breast is less important than *who* makes that decision and how it is implemented. A woman who acceded to her husband's wish that they bottle-feed the baby so that he could share that activity, held the baby facing away from her when she fed him. Much later she realized that she did not want the baby to see her being an inadequate mother, for she believed a good mother breast-fed her babies. Such self-denigration was not new for this woman, nor for her unconsciously conspiring husband. She often let him make decisions she later regretted. He said he wanted to share the childrearing, but actually he wanted to do it all. He needed to be better at everything than she was, including being a better mother. A system in which he made most of the decisions had worked well enough for them before they had the baby, but it did not work well afterwards. She was unhappy, and the baby was unhappy with her. Her awkward way of holding him made it hard for him to digest his food, and he cried and fretted until his father came home from work and fed him properly.

A friend pointed this out to this woman and showed her how to hold the baby. Although it was hard for the mother to change, she eventually did so and, as the baby became more peaceful and content, she became more confident and relaxed. Oddly enough, so did the father. His lack of trust in his wife betrayed his ambivalence about being dependent on a woman he did not respect. Her growing confidence reassured him about his choice of her.

If a couple decides to let their baby cry for exactly ten minutes each night before he either goes to sleep or they pick him up, the issue is not whether ten is the right number of minutes but how that decision is made, who picks him up, and what happens next. This shows how things get done in this family, what roles each member, including the baby, plays, and how effectively this family system meets the needs of all its members. It is also possible to predict the kinds of systems a family will develop. If the child is the exclusive focus of the family during the early months of childrearing, a child-centered system is likely to evolve. If the family makes an effort to keep the child quiet when the father is around, a father-centered system may prevail. If the family protects the mother from the baby's total dependency on her, a mother-centered system would take hold. These may not be the best family systems but they meet the underlying psychological needs of family members. Family systems do not have to work well to work.

It is hard to believe that our spontaneous and instinctive reactions to new babies could mean so much. It all happens so fast and, seemingly, so randomly. But the responses of today are the systems of tomorrow. What works with this situation will be tried again and, if it works again, tried yet again. Our behavior becomes set, patterns become automatic, then habitual. We are usually too busy to notice what is happening because we are only thinking about keeping everybody—our baby, our family, our friends, ourselves—happy.

Subsystems—The New Math

Families take on new shapes when they add members. The straight line between two people opens up to form triangles, rectangles, squares, parallelograms, hexagons, and so on. Then, because children tend to tie us in new ways to other family members and to friends, there are circles within circles and spirals of potential interactions. This new geometry gives us dynamics that did not exist before and pairings that were not previously possible.

Subsystems are the structural arrangements that evolve in families as a way of dealing with each other. They can be negative coalitions, as when two people scapegoat a third. They can be positive alliances in which two or more people join together to offer support or problem solving for the group. They can also be pairings of a temporary or permanent character, where some people always or occasionally work together while others never do. People who say they have good family relationships may be betrayed by their actions. People who never talk, look at, or touch each other probably do not have strong alliances. Those who continually fight, scream at, or hit each other have a strong, destructive bond. Families with relatively little verbal interaction can still be very powerfully connected. Any observant individual—a family member or an outsider—can uncover the nature of these subsystems by watching a family interact.

The Parental Subsystem

He comes home every night between five thirty and six o'clock. He kisses his kids and asks them what they did today. They follow him, reporting on their activities as he moves into the kitchen to greet his wife. He kisses her and then moves upstairs to change into some old clothes, responding as he does so to his children's stories about their day. Then he returns to the kitchen to mix a large pitcher of martinis. In the meantime, his wife has organized the dinner, which they will eat at approximately seven thirty, combed her hair and tidied up. Husband and wife move into the den where they sit down in their chairs, sip their martinis, and talk for the next hour or so. The children do not accompany them. It is understood that this is the parents' hour.

Private time is a vital ingredient for the marital relationship. It provides "refueling" for both parents. It brings the working parent who is away all day back into the family, and it provides breathing space for the stay-at-home parent. People who spend all their time with little children get depleted. It takes enormous concentration to figure out and respond to the needs of children. Stay-at-home parents need to build up their reserves by interacting with another adult, hearing about adult problems, and responding to adult concerns. Working parents, who have spent all day away from their children, need to feel they are part of the family, that their outside perspective is valuable, that the events of their days are of interest, too. When both parents work away from home, the parental coalition serves as a bridge back into the family, reassuring each of them of their roles and identities, as well as confirming that they are real people, attractive, intelligent, interesting, and doing a good job as parents, workers, lovers, and so on. When both parents work at home, the parental coalition helps them affirm their identities as separate from the family identity.

There are all kinds of parental partnerships. One couple never talked in the formalized style of the couple above, but their children always knew not to interrupt when their parents were "having a chat," which they did three or four times a week, usually in the kitchen before each left for work. Another couple never talked at all but their thrilling sex life, after the children went to sleep and at naptime on Sunday afternoons, supplied the confirmation and support they needed. A divorced couple, who had joint custody of their children, spoke on the phone once or twice a week about each of their three children and their own work. Single parents cannot form parental partnerships, but they can develop alliances with other adults that provide the same kind of refueling, reinforcement, and reassurance that a parental subsystem does.

Parents have to complement each other in childrearing. This is generally a matter of dividing responsibilities, a luxury single parents may not have. In many of the more traditional parental relationships, the mother takes care of the children and the father provides economic support. In a growing number of families, the nurturing and providing roles are divided equally, and in still others, the roles are completely reversed. Parents who choose a less traditional division of roles find the transition easier if they had a model in their family of origin. The sons of women who work, for example, can share childrearing with their working wives much more readily than the sons of women who do not work. But the strength of the parental relationship is particularly important if neither parent has a model for their new role. Men and women who deviate from parental models, or who do not have peer support for new roles, need to bolster each other in finding and accepting such roles.

The kinds of roles ultimately worked out are less important than *how* they are worked out. Often, our ideas about childrearing are not reflected in the reality. We thought we'd share everything, but we find that one of us always changes the baby's diapers, one of us always holds the crying baby, one of us always takes the baby to the doctor. One young mother expected to deal with all her baby's nighttime needs but found, to her surprise, that her husband handled it instead. Whatever works is best. We make hundreds of adaptations to each other and the baby in the early months. Some of these become habits that are automatically repeated in new situations and with new babies. They also form the basis for each family's individual definition of the mother and father roles. The understanding and acceptance of each parent's role is the core of the parental partnership.

Threats to the Parental Subsystem

Triangulation is a process that may occur when a problem or a conflict between two people is deflected into a third. It is the avoidance of confrontation; anything unpleasant is directed at the third person or object. A childfree couple, for example, might use a friend, someone's lover, a relative, or even drugs or work to avoid each other. If there is strife in a marriage already, or if it develops around the addition of a member, parents may be too upset, confused, and frightened to do anything but blame the baby. We won't try to convince you that a tiny baby senses this conflict and becomes colicky, sleepless, or withdrawn. We have noticed that there is some correlation between a particularly demanding or unhappy child and parents who seemed relieved to worry about the baby rather than themselves. And, certainly later in family life, a "bad" or "sick" child is often a sign of a "bad" or "sick" marriage.

(A bad marriage does not necessarily mean a bad parental coalition. The parents could be held together by their powerful insistence on blaming their child for their own marital problems.) In any case, triangulation can occur whenever the emotional relationship between two family members is so rocky that incorporation of a third party is the only hope for stability.

The outside world can also present a threat to the parental partnership. Incursions from relatives and friends full of advice about childrearing can undermine the trust parents have in one another. Grandparents are the most likely offenders.

A woman whose daughter went back to work a month after her baby was born while the husband stayed home to care for the child, told her best friend that Ken just wasn't much of a "provider" so her daughter had to go to work. Meanwhile, *his* mother told her bridge club that Ken was unhappy, that his wife was not very "motherly," and that he had to take over. Mary and Ken knew what their mothers were going to say before it even happened. They also knew that they were doing what was right for them. They were tailoring their roles and responsibilities flexibly to a changing time, their time. They were not reflecting their parents' standards from a different time. But they were not immune to what they accurately perceived as their parents' feelings of rejection. They had to maintain their own positive view of their parental partnership, and they had to convince their mothers that what they had done as mothers was right, too. They had to convince that generation that they had learned how to be good parents from them.

The Parent-Child Subsystem

There are two types of relationships between parents and children: that between each parent and each child, and that between each child and the parental subsystem. The bond between a child and the parental subsystem is demonstrated every time parents help their child, as when one parent supports a newly walking toddler across a room to the other parent. This dynamic is seen over and over again as children learn the rules for mastering their physical world. Later, parents team up to teach children the family's rules and societal rules in the same concerted and creative way.

When there is conflict in the parental subsystem the child may be scapegoated, creating a triangle in which the parents together or separately will blame the child for their own problems. When parents are fighting or angry at one another, they often regulate the tension between them by suddenly noticing and attacking their child's behavior or actions. An outsider or the informed insider can literally see this happen over and over again. A perceptive child will often take advantage of weakness in a parental relationship by playing one parent off against the other, asking mother for what father won't allow and vice versa.

The relationship between each child and each parent is part of the family's secret life. No longer can any one person know everything about the family because no one person can know what goes on between any other two people. The arrival of a baby means that each parent has a relationship to the baby of which the other parent isn't part. This can strengthen the family group by introducing another line of support and another combination that will eventually help solve family problems. Large families have the advantage of a greater number of subsystems and options. However, it can also weaken the group later on if one parent forms a strong alliance with the child that excludes the other parent completely. The child is caught in the middle and spends much of his or her time taking sides, thereby weakening the bond between the group as a whole.

The strength of each parent-child relationship is based, to a large extent, on the parent's degree of honesty, love, and respect for the child's individuality. One of the most important elements in meeting the needs of children is the ability to empathize with them, to remember, if only in a general way, what it felt like to be a child. This is especially important during the early years when a child's verbal communication is limited. If we can remember or re-create feelings of helplessness or discomfort, it is easier to comfort a child, even though we may not know specifically what he or she is feeling. In later years, the actual memory of how we felt when our youngest sister was born, how our parents reacted to our games or misbehavior, what we liked to play with our friends, fosters a strong bond with our own children.

Single parents sometimes forge an unconscious coalition with a child to meet the needs of their special circumstances. In one case, the young son of a single mother was exceptionally good. Of course, he may have been constitutionally "good" anyway—not everything can be attributed to psychology. But it is interesting to note that his mother "needed" an especially well-behaved child. She was a live-in nurse who cared for people after hospitalization or childbirth. Because she had a child, many potential employers were not interested in her services. Only by guaranteeing that her child would be no trouble could she find jobs. And he was good. He would sit in his playpen and beam at the world. He seemed cheerful and contented. He developed quite normally, although he spoke early and walked late, both conveniences to his mother. He was a curious child but never so curious that he left the room, house, or yard where he was supposed to stay. He was toilet trained in a few days. He was a very, very easy and good child. He seemed to understand that his behavior determined the survival of his small family. His mother would take care of him if he did exactly what she wanted. They formed a coalition of two against the world.

Threats to the Parent-Child Subsystem

Overidentification with a child, seeing that child as an extension of yourself, can negatively affect the parent-child relationship and the child's development of autonomy. For example, one young woman carried her baby around constantly and never really left him alone. She explained that the baby needed to be held, but that didn't seem to be the case. It seemed more likely that she herself needed physical affection and couldn't express herself in any other way. Unfortunately, her confusion over who needed what created an unbalanced family system. Her child became extremely dependent on her and distrustful of others, and her husband felt rejected and left out. He felt that neither the child nor the mother needed or even liked him.

It is difficult to be a good parent if we act only on our needs and not the child's. Although children offer parents the chance to relive and rework childhood, confusion about identity can hurt the relationship both between parent and child and between parent and parent.

Equally dangerous is the possibility of identifying the child with one of her siblings, treating the child as if he or she were our younger brother or sister. This is a form of transference. A woman who hated her younger brother came into therapy because she feared that the child she was carrying would be a boy. Her first child had been a girl, much like herself. She wanted to spare her daughter the kind of relationship she had had with her own brother. She also wanted to protect the unborn child from her hatred and free herself of the guilt she was already feeling. The therapist insisted that she bring in both her husband and young daughter in order to strengthen the relationships that already existed, especially the parental partnership, since she mostly seemed to fear becoming a child herself and losing her sense of being a parent. Indeed, that was the weak link that therapy was able to bolster.

It seemed that her husband had had some business reverses that threatened his own image as provider, making it more difficult for him to help his wife during this pregnancy. Much of the therapy hinged on the couple's recognition of their success as capable parents of their bright, happy, little girl. The therapist also helped them understand how old business, in this instance unresolved guilt feelings about continuing sibling rivalry, can become a current issue when there is too much stress on the family system.

If there is no parental partnership, as in the case of single parents, or a weak parental partnership, the parent-child relationship could be used as a substitute. Although the parent may benefit, the child really needs a parent more than a friend. This type of relationship is more evident in later years in parents who pride themselves on being "friends" with their children. There is nothing inherently wrong in friendships with our children, but if we insist on using children to compensate for relationships with other adults, we rob the child of the support, the role model, and the protection he or she needs from a parent.

The Child-Child Subsystem

Babies recognize and respond to brothers and sisters very early. They can separate them from the family group because they are so much closer in size. And siblings have lots of feelings about a new baby. We are all familiar with the older sibling who responds to the birth of a baby by acting like a baby, too. In an attempt to capture some of the attention the baby is getting, this child may "forget" that she or he is toilet trained or might demand to be picked up and carried around again. Parents usually respond to these transparent messages by spending more time with their "neglected" children until the threat of competition disappears.

Parents affect the sibling relationship through their own experience with siblings. The mother of two daughters, for example, who comes from a family of two daughters, will have expectations for the relationship between her children based on her childhood relationship with her sister. One mother who had a very distant, cold relationship with her sister hoped that if she had two girls they would be close. Her first child was a girl and, as if to give her fantasy every chance, she became pregnant again just ten months later. The second child was a girl and the sisters did become close. We can't say that closeness in age determined the type of relationship they developed, but that factor, combined with parental expectations, certainly had some influence.

Our sibling order and the relationships that grow out of it affect our future relationships with people outside the family. Although there are many variables concerning sibling order, many of us find that our friends and lovers have the same or complementary sibling position that we do. Oldest children are attracted to other firstborns, and children who grew up with older siblings feel more comfortable with older friends. We form natural connections with them. However, intelligence, physical size and special circumstances in any particular family may negate this principle. A larger, stronger, younger brother may become the protector of his older brothers and in some ways their elder. A mentally retarded firstborn child will seem like a younger sibling, and the secondborn in the family will take on the characteristics of leadership and authority usually found in a firstborn. But on the whole, sibling relationships are very important to the development of family systems, to the relationships with peers later in life, and in the future families our children will form.

Threats to the Child-Child Subsystem

The greatest threat to positive sibling relationships comes from parents. Parents who favor or scapegoat one child or form an exclusive coalition with one may cut that child off from a trusting sibling relationship. Although siblings will often stick together anyway, they may risk a loss of parental love through loyalty to each other. This is demonstrated in some divorce cases where parents use the children against each other. The children cannot win. They're going to lose one parent and one or more siblings whatever the outcome.

Parents also affect these relationships less directly. Our own sibling relationships are not lost on our children. If we do not get along with our own brothers and sisters, our children may not think that it is very rewarding or worthwhile to expect much from their own brothers and sisters. If we do turn to our siblings for advice and support, our children will probably do the same. If a wife is close to her brother and her husband thinks her brother is boring and doesn't want to spend time with him, the children have a choice. They can agree with either their mother or father, and they can model their own relationships after either of these parental models. Whatever the children do, their choices can be observed in how they play, fight, and get along together.

The Intergenerational Subsystems

The strongest family relationships are sometimes forged between two generations—grandparent to grandchild. These depend, to a large extent, on how often grandparents are seen and the proximity of the two families. Parental expectations will affect intergenerational connections much in the same way that they affect sibling relationships. A parent who was very close to her or his grandparents may hope that her or his children will have a similar experience. A person whose own child had a strong bond with a grandparent may hope to have that kind of relationship with a grandchild.

A man who had two children of his own nevertheless had a very special relationship with his brother's youngest son. The boy was very athletic. In fact, he was the only one of his generation who had any interest or ability in sports. The uncle had also been athletic and, although his activities were now limited by age and responsibilities, he had not forgotten his record in the high jump or lost his love of basketball. The boy's parents had no interest in sports so he turned to his uncle for encouragement and support. His uncle took him to all the games, watched him practice, and bought him equipment. This relationship didn't take the place of the boy's relationship with his own father, but it gave him something extra. And for the uncle it was a different expression of the dynastic imperative from the one he shared with his own children.

Threats to Intergenerational Subsystems

Distance is certainly one threat to the formation of bonds with other relatives. It is much easier to form affectionate helping relationships based on common interests when there is physical proximity. However, if the parents or the boy described above did not like the uncle, even geographic convenience would not help the relationship. So family distance, literally or psychologically, can certainly be a threat.

A lack of generational boundaries is another threat. If grandparents act as parents in their relationships with grandchildren, the line of authority that connects parents and children becomes unclear and confusing to the child, and the whole family structure is weakened. A parent who does not want to be a parent may obliterate intergenerational boundaries by becoming a child. For example, a woman whose husband traveled a lot would pack up her children and move to her mother's house until he returned. Her mother was a nurse, and this woman had always been her patient. She had never really learned how to take care of herself or her children. She was able to manage when her husband was there to help, but without his support she became a child again. Her mother, therefore, could not become a grandparent because somebody had to be the parent in this family.

Adding Up the New Math

All these relationships illustrate a family's psychological structure and processes, and they are critical to an understanding of family functioning. Families are problem-solving groups that require clarity of leadership, authority, and communication. Structure, coalitions, alliances, and pairings are the most visible elements of family systems. Who sits next to whom? Who always sides with mother? Who joins with whom to criticize or poke fun at dad or one of the children? By watching a family group, even our own, we can actually see the shape of the family's interaction, where it is strong and where it breaks down.

In one family the strongest relationships developed along sex lines: men versus women in subgroups and pairs. Mother and daughter had a powerful alliance, father and his brother had another, grandson and grandfather had a third, and the oldest daughter and the new baby girl seemed on their way to forming a fourth. There was a weak parental partnership and considerable rigidity, so there was little affectionate interaction across sex lines from mother to son or grandfather to granddaughters, and so forth. The support and stability generated along these lines was negligible, but the same-sex relationships tended to work well.

At times, the family system did break down, leaving people irritable, frustrated, and unable to act, usually whenever the mother and father or another weakly linked pair had to work something out together. Thus, the older daughter could not seem to baby-sit responsibly for her brother, although she was fine with her baby sister. And the parents could never make a joint decision about family entertainment. They always had to cancel reservations or turn down invitations when the entire family was involved. These breakdowns were always handled the same way. After some distress and procrastination, the grandfather would be called in to baby-sit or help out with any male family members, or the parents would get the idea that it might be better for just the "boys" or just the "girls" to go on some expedition. Thus, conflicts and problems within the family were accommodated or compromised rather than genuinely resolved.

But a question remains: why can't some parents function adequately as leaders, as the executive subsystem of the family group? Why are dysfunctional coalitions formed? Evidently, they meet some underlying needs or are a response to unconscious forces that the family systems keep in check. This becomes apparent in the great stress that develops when a change in the system is required. That stress is a signal that more than behavior is being rearranged. Family interaction and structure represent the ways in which we suppress, express, or redress hidden motivational forces that threaten to upset our equilibrium.

Equilibrium and the Battle of the Hidden Forces

A new baby brings out new needs and a consequent rearranging of underlying psychological feelings. Most new parents are not aware of all their unconscious reactions. The arrival of a new baby can be energizing and also exhausting. Exhausting because lack of sleep and time is underscored by profound changes on a deeper level—changes that drain us of psychic energy just as the baby drains us physically, changes that lead to new family systems.

The Child-in-Us System

Ruth Nowita was still very tied to her own mother when her first child was born. She was not prepared to be a mother. Her husband, Dennis, was not prepared for her to be a mother. His mother had died when he was very young, and he had found a mother in Ruth. He was not ready to give her up or to be a parent himself. They were both stunned by the demands of their healthy and relatively undemanding baby boy.

Their response to the situation and the surprising feelings it evoked was to form a very strong, defensive parental coalition. Although they had been close before, they became obsessively and exclusively close in the first months after the baby was born. Ruth's mother took care of the baby while Ruth worked—and while she didn't. Ruth would come home from her part-time job, take a cursory look at the baby, sit down in the kitchen, and start talking to her mother. They would chat until Dennis got home. If the baby cried or woke up Ruth's mother took care of him. Ruth would give him a bottle, but she didn't hold him while doing so. She'd prop the bottle up on a pillow in his cradle so he could get at it and feed himself.

When Dennis came home, Ruth's mother left. Ruth began fixing dinner, and Dennis would sit in the kitchen talking with her. He would usually go into the baby's room and tickle him or watch him for a moment, but he never picked him up, and neither of them brought him into the room where they were. One of them would change his diapers, bathe him, get him a bottle, rock the cradle a little. But they rarely picked him up, cuddled him, or played with him. They were adequate parents, they met all his physical needs, but they really did not seem to notice him very much. All their efforts were directed at being a couple, not a family. Although they occasionally talked about the baby, they never talked to him. If he cried or fussed, they would see that he was clean and warm and fed, and then they would just leave him.

The baby grew into a self-sufficient but anxious and somewhat passive child. He learned early that it wouldn't do any good to demand much. He became a very watchful and careful boy. He never asked for anything and he was very distrustful of other people. He learned how to entertain himself, and he learned that he could have all of the little bit of love his parents had to give him if he was quiet and unobtrusive. Ruth and Dennis didn't have any more children. They said they'd decided no one could be as perfect as the child they had, so why bother. They were probably right. Ruth and Dennis were simply unable to add the roles of father and mother to that of husband and wife. In response to their child's needs, which they perceived as overly demanding, they defensively tightened their roles as husband and wife and retreated to their childless state. Ruth's mother made this regression possible by being available to mother the child. Ruth and Dennis were unable to take on the responsibilities that would foster family growth. They couldn't help their child grow because they were not ready to grow themselves.

The birth of a child is the birth of the child in us. We become aware of a baby's needs through the recollection of our own needs, and that enables us to care for an infant who cannot verbalize those needs. But some new parents, like Ruth and Dennis, are overwhelmed by a child's helplessness and become helpless themselves. This process doesn't occur because they are really helpless, but rather because both parents are still tied to their families of origin and do not believe that they can take care of themselves, let alone others. Neither Ruth nor Dennis had been able to separate from past identifications or develop enough autonomy to accept the parental role. They were able to handle their own relationship, but they could not deal with the dependency needs that the baby aroused in each of them. They made an unconscious decision to care for each other at all costs. Twenty years later, when their son left home, they were much the same. They suffered no empty nest syndrome for he never really had been a part of their family.

A strong, exclusive parental coalition is only one reaction to unexpected feelings of dependency. One man nonchalantly dropped off his wife at the hospital before each one of her three deliveries. He could not bear the thought that she or the baby might need him. Although this is a rather extreme example, fathers in particular tend to turn to work or some special project to avoid the feelings of helplessness that babies arouse. A father who is overly dependent on his wife may be envious of the baby who is consuming so much of her time. He may turn to another woman for the care and attention he is no longer getting from his wife, or he may punish his wife in more subtle ways for neglecting him.

A man who constantly turns his baby over to his wife may be punishing her. To justify his fear of fatherhood and to mask his own dependency, he becomes helpless. He cannot take care of the baby. He cannot comfort it. This can easily become a problem unless one of the parents recognizes what is happening and moves to intercede. The mother, for instance, could hand the baby back to him, encourage him to hold the happy baby more often, and leave the father alone with the baby. The father himself could ask to be left alone with the baby—the presence of the mother is intimidating to many people trying to comfort a child. He could also spend time holding the baby for no reason other than his own pleasure.

A mother's realization that she is going to have to care for this helpless creature, that she doesn't know how, and that she is no longer going to be cared for herself, can lead to postpartum depression. Women are four to five times more likely to have a mental breakdown with a new baby than at any other time. Although a helpful husband or mother can ease the situation after the birth of a child, a particularly dominant or successful replacement will make the new mother even more despondent. That help must be directed toward the mother, not the baby. She has to become confident about being a mother herself. Again, patterns develop from these early conflicts. If a new mother cannot shake off her depression and despair, if she doesn't trust herself as a mother, she may become a chronically invalided member of the family system, one who is there to make others feel competent and trustworthy.

The Tyrant System

We can see the beginnings of a dysfunctional family system based on power in the above example of the father who couldn't hold his child. If the mother takes the baby and makes it quite clear to both father and child that only she can give comfort, a harmful mother-child coalition may develop. Women generally have great power in childrearing, and taking over can become a habit. The mother may make all the decisions for the family. She might begin by allotting chores and roles and, in the process, rob other family members of any responsible position whatsoever. Tyrant systems develop only when other family members shirk responsibility. No one can become a tyrant unless others are willing to support that individual or fear a confrontation with the tyrant.

Sometimes the new baby can become the tyrant; he or she will call all the shots. Parents have very little power when a baby enters their lives. The baby dominates their lives, determining their sleeping habits, mealtimes, and the amount of their free time. In part, this is necessary and desirable. The baby does have to be cared for, and some babies need more care than others. But at some point babies can become tyrants. If there is a power vacuum in the family, the baby may fill it. If, for instance, the parents are competing with each other rather than complementing each other in their roles as parents, the baby may just take up the space neither will give to the other. The same process can occur if the parents are always fighting over styles of childrearing, the rules of being a family. In the meantime, the baby will make the rules. Parents can be so intent on their own battles that they do not even notice how completely the child has begun to run their lives.

Like all systems, this one can become self-perpetuating. The parents may not be able to resolve their differences, form a workable alliance, or take responsibility for making decisions. They may fear that, if one parent takes over, the other will leave, blame, or ridicule the one in control. They may be so closely tied to their families of origin or each other that they cannot act on, let alone discover, their own desires. They are simply unable to assert themselves. And they get very tired. Fighting with each other, feeling confused about their goals, and caring for the baby wear them out. They complain about their inability to satisfy or control their child. They say the child is particularly demanding and spirited. They accept their situation because it has become familiar, and they do not want to risk change. So the tyrannical baby becomes a mainstay in their family system.

The Coming-Home-to-Roost System

Jonathan, the father of three-year-old Jason, began fighting with his own father because the grandfather often gave Jason pocket money for no apparent reason or occasion. The grandfather argued that the small gifts were harmless. Jonathan countered by saying that Jason would never learn the value of money if it was handed out so easily, and he ordered Jason to return the money. The grandfather shrugged off the conflict, but Jonathan found that he was absolutely livid, seemingly out of proportion to the actual issue. He began to think about his own relationship with his father, especially in regard to money.

Several years earlier the father had helped Jonathan and his wife Alicia buy a house. He provided money for a down payment, and it was understood that he would pay property taxes and insurance and help with improvements if they covered the mortgage. But whenever taxes were due he hemmed and hawed. He encouraged them to remodel, and then he gave them the money to cover expenses in such irregular installments that they lost their credit rating. They always had to beg him to keep his promises. And they always said they'd never fall for his promises again.

But they did. He bought them a car but never paid for the repairs. He agreed to pay for site preparation and installation of a hot tub they wanted. He did finance the preparation, and the tub was lowered into the ground, but it remained there for a year until he finally came through with the installation funds. They continued to say "never again," and complained bitterly about his broken promises. All of which fit into this family's Coming-Home-to-Roost System. They were all struggling with the issue of autonomy.

In examining his anger toward his father, Jonathan realized that the real problem was not the money Jason received, but his father's attitude toward him. In this family, strivings for autonomy were bogged down by regret. The older man repeatedly offered to underwrite his son's autonomy, explaining that all the money he had would go to his son eventually. Then he began to regret letting his son go and reneged on his offers. Jonathan followed the same pattern, only in reverse. He claimed that he didn't want his father's help, that there are always strings attached, that he wanted to be his own man. Then he regretted letting go of his father and accepted yet another dollar. The family was held together by their mutual regret over their lack of autonomy.

A child's growing autonomy will affect his or her parents' autonomy. Women who prefer a symbiotic relationship with a dependent child to the independence of a curious, searching toddler will have to reevaluate their own needs. Fathers, to whom toddlers turn for help in exploring external realities, may find themselves, like this father, checking out their own journey outside the family. Family systems are visible at these transition stages when change makes it possible to examine the entire context in which the change occurs. Lucky families, like this one, can make such opportunities meaningful. These people sold the house and bought one they could afford on their own. They still lived nearby and often visited the grandfather, but they no longer accepted gifts from him. But that wasn't hard; he didn't make any offers.

The Social Security System

All families wonder if there will be enough love to go around when a new member enters the family. The most blatant expression of this is an older child's reaction to a new baby. Mere assurance that the child is loved just as much as ever is often not enough. If that is true, why would parents spend so much time cooing over the new baby? Children do not understand the difference between quantity and quality when it comes to love. But then, who does? We adults may understand, but that doesn't mean we like it. It is hard to experience shifting love patterns, to see our husband love our baby or our daughter love some stranger. Where does it leave us?

For some families, these threats and fears lead to a system based on an *unequal* distribution of affection. If a family is not secure enough to believe that the redistribution of affection is possible, they will choose one person to be the outsider. By choosing someone else, they do not have to worry about being left out themselves. It is an unconscious process that protects their place in the family's affections. There can be more than one outsider; sometimes a whole branch of the family will be considered outsiders. Of course, outsiders also have some security in such a system. They know who they are, where they stand. Although a new baby is not necessarily the outsider, the arrival of a baby stirs up the existing love relationships in ways that precipitate the kind of insecurity that can lead to the scapegoating of the newest and most vulnerable family member.

Families threatened by too much closeness sometimes develop an insider system. They choose one person who is more wonderful, more lovable than any of the others to idolize and admire. Through this process, they raise the self-esteem of the whole group. Although this puts a lot of pressure on the loved one, this assigned role gives that person an identity and an unquestionable place in the family. He or she belongs and, therefore, so do the others. The presence of a nearly perfect family member makes it easier for the family to believe in itself even if the confidence of the individual members is low.

The Cutting-Your-Losses System

"You mean you're going to let them *circumcise* him?"

That's what Clare MacKay Steinberg's brother shouted when she told him about the bris. Clare's brother, Gregg, was the only member left in her family of origin. Their parents were dead. Clare was older, and the new mother of a little boy who was to be circumcised on the traditional eighth day after birth in a religious Jewish ceremony. Clare did not really want to go through the circumcision herself because she thought it was barbaric and no longer necessary for health reasons. Clare explained to Gregg that her husband, Jeffrey, who was Jewish, didn't feel right about having an uncircumcised son. Gregg said it was the baby who wasn't going to feel right. Gregg himself was circumcised and felt the procedure had caused great physical and psychic pain.

"What do you mean, *no* guests?"

In the meantime, Jeffrey was telling his parents that he and Clare would have the circumcision, but only for the immediate family—no uncles, aunts, friends, brothers, and sisters. His mother was horrified. He explained that, since Clare wasn't Jewish and they were both tired and not feeling very festive, they would rather have a family party at a later date. His parents were ashamed. No real bris? Their grandchild?

"He not only won't be Jewish, he won't be American."

In their last conversation before the rabbi arrived, Jeffrey told Clare that most boys were still circumcised, that their son would be one of the boys, and that children always lived through experiences like this. He was trying to convince himself as much as her. Although they all lived through it, Jeffrey, Clare, and the baby cried throughout the ceremony and for some time after Jeff's parents and the rabbi left. Clare and Jeffrey were relieved that it was over and, when asked a few days later if they would have done it over again, they both said yes.

But they didn't. When their second son was born three and a half years later, he did not lose his foreskin. During those years, the family developed a system to protect themselves against loss. They might have lost a foreskin once, the affection of their families of origin temporarily, trust in each other for a while, but they were not going to lose again. The focus of their system became the child who never lost another battle. Through a protective system that centered on the firstborn, the parents were able to build their confidence and bring their families back through their affection for that child. It worked so well that the noncircumcision of the secondborn, which even Gregg thought was a mistake because the brothers would be different, was accepted with surprising grace all around.

No system operates in response to just one underlying psychological force. There are always other issues and forces involved. Although loss or separation was the dominant force present in the system described above, there was also a power struggle between the families of origin and the values and rules that each parent brought from the past. And dependency was also an issue because Clare and Jeffrey had to learn to take care of each other without help from their families. They had to trust each other and believe that they were right. They had to be able to separate from their families without losing the love of those people or of each other. They had to establish themselves as an autonomous family with their own special identity.

It is possible to define family systems, especially failing ones, by the complaints of family members. In each system we've described, the families were obsessed by some problem connected to an unresolved, underlying force. The couple who cannot acknowledge their own dependency needs all but ignore their dependent baby. The family that cannot make responsible decisions complains about their demanding child. The father who is angry about money may really be worried about his own lack of autonomy. The people who worship one family member may long to be worshipped themselves. That central complaint, that constant source of aggravation, may be the route into the system and the clue to what lies behind it.

The experience of having children provides us with a second chance. Raising children won't solve all our problems, and it will certainly inspire new ones, but it does bring out issues that are still unsettled. It gives us a chance to meet our own parents on a new footing and develop a more equal relationship. It enables us to rediscover our own childhood. With some information about our family of origin's development we can better understand our own responses to our children and our current family's development.

But even more important in terms of the survival and indelibility of families is the awareness that children can show us how systems influence our behavior and regulate unconscious needs. Raising children gives us the chance to rework the past, to make changes in our behavior if we don't like what we see, to hold onto systems that work. Families without children will also see the repetition and have a chance to make changes. But the changes will only last for one generation. With children we can set up systems that will be passed on.

9

❀◆❀

Stage Four:
The Best Years of Our Lives

In Stage Four children become active participants in the life of the family. Although children join the family system on the day they are born, they do not act independently to regulate psychological forces within the family. But when they reach school age, they are capable of taking on roles and affecting the relationships between family members. Their fascination with order and their concern for stability in the home is demonstrated through their loyalty to family rules. Their individual social and intellectual development and their experience of the world beyond the family combine to give them a special stake in the family system.

In Stage Four, the task of a family with children is to integrate those developing personalities into the family personality. For childfree couples who have been married for five to ten years the task is to integrate each partner's changing personality into the family personality. In both cases the family personality will undergo change. When there are children, their demands to be part of the family and to be considered in the decision-making process affect the whole family. In the adult family, the demands of careers and other outside activities have to be integrated into family life. All families have to find boundaries and solidify identities within the larger social context. The formerly intimate and self-sufficient circle is now being invaded by outside influences, such as school and the workplace, and by internal pressures, such as each individual's search for identity. No wonder the perimeters of the family are so important now. The family has to save a place for everyone inside its borders while helping everyone find a place outside.

When young children are in day-care centers or nursery school, as they may be in Stage Three, they do not affect the family in the way that they do when they enter elementary school. This is the beginning of Stage Four for families with children. Because infants and young children change so rapidly and are so demanding and interesting, we tend to lose sight of the fact that the family itself changes little in this period. The systems that families develop in response to the hidden psychological forces that children arouse remain relatively constant until children enter school. Whatever worked to wean the first child will be tried when a second or third child comes along. The same basic problem-solving techniques will be used for walking, talking, toilet training, and other developmental points. The system will be constantly refined and broadened to accommodate that development, but the responses to all conflicts that arise during that period will be structurally similar. As long as children are unable to make decisions for themselves or to control events, the psychological forces that are the core of family systems will remain in the same general juxtaposition.

In families with children, there are both physiological and psychological reasons, as well as chronological ones, for the passage from Stage Three to Stage Four. The child of six is beginning to control her or his world. Previously, limited muscle coordination and speech facility prevented a child from moving confidently and independently through the world. Physical control makes it possible for the child to develop other kinds of control. Children can now recognize that they have an effect on others, that they can be part of groups. They are developing cognitive abilities and learning about emotions. They are also learning about other people, other families, other values. In order to assimilate all these changes, children develop a special investment in the family system. They seek both stability and consistency. They want rules so that they can meet the challenges of their own development and still know that they belong to the family.

The impression of Stage Four is usually lasting. It is the time of expansion and rapid individual development for both adult families and families with children. It is the time we remember best when we speak of childhood. We are all learning new skills and taking on new responsibilities and roles.

For parents, this is an exciting and fulfilling time because they can expand their roles in relation to their children, themselves, and other adults. They are no longer just mother and father, or husband and wife, tightly linked to the family circle. Because they identify with their children, their children's quest for information and knowledge about the outside world pulls them back into that world.

And, as their parental responsibilities ease, they can renew and strengthen their identities as spouses, career women and men, friends, and so on. Furthermore, it is often a blissful stage for parents because their children tend to like them and admire them, and all parents thrive in the absence of real parent/child conflict.

For children, this is an important time because they begin to see themselves as distinct and separate individuals with roles and responsibilities both in and out of the family. They feel important, as if they matter, which indeed they do. Their inquisitiveness, seriousness, and respect can revitalize and anchor the family during this stage.

The Child in the Family

Between the ages of six and about eleven children are a very conservative force in the family. They know the rules, and they want everyone to follow them. They know when meals are served, and they expect them to be on time. They know when they are supposed to leave for school, and they are ready. They are concerned if their parents don't keep promises to them or to others. They worry if their parents are fighting. They have a very rigid sense of right and wrong, of justice and fair play. Although their literalness, their lack of appreciation for anything that is not black or white, can be infuriating or laughable, it is important to the whole family.

Children are trying to clarify their own rules and develop their own ethical codes. When they admonish parents about yelling or unfairness, they are not being disrespectful; they are simply searching for consistency and equality. Children find it very difficult to follow the old parental admonition to "do as I say, not as I do." After all, these parents are the models. Children are beginning to bump into other value systems, the rules of other families and other groups. Their attempts to sort out what is just pervade and benefit the whole family. Parents, and other family members, often need to be reminded to play fair.

Children are also very concerned about protecting the family and making it a safe place for everyone. They will work together unconsciously, as the Knoll children did, to keep the family stable. The Knolls went out for dinner every Friday night. The parents, Sally and Sam, both worked. They were in their thirties and had been married for five years before Pete, now nine, was born. Emily was born two years later. For the past year or so they had saved Friday nights for a family outing. Before this, Emily had simply caused so much trouble that Sally and Sam didn't enjoy taking her out—although Pete had always behaved very well in public places.

When they got to the restaurant, Sally ordered first. She would always say, "I'm not very hungry tonight, so I think I'll just have a salad," or "I'm on a diet today, I think I'll just have a salad," or "I'd like something refreshing tonight, so I'll just have a salad." The children, and often Sam, too, would join in the chorus, saying, "So I'll just have a salad," with her. It became a great joke that they all enjoyed because it pulled them all into a cohesive family group. It provided a sense of belonging and had a special meaning for each of them. For Sally, it meant recognition from her children and husband; for the children, it meant vocalization of something they knew about her; for Sam, it meant being in tune with his children. It was not something they would have done if an outsider had been present. It was a family ritual.

The children always ordered hamburgers, no matter where they went or how often their parents encouraged them to experiment. Like most children this age, they were not interested in trying exotic foods. They liked what they knew, what they had had before. Their tastes in food mirrored their attitude toward family systems—they were comforted by familiarity. They didn't want change. That's why they liked their mother's salads, although she deviated from their norm by ordering different kinds of salads. But they always ordered two well-done hamburgers with the works, although Pete sometimes wanted extra mayonnaise. It was all right to hear about other foods, to see and taste them, to experiment a little—usually accompanied by feigned gagging—but they would always order what they knew they liked. It was almost as if they wouldn't be the same if they ate different foods. We are, they might have been saying, what we eat.

Sam did the most experimenting, but he did it in a particularly agonizing fashion. He always led the waiter or waitress through the whole menu, getting an exact description of everything that seemed interesting. The children squirmed and giggled during this performance. On one occasion, he had finally narrowed his choice to two strong contenders when Sally began to get impatient about his indecisiveness. She snapped at him to hurry up. Just as she did so, Emily knocked over her glass of water. Sam joked that since she'd thrown cold water on his first choice, he'd have his second. Everyone laughed, and Pete mopped up the spilled water with his napkin.

It was a very insignificant incident, yet it showed that the children knew how to defuse the antagonism between their parents, play their roles together, and support the roles that their parents played in the family system. In teasing their mother about her salads they gave her a special place in the family, a recognizable characteristic. At the same time, they also strengthened the coalition between their father and themselves. In giggling and squirming while their father ordered, they supported his ineptitude, a role he evidently enjoyed. They also supported their mother's impatience, which may have been an aspect of the dynamic between the parents.

And they worked together. Emily, the more aggressive and active child, took the lead by spilling the water. Pete, who was older and known to be more responsible by everyone in the family, covered her tracks by mopping up the water, thereby averting any anger either parent might direct toward Emily for her carelessness. Of course Emily was not really careless at all. Like Pete, she could not have cared more. Both children were taking care of their parents in order to assure that the family would remain a safe haven for all.

Mother, May 1

In Stage Four children learn how to play various games—the school game, and the mysteries of reading, writing, and arithmetic; the family game with its roles, responsibilities, and special rules; the work game that adults play and the changes that it creates in the home; and the game of social consciousness and peer relationships for all. The family gives the child a base from which to explore his or her own growth. The child gives the family a new voice and consciousness for its moral and intellectual growth.

Children's fascination with rules shows up in their play at this stage. Preschoolers are interested in toys. They do not understand the concepts of winning or losing, nor can they remember the rules involved in games. Older children are interested in games. They are eager to apply rules and play parts. Games range from marbles, cards, and sports to games like "house," "store," and "war," where children experiment with adult roles. These games give children some experience in being in groups, in learning that they have an effect on others and on the game itself, in discovering how the game and the group affect them.

During this stage, children often resolve the conflicts raised by their rapid growth and development through an internal game— fantasy. Fantasy serves as a defense against emotions children haven't yet learned to handle, as well as an opportunity to try out adult roles in secret. Children no longer limit themselves to being cops or robbers or cowgirls. Their interests and outlook broaden. They spend time in front of mirrors wondering if they will grow up to look like movie stars. They dress up in their parents' clothes and act out their parents' lives. They dream about what they read in books and see on television, and picture themselves as space travelers, adventurers, heroines, and spies. They imagine themselves in the roles of other adults they are now meeting—teachers, doctors, and other children's parents. All their new learning is applied directly to their fantasy lives.

Children also use fantasy figures in more mythical ways to protect themselves from frightening feelings. When children get angry at their parents they fear that their anger will destroy their parents. To offset that fear and defuse the guilt and anxiety it produces, children often fantasize about monsters. Similarly, sexual feelings toward parents, themselves, and others may be turned into romantic or heroic fantasies.

A child's preoccupation with fantasy may indicate some emotional stress. In turn, this may be a clue to stress in the family systems. For example, some children create mythical, fairy-tale families to defuse their own fears about their parents' unhappy relationship. Constant daydreaming can also be a sign to parents that the child's own growth is so overwhelming that she or he needs extra support and attention.

Some children tell their troubles to fantasy friends or insist that the "friend" is responsible for some misbehavior the child can't acknowledge. One little boy, Ben, talked to the family pet, a cocker spaniel. He told the dog everything, often in his parents' presence. They tended to dismiss these conversations as immature and silly, but had they listened and observed more closely, they would have learned a great deal about the family and the conflicts Ben's fantasies addressed.

The dog actually played a pivotal role in the family. The mother had bought the dog against the father's wishes. She felt that a boy should have a dog, and she and Ben were solely responsible for the dog and lavished much affection on it. The father felt that they cared more about the dog than him and, in truth, Ben had a very special bond with the dog and, through the dog, with his mother. In a way, mother, Ben, and dog had formed a coalition against the father. This coalition was rooted in their resentment about a move he had insisted they make against the mother's wishes. The father's inability to include them or consider their wishes in making that decision had led to his exclusion from the affectional bonds of the family.

The Parent-Child Subsystem

Changes in a family's subsystems reveal the broader changes in family structure that are generated by a child's development. Most importantly, children can now affect the relationships they have with parents, grandparents, and siblings. They are no longer silent partners in the formation of subsystems. Furthermore, they are making contacts outside the home that can change or weaken those inside the home.

Because children are no longer as dependent on their parents for physical caretaking, the child-parent subsystem changes. Children begin to strike out on their own, and parents must learn to let go. But all these changes are frightening, and we often try to cling to old patterns. Although we can tie our own shoes now, we may still want a parent to tell us to do so. Or, we may suspect that a parent still needs to help us do so. Up to a point, periods of regression are normal for both children and parents because they ease the conflicting emotions produced by so much change. However, when children continue to depend on parents for help with tasks they have mastered in a previous stage or when parents continue to encourage such dependence, it's a sign that the relationship is meeting other needs.

On the other hand, a relationship that changes very abruptly shows the influence of yet other needs. For example, if our parents no longer offer to help us tie our shoelaces, or if we refuse the help they do offer, we may never really learn how to tie them properly. Parents must be alert to their children's developmental capabilities, and children must feel that their own rapid development won't make their parents feel left out or abandoned.

The parent-child relationship also changes as children begin to form relationships with other adults, particularly teachers. If children are aware that their parents fear these competitive relationships, they may develop learning problems or discipline problems. They cannot recognize the authority of the teacher because to do so would betray a parent. Persistent misbehavior at home and at school may be a sign of an internal struggle to resolve authority conflicts between parents and teachers, as well as the conflict between their own desire for independence and a parent's unconscious desire for their dependence. A strong affiliation with a grandparent or some other slightly removed relative at this stage often gives a child a safe way out of the family.

Sometimes a bond with the mother will shift to the father or vice versa. In one compulsively achievement-oriented family, both parents and the two older daughters were highly motivated intellectually. The youngest child, a boy, was a sweet, loving child, and his father's favorite—until he started school. He had a learning problem; he couldn't seem to grasp the material quickly enough. His father was in despair because he was so angry at the boy and knew that he was being unfair and ruining his relationship with his son. To take up the slack, the mother became very protective of the boy. They formed an alliance, and the whole family entered therapy. In the early months everyone except the mother kept the boy at a distance. They all talked, analyzed, intellectualized, and agonized in a highly competitive, fluent style while the little boy sat and smiled shyly around the room. Occasionally he would edge over to his mother's chair or climb into her lap. Although she went on talking, she would always hold and cuddle him, whisper to him and giggle a little with him.

At first, the therapist tried to engage the boy in the conversation and encourage the others to talk to him, but eventually he decided to take his cue from the mother. In the next session, while everyone was rattling on, the therapist motioned the boy over to him, put the boy on his lap and held him. The boy went back to his mother after a little while, but several sessions later he came over to the therapist himself, and this time they talked for a little while. For some time only the mother and the therapist seemed to have this kind of bond with the boy, but one day the younger daughter motioned to the boy and, after a little hesitation, he sat on her lap and talked to her.

It took a long time—over a year and a half—before the boy was sitting on his father's lap and rebuilding the relationship they had had. In the meantime, he'd developed alliances with everyone in the room. Sessions still consisted of the same heated conversation in which everyone analyzed everyone else, but now there was this little snuggly presence moving from person to person, connecting them and himself in the process. In another few months, the little side conversations between the boy and each family member became more public, more a part of the general conversation. He gained confidence to be a member of the group just as they realized they wanted him to be.

In another family, a girl who had always been "daddy's girl," became "mother's girl" after she'd started school. Daddy felt a little guilty about it, and sad as well. He recognized the fact that his feelings for her were not totally innocent—natural perhaps, but not innocent—and he was afraid that this had driven her away. But he also realized that the new bond with her mother was a normal, predictable change. Oedipal feelings notwithstanding, she had simply become interested, both through her association with other girls at school and through a new awareness of her mother, in her own femaleness. She was doing what all girls her age do—making a same-sex identification, becoming involved in the female role. To do so, she had to watch her mother very closely. She followed her around and loved to dress up in her mother's clothes and stumble about in her high-heeled shoes. She had a little briefcase much like her mother's and, after dinner, when her mother sat down at the kitchen table to do some office work for the next day, the girl would bring in her homework and set it up across from her mother. Sometimes we tease children about behavior like this, but it serves a very serious purpose.

Before Stage Four, children have very little awareness of their parents as people, and particularly as men and women. Now, they are full of curiosity. They want to know what it is like to be a man or woman. They want to know what their parents were like at their age, wondering if they themselves will grow up all right. They ask dozens of questions about their parents' childhood experiences, and they like to hear stories, especially from grandparents, about their parents' childhood. They are extremely curious about sex, what men and women do together, and they want to hear all about the crushes their parents had on camp counselors, teachers, and movie stars of the same sex. They are very intent on modeling themselves after certain favorite adults, and a strong parental partnership can be extremely beneficial at this time.

The Child-Child Subsystem

There may be a lot of bickering between brothers and sisters during this stage. As older children begin to spend more time with their peers, they are often annoyed by tag-along younger siblings who are not yet ready to function independently and unwilling to lose their former playmates. Older children constantly beg parents to get a younger brother or sister off their backs. What they don't want now is a reminder of their own dependent state, which is not entirely past. On the other hand, younger children complain about hand-me-downs and the special privileges older children now have.

This rivalry between children is rivalry for parental affection and approval. We tend to forget that children do not just fight because they have grievances against each other. Their battles are also a way to distinguish themselves from each other in their parents' eyes. The parent-child subsystem is particularly important in offsetting this potential problem. Parents must develop different relationships with each of their children. If parents treat all their children in the same way, saying things like "It was good enough for your sister and it'll be good enough for you," children feel that they are not recognized as unique individuals, separate from their siblings. Although this leads to antagonism between siblings, their bickering actually is an expression of their anger at their parents.

Parents must also learn to recognize that each child has special needs that are related to his or her particular stage of development. For example, an eight-year-old is beginning to make his or her own friends and develop interests apart from the family's and particularly apart from those shared earlier with a younger sibling. The older child wants some privacy, wants to test his or her independence. A younger child of five or six, however, is still attached to ideal models—parents and older siblings with whom she or he can be identified until ready to establish a separate identity. Children want to have these differences recognized, too.

Nonetheless, children will stick together when there is strife in the family, and they will unite against a parental coalition. Although they may disagree about the larger world and argue about friends and activities on the outside, in the small, inner world of the family they have mutual interests. Like Pete and Emily, cited earlier in this chapter, who colluded over spilled water, children will work together to keep the family stable so that they can have a home base from which to explore their own growth.

The Adult in the Family

The growth of a child resonates throughout the family. Where parents in the previous stage were connected, often day and night, to their children, they now begin the process of reconnecting with themselves, with the people they were before, and with the couple they were before. When children enter school on a full-time basis, parents have more time to explore new opportunities. Furthermore, children's eagerness to expand their horizons often stimulates a similar reaction in parents. Career men and women find that their child's entry into the world of learning parallels their own desire to make a career or job change. Some adults return to school themselves to get new or further training at about this time. Although many parents find their increased freedom exhilarating, they also identify with their children's struggles to learn, and this can generate unconscious feelings of fear and uncertainty about their own direction.

When children are in grade school, their parents are often in their thirties and experiencing some mid-life crises and inner doubts about their own goals and future. And as their children bring them into contact with other adults—other parents, teachers, doctors—who have different values and life-styles, they may feel threatened by the influence these new people and ideas have on their children. Although this stage is usually a happy period in family life, it can be quite difficult if a parent's self-esteem has been shaken by a child's lack of dependence. However, entry into the outside world is very rewarding, and many parents anticipate the chance to realize their potential eagerly.

Couples who have neglected their marital relationship and put all their energies into parenting may experience marital difficulties during this stage. Loss of the full-time parental role, or at least full-time identification with that role, can leave parents feeling bereft, and a strong marital bond can ease this sense of loss. If that bond has withered, many parents feel abandoned, particularly if their children were a welcome distraction in a troubled marriage. Without that distraction, many couples begin questioning their relationship as they turn to one another and find no common bond.

Even in childfree families, the combination of seven to ten years together and a self-questioning stage of individual development leads many people to doubt their partnerships. The seven-year itch is quite real for many couples. We tend to blame our partner for our own lack of success, for not keeping up, or for not being content with the status quo. We begin to wonder why we are together. Often, these doubts lead to experimentation, in fantasy or in fact, with other partners. And our growing dissatisfaction can raise anxieties that are transmitted to our children. No wonder children have to work so hard to keep things stable. The predictability they need and expect is often threatened by the individual changes in other people.

The Parent-Child Subsystem

Although parents generally recognize their function as role models for their children, they often are not aware that they identify with their children as well. And the effects of this reverse identification show up in the parent-child relationship.

When a child goes to school, she or he is up for scrutiny. Although none of us likes to acknowledge this, most parents know it and most children feel it. The child is compared to other children, often for the first time, in a setting that parents cannot control, try as they sometimes do. Suddenly they, too, are up for scrutiny through their child, and they feel exposed when their child's performance and behavior is judged by other authority figures. Often, they begin to monitor their children's exposure to outside influences—other children, school, television—as a reaction against their own fear that their influence may be inadequate.

At this point parents may feel very ambivalent. On the one hand, they want to hold onto their former relationship—one in which they knew all about the child and had all the influence. On the other hand, they begin to see their child as others in the outside world see him—in an impersonal, judgmental context—grading and comparing the child to others, as if their relationship was not personal or intimate. This internal struggle makes it very difficult to maintain a parent-child bond that allows the child both independence and support. In short, parents tend to lose sight of the fact that the child is still a child.

In identifying with their children's experiences, parents begin to recall their own childhood experiences, and they often confuse their own youthful emotions with their children's current feelings. In the case of the underachieving little boy in a family of overachievers cited earlier, the father was dismayed that the boy was not as intelligent as he had been. Another father whose little boy had learning problems nagged and harassed his son for a different reason. He too had had learning problems, and his son's difficulties exposed his own weaknesses, causing embarrassment and shame. He found it impossible to reestablish the previously strong bond he had had with his son until long after the boy's learning problems had been solved and buried (possibly to turn up in the next generation). In the interim, the boy's mother shielded him from the father's disappointment, and that bond carried the boy through the early part of this stage.

When parents worry that their children's behavior may reflect negatively on the family, they may use an alliance with a child to cover up their own fears of inadequacy. A common example is the parent who does a child's homework to ensure the child's success and thereby bring credit to the parent and the family. Although this alliance appears to be based on the help the adult offers the child, in fact the child actually helps the adult. The child knows that she or he is supposed to do homework alone. In accepting the parent's help the child unconsciously protects the parent.

If a parent is experiencing some uncertainty about life or marriage that creates a rift or weakening in the marital relationship, the child may be called in as a substitute. The child may become that parent's confidante, or an ally in any battles between the parents. Similarly, the parent may focus totally on the child in an attempt to avoid or cut off any interaction with the other parent. Such a coalition can destroy or weaken the child's bond with the other parent.

One mother told her daughter all about her affair with another man so that the girl could cover for her. Although mother and daughter had been very close before this revelation, the daughter began shifting her loyalty to her father. She never told her father about the mother's affair, but they began to talk more than they ever had, and they spent more time together when the mother was away on business. The father encouraged this new alliance because he felt that something was missing in his marital relationship, although he wasn't aware of his wife's affair on a conscious level. When the mother realized that her daughter and husband had bonded in a way that could exclude her from the family circle, she broke off the affair and returned to the fold.

However, the marital problems that were at the core of this family system were not addressed or changed by her action, and a few months later she was involved in another affair. Again, she misused her renewed coalition with her daughter. Again, the daughter shifted her allegiances to her father. Again, the father encouraged his daughter to supply what his wife could not. This family pattern was repeated several times because neither parent could confront their marital difficulties or recognize how their coalitions with their daughter shielded them from any confrontation. When the daughter became a teenager and started forming strong bonds with her peers, the parents began to realize that something was wrong. Finally, they were forced to face their marital troubles.

The Parental Subsystem

Even parents with marital conflicts or disagreements can have strong parental coalitions. It is possible to respect each other as parents and to carry out complemetary roles in childrearing without really getting along as husband and wife. One couple who "stayed together for the children" went their separate ways as individuals but retained a consistent investment in their two children. This family had had a very tumultuous Stage Three because they fought endlessly about the children. They disagreed about the proper way to handle each new event in their children's lives, and they often blamed one another or the children for problems, conflicts, or mistakes.

Since they shared childcare equally they were able to return to their jobs full-time when the children entered school. Through work they found the confidence to recognize that they had very different interests and personalities. What they did have in common was a desire for children and a concern for the children's well-being. Their system of fighting and blaming the children for their own disgruntlements, which had developed in the previous stage, could be changed once they realized that they were better parents than married people.

Some couples neglect their own relationship after their children begin school because it doesn't seem as important when the children are no longer totally dependent. However, because parents tend to identify their own childhood experiences with their children's experience during this stage, it is particularly important for parents to work together to combat overidentification. Each parent must be alert to the potentially destructive consequences of overidentification. Is the other parent locked in battle with a child?

Does he or she avoid or slight one child, or favor another in an exclusive yet static bond? These are all important clues that both parents must learn to recognize. Furthermore, parents need one another's support in setting limits if a consistent, predictable, yet flexible climate is to pervade the family. Although children are now involved and responsible members of the family, parents are still the leaders.

The Family in the Family

During this stage the family identity solidifies. All family members know their roles, understand the family's rules, and recognize how these aspects come together to promote family harmony and solve problems. This process—the exercising of family systems—fosters a sense of identity and unity that the family did not have before everyone learned to play the game.

All at once the family starts identifying itself as a group that "likes sports," "plays backgammon," "goes camping," "watches television," and so on. They characterize the visible aspects of their lives by describing themselves as a family that "lives in an apartment," "lives down the street," "is small," "is large," "is tall," or "is blond." Similarly, they define their inner qualities as a family; they are "affectionate," "smart," "funny," and so on. Although children initiate these descriptions as they come into contact with other families and people, everyone in the family is ready to separate themselves from the crowd, to see themselves as unique, to feel part of something special.

These conscious identifications tend to be positive, but negative identifications are made as well: "We are the family that lives on the other side of the tracks," "We are the group that fights all the time," "We are the group that never does anything together." These are powerful identifications, too, although they are not always acknowledged. They also provide a sense of unity, of belonging, but they can be destructive to the family structure. Families may not be able to escape or surmount the unhealthy and unrewarding patterns they have developed as a result of these identifications.

Within these group descriptions, which give families both a rallying point for themselves and a place in the world, are the special identities of individual members. Children can now play the roles that uphold family systems, such as tyrant, victim, or everybody's favorite. They are also able to label and hold onto identifications that acknowledge something special about various family members in addition to their more functional roles. So we find the crowd-pleaser, a boy who can always be counted on to entertain and amuse the family. Although this identification may be tied to his more specific role of entertaining others to distract them from conflict or trouble, it isn't necessarily so. The family may simply accept him as an entertainer because he's good at it and they enjoy encouraging him. A clearer example of affectionate labelling might be the little girl known as pie-face by her family because of her sweet tooth. In that family, interestingly, every generation had its pie-face. The labelling united them and made an indelible impression.

There can be real exhilaration now in families as each person finds a place, and everyone feels familiar with the way that place fits into the family system. Certainly, ideas like role and system are not consciously understood by family members, but it is due to the meshing and the maturing of these concepts that confidence and tranquillity descend over many families now, making this a sort of honeymoon period in family development. The relative stability that children need and fight for, and that adults are only too eager to enjoy after the rigors of early childrearing and the pangs of self-doubt in mid-life crisis, offers a welcome respite for all.

Remarriage

Therefore, it's not surprising that remarriage is often harder than expected during this stage. Families, whether they are two-parent, single-parent, or recently divorced, have just become comfortable with their patterns and shape. They have just made an identity for themselves, learned their roles and systems and defined the rules. Suddenly, they are thrown together with people who have another identity, just as new as theirs, if both families are in the same stage. Furthermore, these two families are expected to become a group, without any common history or experience together and probably no common roots—such as relatives, neighborhoods, schools, or activities. Although the signs were favorable at the outset, when everyone looked forward to blending the families, just a few months later, rules we never dreamed of and roles we can't conceive of are standing between our two families.

Each family has just developed its own style. The blending, no matter how desirable, raises questions about whose style will predominate and what will be lost in the process. Ideally, we want to develop a new system that is based on the new people and new needs of the family. But that takes time. Meanwhile, each family will find itself inadvertently maintaining its own identity. That is, after all, what we know. In spite of ourselves and our best intentions, change is threatening. We create a family identity to set our family apart from other families. We may want to let that go, but the process is harder than we anticipated.

Remarriage at any stage inspires a strong sense of hope in everyone. We cannot help hoping that the new family will take over and resolve all the problems in the old family. We anticipate success this time. We will not make the same mistakes. We will create something wonderful that will make each one of us special, beloved, and part of an extraordinary group. In fact, remarriage is very similar to marriage; we anticipate that the new family will supply what was previously missing. And, like marriage, the old problems will still exist and new ones will surface. It won't be perfect, and the disappointment, the fear of another failure, can discourage families before they have really given it a chance. It can take two or three years to form the systems, subsystems, and special identity that create a family.

The Winds of Change

In all stages of family development hidden psychological forces are rearranged by changes in the members and the membership of the family. In Stage Three, parents' reactions to the forces of power, dependency, autonomy, love, and separation in themselves and in the children formed the family systems. In Stage Four, children create the changes. Now their reaction must be heeded, making the systems both more complex and more complete. Not only does the family have to integrate each child's separate and different personality, it also must grapple with the different issues each developing child has to face. As the child goes out into the world and begins to blossom socially, intellectually, and emotionally, the psychological life of the family will change. And the family system has to accommodate these changes.

The Cutting-Our-Losses System

Children feel a certain separation anxiety about starting school and parents often share it. When our children enter school we recall our own feelings about leaving the safety of our home and beginning first grade. We may have been frightened, guilty about leaving mother at home, anxious about meeting new children and having a new authority, the teacher, in our lives. Therefore, we may assume that our child shares the same fears, or we may translate our child's general doubts into our own specific ones.

Our separation anxiety is intensified by other concerns—what we will do without our child; how our child will do under the influence of a new authority figure. Both these concerns are connected to lost roles. Children are less dependent on their parents for protection and caretaking; other adults now tell them what to do. After six or seven years of total identification with the parenting role, parents may become uncertain about their identities. They may wonder, "If my child doesn't need me anymore, who am I?" And in losing some of their former authority, they may feel quite powerless in contrast to the new authority—the teacher. Many parents identify the teacher with a critical authority from their own past, a parent or teacher who scrutinized and judged their performance as children then and parents now. Or, if the teacher is younger and less educated or experienced than they, parents may see the teacher as one of their younger siblings with whom they were always in competition. The problem of parental overidentification can be quite severe when children enter school.

Children can also overidentify with a parent's separation anxiety. School phobia is a classic syndrome in children who fear that one or both parents will fall apart when they start school. In turn, this fear generates anger on the part of the child—anger toward the dependent parent who won't let go—and the child also fears this anger will destroy the parent. This unconscious interpretation by the child often surfaces in a parent-child relationship in which the parent has virtually abandoned the child long before because parenting was just too demanding. The child hates the parent for not being responsible, and is, in turn, super-responsible toward the parent. The child who is afraid that the parent will fall apart may believe that the parent lives only for her or his love and will feel rejected if she or he leaves.

The Moltanaldo family entered therapy because the younger boy, Caesar, could not go to school. Every morning he would get up and get dressed just like his older brother, Barry. The boys would eat breakfast with their parents, and then Caesar would start throwing up. The father, Rodolfo, would hastily leave for work, and

Barry would tear out the door to meet his friends and walk to school with them. The mother, Celia, and Caesar would be left alone. She would help him back to bed and stay with him, reading to him and playing games until he felt better. Then they would go out to do some shopping or laundry and return home. If Caesar didn't eat breakfast, he had dry heaves. On weekends he didn't get sick, but he wasn't very eager to go out and play. Generally, he stayed home, and his presence intensified the tension between his parents. They frequently argued about his problems and their inability to handle them. Celia and Caesar had been to several medical clinics before psychological counseling was recommended.

Celia and Rodolfo Moltanaldo were Italian immigrants who had adopted Barry after Celia was told she could not have children. They were just delighted with Barry, who was a happy, strong, and bright child. Rodolfo would hurry home in the evenings to play with the baby. The family did everything together and felt extremely happy and successful. They found New York exciting and energizing, and they did not seem to miss their small-town roots.

Twenty months after the adoption, Celia became pregnant. She and Rodolfo were startled. They were pleased that they could have a natural child, but they were not prepared to add to their already perfect family. The pregnancy was a difficult one, and the baby was colicky and unable to sleep. Celia was overwhelmed by fatigue and the baby's needs. Rodolfo put in a great deal of overtime to meet the added expenses, and he was rarely home to help her. All the joy and hope they had felt about family life began ebbing away. They become depressed and isolated from each other and from the outside world. Although Barry remained cheerful and responsive, he was always eager to go to school and leave the family. Caesar had always been slow, withdrawn, and sad. When it was time for him to go to school, he seemed to have no energy at all.

One of the family's central problems quickly emerged in therapy. Mr. and Mrs. Moltanaldo were unable to support and nurture each other as they had before Caesar's birth. Their marital relationship and their parental partnership had weakened considerably. He worked all the time, and she felt trapped at home. Although she could have returned to work to gain some freedom and ease the financial burden that he faced, this obvious solution did not occur to them. They had developed a system to protect them from a separation anxiety that had nothing to do with the present, although Caesar's problem had brought it to a crisis.

Actually, the Moltanaldos were reliving their separation from Italy. Caesar, their "Italian" child, their real child, had raised this issue in a way that Barry never could. They had tried to put the past behind them, but it was still very much a part of them.

Celia was almost phobic about venturing out on her own. Her dependency on her own family in Italy, from whom she had literally run away, had reasserted itself when she had a child of her own. Because Barry was adopted, he did not seem to bring out the homesickness in her that Caesar did. His dependence on her and his reluctance to go to school were motivated in part by her reluctance to lose him. Although she recognized in Caesar's sadness her own sadness as a child trying to escape an overprotective family, she felt powerless to change the situation.

Rodolfo's absence reinforced her sense of powerlessness and isolation. Although he said he had to work so hard because he wanted his children to have a better childhood than he did, he was actually giving them the same kind of childhood he had had. His father had died when he was three, and his mother had had to work. He had been lonely and very deprived. His family had been desperately poor, he had missed his mother terribly, and he was determined that his boys would never suffer in that way. So he unconsciously supported Caesar's inability to leave home because he identified his own youthful loneliness with Caesar's desire to be with his mother. Unfortunately, because he worked so hard he was never home. In a sense he "deserted" his family through work, just as his own father had "deserted" him through death. He referred to Celia's demands for attention and companionship as "mission impossible," probably because they aroused his own unfulfilled dependency needs. Rodolfo and Celia's reluctance to confront their histories doomed them to recreating that history in their own family.

In many ways the boys symbolized this pattern. Even their names were a clue. Barry, the adopted son, the all-American boy, was outgoing, aggressive, and inquisitive. He represented his parents' hopes and dreams in this new country. Caesar, the natural son with the Italian name, was depressed and sad, unable to get out, to communicate with others. He was a reminder of things past, of Italy, of community, but also of poverty and suffocation. He represented the family's troubled side. Barry was their positive side.

They all envied his zest and confidence, but they believed, mistakenly, that those qualities were a result of his different genes rather than their own strength and sense of hope.

To rebuild that strength, the therapist helped them reinforce three different subsystems within the family system. First of all, the parents had to renew their marital bond. This was encouraged in two ways. Rodolfo came to recognize that his working pattern separated him from his family and was largely a reaction to his own fear of being an inadequate father since he had had no role model as a child. Celia, on the other hand, needed some distance from her family. She started going to P.T.A. meetings and taking part in church activities. But, more importantly, she took a part-time job, which lessened her dependence on both Caesar and her husband. Finding a place for herself in the world gave her more confidence about her place in her family. It also gave her something to share with her husband, and that led to greater intimacy on many levels. They began having dinner together one night a week. Sometimes they went out, but often they ate alone at home after the boys had gone to bed.

The subsystem between Rodolfo and his sons also had to be strengthened. Trust in the father makes it possible, symbolically, for children to "leave" their mothers and become individuals. In the Moltanaldo family, Celia actively, if unconsciously, discouraged any intimacy between her husband and sons. She would sit next to the boys during therapy sessions, often positioning herself between them and Rodolfo. She would tell the boys to stop "interrupting" when they sought their father's attention or asked him to play with them. When the therapist pointed this out, she realized that she created barriers that made it difficult for her hesitant, unsure husband to become a real father. Father-son activities were scheduled for the first few weeks so the boys and their father could get used to being together. Then their activities together became less formal and more spontaneous.

The third subsystem that needed work was the one between the brothers. They had been split apart by the family system. Yet Barry could help Caesar negotiate the world of school and playground, and Caesar could help Barry stay in the family. Celia's relaxation of her hold on Caesar and the therapist's and parents' assurance to the boys that they could help each other cleared the way for this to happen.

Although Barry did not seem to be suffering from separation

anxiety the way Caesar was, his eagerness to get away from the family was very similar to his parents' eagerness to escape Italy. An inability to be separate, independent people without totally burying the past characterized all three of them. Only Caesar held the history, and it was a very heavy burden for him. The family had to incorporate their connectedness, past and present, in order to build a support system that would enable them to separate without pain.

The Coming-Home-to-Roost System

Trivial as it may seem, "sleep-overs" can reveal a great deal about the hidden psychological forces during this stage. In Stage Three, when children are infants, toddlers, and even preschoolers, these sleep-overs don't pose much of a threat. But in Stage Four that changes. Although it's hardly a real threat for most families, often there is a little flash of feeling that is related to family autonomy and identity. It is inspired, of course, by the children's growing interest in rules and values. They are absorbing what they see and learn outside the family and bringing it home. And they are taking the home outside with them. They are comparing themselves and their families to others. And they are often surprised or smitten by the way other families function. They wonder why some families behave in a certain way, and they wonder why their own families behave differently. In other words, they are beginning to recognize that families work in different ways.

But children are not the only ones making these observations. When another child sleeps over at our house, we adults notice and experience it differently than we had when our children were younger. We may be aware of these new feelings only on the first few occasions, but to some degree they exist whenever our child brings a new friend home. We feel self-conscious. We are aware that the house is dirty or that dinner is late. We try not to fight in front of this child. We wonder whether or not to kiss this child goodnight. We don't know if we should let the kids watch television, eat ice cream, or stay up as late as our children usually do. When our child sleeps at someone else's house, we have unreasonable fears that she or he won't be fed, won't want to come home, or won't remember to be good, well mannered, bright.

We become very sensitive to the differences in class, race, religion, style, and operations between families. We find ourselves judging and wondering how we are being judged. And our children notice and sometimes call attention to the fact that we are behaving differently, saying things like "Why are we eating so early tonight?" or "Why can't we have hamburgers like we always do?" or "We never eat in the dining room unless somebody's sleeping over," and "Why are you doing the dishes, dad?"

Our concern about the opinion of others and our concurrent interest in forming opinions about them are just small examples of the way we test our autonomy as a family and become aware of our own borders. When a stranger enters our house we become aware of our own rules. And the stranger's reactions to those rules will probably affect us to the degree that we feel they do or don't work. The systems we have evolved to set ourselves apart from others and keep ourselves intact may be called into question by comparison with systems that seem more effective. We may decide, through sleep-overs or other comparative experiences, that the outside world isn't really such a dangerous place. On the other hand, we may feel that it is extremely dangerous and retreat into our own small circle for a few more years.

The Tyrant System

Families who have developed a tyrant system will experience some shocks during this stage. Whether the tyrant is a benign dictator or a ruthless power-monger, his or her power may be threatened by the family's sudden exposure to the many influences from the outside world. School presents a major challenge, both as an institution that usurps some of our authority over our children and in the form of the teacher who represents this authority. The adult who has been making decisions for every family member no longer has absolute control. Children, exposed to other authority, will begin to challenge that control at home as they come under the influence of other adult role models. This can result in shifting coalitions within the family as the child allies himself or herself with the less powerful parent or forms a coalition with siblings to challenge both parents.

This is not necessarily a malevolent process. The tyrant may be quite ready to turn over or share the decision making with other responsible family members. As parents we cannot forget that positive leadership in the family can be democratic. Most children respond very well to firm but flexible leadership in which their needs and individual differences are respected. Children need to be involved in decision making during this stage.

If the family tyrant is a child, school experiences and association with other children may change the system. For one thing, the teacher will not react to the child's power plays in the way parents do. The teacher has no particular investment—unless she or he happens to identify with this child for some special reason—in meeting the child's demands. The teacher is not in conflict with a spouse over this child. Although the parents may not be able to take control, the teacher is not part of that system. The teacher does not have to worry about losing the child's love if she or he refuses to respond to the child's wishes.

This same process occurs with other children. They don't know that this child is special. They do not know that the family kowtows to this person. Brothers or sisters may accept the tyrant's domination, but other children won't. And the child, if she or he wants to play with the other children, learns that the techniques that worked in the family, such as withdrawing, crying, or having a temper tantrum, do not work with the other children. As manipulative techniques are given up at the playground, they may also be given up within the family, creating the possibility of change. However, children with strong power needs often learn to manipulate their peers just as they manipulate their families. Family roles do become the roles we play in other groups. But this process takes some time, possibly time enough for the family—if they are ready or able—to develop a broader-based pattern for sharing responsibility.

Sometimes, a family group will operate as if there is a tyrant when there actually isn't. For example, Jennifer and George came into therapy because Jennifer was concerned that her daughter, Annie, didn't like George. Jennifer said that George was harsh and even jealous of Annie and that Annie was afraid of him. George thought that Jennifer was exaggerating. He felt that Annie was spoiled and that Jennifer was overprotective. He thought that he and Annie got along fine and that Jennifer would relax once they married, which they planned to do.

In the course of therapy it turned out that both Jennifer's father and first husband had been tyrannical, brutish men. Jennifer had played the martyr to both of them. George was not a brute, and he treated her very differently than her father or husband had. But she could not break out of the old, safe, if unrewarding pattern. So unconsciously she located her old feelings in her daughter, deciding that George was being brutish to Annie, with whom she identified. George was not mean to Annie, although he did recognize that Annie was not particularly fond of him. He had a history of being unloved. His own mother had run away with another man, leaving his father with four children.

George and Jennifer seemed to be experiencing their relationship through Annie. In fact, they were unable and somewhat unwilling to talk to each other or establish a very intimate bond. Rather than deal with their own doubts and fears about getting married, they focused their problems on Annie. Although the therapist continually encouraged them to talk about their own relationship, they always changed the subject. Invariably, a session would end with a review of George's strictness and Jennifer's protective attitude toward Annie. Neither of them was able to build a new kind of interaction with each other. Their inability to work out a system that would allow them to marry and become a new family resulted in their breakup a few months later.

The Social Security System

Family systems centered on love relationships are naturally going to undergo change when there are more people, people beyond the immediate family, to love. As in the previous stage, there is always some fear that there will not be enough love to go around. It is only through experience that family members learn that they have a place, that love can reach all around a family circle, and that affection for each other can be lasting. Both children and adults have love "affairs" outside the family now—from children's crushes on teachers and fantasy figures, to adults' growing interest in jobs, co-workers, and friendships with peers. But love in the family, the giving and receiving of affection that assures us we are part of something special, can really develop now that children recognize that they, too, can be loving as well as loved.

The Child-in-Us System

Perhaps it is the psychological force of dependency that we see most clearly during this stage. Children are becoming independent, and parents have to learn to trust them to take care of themselves. This is hard, especially when parents identify with them—like Marilyn's mother.

Marilyn was beat up by the little girl down the street. She came home with a bloody nose. Or, rather, a bloodied nose. The blood had dried. Marilyn's mother was furious. She wanted to go and punch the other girl's mother or shake the other girl and tell her never to hurt her daughter again. Marilyn's father just laughed—evidently forgetting that he had been halfway out the door when Marilyn had been in her last scrape. He told Marilyn's mother that children had to fight their own battles. Marilyn's mother began to calm down, but she was amazed at the strength of her own fury. She realized that the fight stirred up memories of similar incidents in her childhood.

In the meantime, Marilyn went into her father's study to use the phone. He overheard her telling a friend (who evidently witnessed the fight) that her cousin Clark was going to help her deal with this neighborhood toughy. Marilyn's father was mystified. Although Marilyn had a cousin named Clark, she'd never met him. And he was much older, probably in college. It seemed unlikely to Marilyn's father that Cousin Clark would be called in for such a mission. Then suddenly he realized that Marilyn associated Clark with Clark Kent. Of course! Superman. Superman will protect her.

This is an example of an interaction that is not part of a system because the system no longer applies. Although Marilyn's parents may have overidentified with her in the past and rushed to protect her, they are now learning that she is a separate person, old enough to fight her own battles and independent enough to have her own battles. The mother is surprised by her own rage but correctly places it in her past, aided by her husband's amusement. The father is startled to hear about Clark Kent but correctly surmises that his daughter has created a fantasy protector for feelings she cannot quite yet handle. Marilyn herself is doing fine. She won't need Superman for long. She's learning to handle her own feelings, fight her own battles, and she knows when to come home.

This stage is a very important one because it solidifies family identity and individual identities within the larger family circle. Families need to develop the confidence that comes from forging a family identity, learning their roles, and knowing how to play their family game because the next stage is much more confusing and frightening. It's an exciting time, too, but the personal and sexual identity crises in adolescents and the corresponding reactions in adults make it a very unstable time. And the lessons learned in this stage—how to balance individual and family development and incorporate the outside world inside the family—will stand any family in good stead when pubescent hormones hurtle them into Stage Five.

Stage Five:
Rebels With a Cause

Stage Five is all about identity crisis—in the adolescent child, in the adult, and in the family itself. The child who is becoming an adult is the model for this stage, someone who is struggling to find an identity that is independent of, and yet connected to, the past. Adolescents must establish themselves in the larger social context while the family must regroup into a smaller context to face the eventual loss of these adolescents. Adults will have similar identity struggles whether or not they have adolescent children. In Stage Five adults are in mid-life, and they must come to grips with their own adolescent fantasies and decide who they are and who they will be for the rest of their lives. In wrestling with these questions, they may discover that they want to change their family's present structure.

When we, as parents, teachers, friends, or advisors of adolescents, tell them that they will outgrow their doubts and confusion they don't believe us. And they are right not to. Why are we so upset when adolescents express pain and uncertainty if we outgrew these feelings? In truth, we did not outgrow them. We simply learned how to avoid or live with our doubts. That's why teenagers, in their search for self, their denial of authority, their rejection of everything they haven't experienced themselves, worry us so. We identify with them. We don't just identify them with the children we once were, as in previous stages. We identify with them as emerging adults—the still unsure, unresolved, unformed adult in each of us. It is what *we* have not outgrown that bothers us about adolescents, not what *they* haven't outgrown. If our own history didn't color our perception of our adolescent children, we would appreciate the fact that their struggles are stimulating and meaningful. Their search can provoke creative excitement in us.

Those very children who were so keen on order, rules, and their family in Stage Four, do an abrupt about-face as adolescents. The honeymoon is over. Suddenly, they are breaking the rules, denying the family identity, and disrupting the family system. In the confusion and anger that adolescent rebellion generates, many of us do not recognize that the family identity is actually being preserved. Although the surface is littered with conflict and dismay, underneath that surface the family is still struggling to be indelible. We all realize that adolescents have to rebel, have to leave the family, have to find themselves. However, few of us realize that adolescents are also trying to stay in the family and keep the family in them. Furthermore, this struggle reaches beyond mere adolescent rebellion.

The family identity itself is changing. The family system has to change to let the adolescent out, but at the same time it must maintain a place for that child in the family. A system that does not allow anyone out results in a moribund family. The drive to be indelible, to carry the family identity beyond the borders of the family, is thwarted. How can the family survive, how can its rules and roles be carried into posterity, or at least into the larger world, if no one leaves home?

On the other hand, a family system that lets its members go before they are ready gives the world people who are unprepared to assert themselves confidently from a home base of strength and support. How is this family going to have an impact if it scatters before it has made an indelible impression on its younger generation? Although some teenagers are more subtle than others in pursuing their own separate identities, to some extent all teenagers are involved in the overthrow of the prevailing family systems. Initially, parents may struggle to retain the old systems because the preceding stage leads them to believe that these systems will work forever. But the system has to change to allow adolescents to find their own identities and parents to affirm theirs. The system has to be flexible enough so that all members can find themselves without threatening the family identity.

Adolescent Identity

There is no choice about change during this stage. As adolescents, we can see ourselves changing and so can everyone else. Our old clothes don't fit any better than our old roles. We have a new body, a sexual body. We may not be prepared to inhabit that body yet, but we have it, and it spurs a need to establish a sexual identity as well as an adult identity. We can no longer predict who we are going to be in our peer group, in our family, in the present, and in the future. We knew who we were as children. We were the sons or daughters of our parents, the brothers or sisters of our siblings, the good kids in the family, the dumb kids at school, the future doctors, jockeys, mothers, or fathers. Now, we have to define ourselves in a larger context with a future that is here. We may want to reject some of the old characterizations by becoming the smart kid, changing our major, and denying our connection to the family. But we don't do so without some trepidation. We have doubts about our success in the real world with our new body and our newfound sense of individuality. And we worry about the family's survival, as well as our own, once we are gone.

Adolescents need to know if the family will fall apart without them. They also need to know if they can survive without the family. Although it is difficult for parents to recognize what is happening when they are being attacked by rebellious teenagers, their children are actually testing themselves as much as their parents. How far can they safely go and still be in the family? Parents are legitimately worried about the safety of their adolescents and set limits to protect them as well as to assert their own authority. Children have to sort out the limits that are important to them at various points. They have to separate their parents' fear of being ignored or left from their own need to step away from the family. This self-testing continues even after young people leave home, until they have enough confidence in their own authority. One woman described going away to college at seventeen and being stunned by a sign-out policy of two-thirty in the morning in the freshman dormitories. She'd never been out until two-thirty in the morning in her life. She'd never even been up until that hour. It took her almost her whole first year in school to realize that she didn't have to stay out until two-thirty. When she lived at home she had continually defied her parents' midnight curfew, claiming they were treating her like a child. But when she left them she treated herself like a child, carrying them with her until she realized she could set her own limits.

That know-it-all attitude that teenagers have, the arrogance and certainty that really drives parents crazy, is actually an early sign of consciousness. The adolescent really does know all there is to know about the new person she or he has become. There isn't really much to know since the awareness of individuality is so new, but it is a heady experience. It isn't very surprising, therefore, that a teenager would generalize from this development and assume that she or he knew all there was to know about everything. But adults are not so sanguine about young people, especially their own children. They tend to leap on the assertions of inexperienced teenagers. It may be their only chance to really crow. They are sure that their children will find out that they don't know everything, whereas they are not sure that these same children will come home on time or study or be loyal.

But adolescents don't really hear what their parents are saying because they are only interested in their own experiences. They respond not to the content but to their parents' tone, and they apply their newly discovered ability to argue and philosophize, to think abstractly. In the previous stage, it was the children who were literal, concerned with the concrete. Their sense of fairness, of black and white, encouraged the family to make clearer distinctions, to pay attention to the rules. Now the adolescent, in questioning the rules and everything else, shows the family that at least some of its authority, some of its values and structures, are quite arbitrary and in need of criticism. Although the adolescent is primarily interested in clearing space for himself or herself, other family members benefit from the extra room.

Adult Identity

The adolescent is not the only one having an identity crisis. Stage Five is the juxtaposition of two of the hardest transitions in life. The child is passing from childhood to adulthood, and the adult is passing from parent to nonparent. Sometimes, the adult's parents are also in transition from an active life to a passive life, adding a third dimension of change in the family. The parent of the adolescent is also aware of physical changes. Just as the child is getting a new body, the adult is getting an old one. Bodies are beginning to sag here and there, energy and stamina decrease. We can't help comparing their fresh faces to our aging ones. We envy their attractiveness, their sexual appeal and potency, their futures. We are sharply aware of what we didn't do with our bodies, our young lives, when we had them. And we question what we are doing now. Since we are clearly over the hill in so many ways, we fail to recognize the ways in which we identify with our children, the ways in which we have not outgrown the very issues they are struggling with.

Delegating

Parents play out many identity issues through a process called delegating. The parent unconsciously urges an adolescent to represent him or her in some conflict that dates back to the parent's own adolescence. This is particularly true when a child faces sexual issues that the parent has never resolved. In some families, teenagers are subtly encouraged to act on their sexual impulses while at the same time they are admonished for doing so. A father, for instance, will listen raptly to his sons talk about girls in school, will laugh and prod them to say more, and then will refuse to lend them the family car to take one of these girls out on a date. The father eggs his sons on, identifying with their sexual drives. But because he could not act on those drives as a young man, and perhaps still cannot, he denies his sons their drives. Thus, he gets guiltfree, vicarious enjoyment from their experience, and they are the ones who are punished for his guilt. Similarly, parents who are afraid of drugs or alcohol themselves will project their fears onto adolescents who may be experimenting with these substances.

Although many parents are legitimately worried about their children, sometimes the fears are their own. Although they use illegality and inexperience in the argument against such experimentation, a bigger problem may be their own inexperience or fantasies about addiction and their own loss of control. Unconsciously, they encourage their adolescents to find out what it is like and also to suffer the consequences. They may do this by soliciting confidences, like the father above, or by playing into that well-known adolescent tendency to deny authority. Without really meaning to, parents sometimes support "bad" behavior by a rabid or irrational insistence on "good" behavior.

Being a delegate for a parent is not all unpleasant. It is a special role, and every role gives us a place in the family circle, as well as a sense of belonging. The child feels powerful because he or she has been chosen for an adult's special attention. To have first place in a parent's affections is very rewarding. The child also has a mission, although it is unconscious and often results in scapegoating. But there are compensations. When a child takes over a parent's internal conflict through the delegate role, tension in the family is reduced, at least temporarily. Furthermore, the parent is relieved, and in a backhanded and also unconscious way, gives the adolescent approval and support.

But being a delegate also takes up energy, energy that the teenager needs in order to find himself or herself. It is a process that leads to resentment because children have to spend their time protecting and using themselves up for their parents. They cannot relate to peers naturally because they have this secret mission. It is even more difficult for them to establish their own identity because they are so busy being a parent's emissary.

Parents are resentful, too, because the children can never really resolve these old issues for them. In fact, parents who delegate are likely to have been delegates themselves. And because they were unable to find themselves when they were children, they are very anxious to establish an identity before it is too late to feel independent and self-sufficient. But, unfortunately, they are locked into an old pattern of behavior, a family pattern that turns out to be indelible. These parents only know one way to reach for their identity—through their children—because that's the pattern they learned when they were children.

The choice of delegate is often predictable. The child who has always had a special meaning for the parent, who looks like the parent, who has the same birth order as the parent, who is named after the parent, usually becomes the parent's delegate. If the parent's problems involve some aspect of sexuality, he or she is more likely to choose a child of the same sex as a delegate. In large and particularly disturbed families one child after another can become the delegate, but this is uncommon. Parents can catch themselves delegating just by looking at themselves, perhaps with outside help, whenever a child's misbehavior or "acting out" seems to be reaching epidemic proportions. We all tend to concentrate on our children at such times, so we don't usually realize that our own anxieties are being subtly transmitted to them.

A family of three came into therapy because the fifteen-year-old son was very depressed and had been doing poorly in school. His mother was extremely upset because she had found, as she was supposed to, a note the boy had written about wanting to commit suicide, and she was afraid for her son. Her husband, the boy's very loving stepfather of two years, feared that the boy resented him and wanted his mother all to himself. Furthermore, the stepfather had been a very good student, and he was surprised that his bright and personable stepson didn't want to follow in his footsteps. They boy himself couldn't talk during therapy sessions. He just shrugged and smiled weakly when they asked him how he felt about himself, his parents, the family.

The therapist suggested a private session for each of them. In her session with the stepfather he expressed great fondness and concern for both the boy and the mother, as well as some awareness that his expectations for the boy were based on his own expectations for himself and were, therefore, perhaps inappropriate. During his session, the boy talked about his stepfather with affection and pride. He also expressed little interest in school and a strong desire for his mother to leave him alone. What he meant by that was not clear until the mother came in for her individual session.

The mother was having an identity crisis which she unconsciously fantasized her son could solve. It was a crisis very similar to one in her own adolescence. As a teenager she had studied dance and become quite accomplished. She wanted to continue with it, but her father refused to help her because he felt it was impractical. He wanted her to be a teacher or a librarian so she could always have a job. Dancing was not a job. Not long after that, she ran away from home, never to return.

She didn't actually become a dancer. She became a very successful record jacket producer after several years of work in both the design and the music industries. She didn't necessarily want her son to be in the arts, but she wanted him to get good grades so that he could do whatever he wanted to do. She would support him no matter what he chose, unlike the situation she had faced with her father. But, actually, she was repeating her father's pattern. She wanted her son to be practical. She wanted him to have good grades so he could choose anything. Because she was in the arts and she was offering him the world, she did not recognize that she wanted him to be practical before he made his final career choice. Her son wasn't any more interested in being practical than she had been.

The whole issue might not have come up if she had not been presented with a practical choice once again. She had married a man who was a fashion photographer. She was restless with her own success and very interested in photography. She was thinking about expanding her business and actually designing and photographing jacket covers. She would need her husband's help to get started, but he didn't think it was a very practical idea. They were both very busy and well regarded in their fields. Why upset what they had? He was puzzled by her talk about opportunities and challenges.

This "talk" between husband and wife was almost an exact echo of the mother's talk about her son and his opportunities. When the mother and, later, the stepfather listened to the therapist's tapes of the two discussions, the therapy changed. The parents began to talk about working together, perhaps forming their own company. As the mother began to fulfill her own ambitions, she grew less obsessed with her son's performance in school. Once both parents were involved in the business, they had less need to be overly involved in their son's business. A few months after the focus on him shifted and he no longer had to carry the burden of living up to their expectations, he started doing better in school.

It is possible for the adolescent to refuse delegation, even when it has positive connotations. Parents can delegate children to be their consciences as well as to act out forbidden or conflicted impulses. The Bronsons were in therapy because the father was an alcoholic, a problem that is often unconsciously supported by the whole family. Thirteen-year-old Mike refused to collude with his parents in covering up an incident that occurred while the therapist was on vacation. Mike had been caught stealing tennis balls from a neighborhood sporting goods store. The manager called his mother, who managed to forestall prosecution by her complete surprise and remorse, plus a litany of the boy's virtues. She and Mr. Bronson swore the boy to secrecy before their next therapy session and, in fact, it was not revealed until some weeks later when the therapist asked Mike if he ever felt used by his parents. When the therapist expressed surprise that the incident had not been mentioned, the Bronsons said that Mike had been so humiliated and embarrassed about it that they couldn't bear to tell on him. But that upset Mike, and he told the therapist that he thought his parents were embarrassed, which of course they were.

It took several sessions for the parents to see that they were counting on Mike to save their self-esteem. They had delegated him to be an ideal child to kindle some esteem in them. Low self-esteem was at the root of the father's alcohol problem and the mother's tacit support of that problem ("I can't be worth much if my husband is an alcoholic"). But, as the therapist pointed out, they succeeded admirably in their parenting roles, raising a boy who took responsibility for his actions and who recognized that the cover-up he'd been drawn into served some other purpose than purported. In releasing Mike as their conscience, his parents were free to become responsible themselves and consequently more respectful of themselves.

Family Identity

Although the individual crises of family members are always critical to family functioning, the major crisis in this stage involves the identity of the family itself. The family systems, or ways in which the family works as a group to meet individual and group needs, are changing. These systems develop in the first few years of family life, and they remain fairly constant as the family grows. In Stage Three, for instance, parents maintain the systems in order to stabilize the developing family. In Stage Four, children bolster, support, and maintain those systems as an adjunct to their developing individual interest in order and rules. But in Stage Five, the systems seem to fall apart. Children who used to greet their parents eagerly after a day at work now ignore their parents while they chat on the phone for hours on end. Parents who used to express affection easily now feel uncomfortable or rejected.

The inevitable changes in individuals throw the family identity into the spotlight. Families do not recognize that they are a family that goes to college until one person does not go to college. They don't recognize that they are a family that does not go to college until one person goes to college. Until their identity is threatened by a change they don't realize they are more than a family of four reasonably happy, red-haired people living on a certain street. It is the change that is responsible.

In a family of doctors, the docile and presumably indoctrinated adolescent who decides to become an actor disrupts the entire family. In a family that hasn't achieved much worldly or other success, the adolescent who seems intent on "making it" threatens everybody. Exactly the same dynamic occurs in the family of a reformed alcoholic. The family identity was intact—"We are the family of an alcoholic," or "We are a family that includes an alcoholic." But who are they if they no longer have an alcoholic in their family? Who are they if they have a reformed alcoholic? Their identity has to change.

The family with a rigid, inflexible identity may be unable to change, and they will blame, scapegoat, or reject the person who is raising questions about their group identity. And, of course, that is exactly the task of the adolescent—to wonder, to question, to test his or her identity. If the adolescent's identity cannot be accepted by the family, the group may splinter in hostility, at least for a time. If the family can allow the adolescent to seek an identity and perhaps choose one that deviates from the family norm, then all family members can go their separate ways and still belong to each other. The family's identity struggle tests their adaptability, flexibility, and unity.

If there is a remarriage during this stage, there may be a clash between family identity and adolescent identity. The task of a new family—to find an identity—is antithetical to a teenager's main task, to find a *separate* identity. This is particularly true when the new families coming together carry a sense of failure from their past experience as a broken family. They want to be whole now. They want to create something that all fits together. There is a tendency to enmesh all family members just when the teenager needs to be set free. And the teen may feel trapped. Before the remarriage she or he had to get away from one family. Now, the adolescent has to break away from two families.

When the creation of a new family is coupled with individual identity searches, this becomes a particularly confusing experience. Initially, high hopes abound. We believe that our new family will cancel out some past mistakes or failures. All the problems, especially in single-parent families, seem solvable. We feel that we will find new meaning in life, that we will put our loneliness and our various conflicts behind us.

These high expectations may hold for awhile, but inevitably some disillusion sets in. We find that we are still the people we always were. We begin to realize that a new wife or child or father will not change our internal structure. We learn that the dynamics between us and blood relatives, as well as between us and new relatives, are repetitions of old patterns, patterns that we wanted to change. We see the old families pitted against each other over rules or family values. We have to find new individual boundaries at the same time that we are trying to find new family boundaries.

We try to do in a year or two what other families, including other families we've been in, have had many years to work out. A marriage between adults with adolescent children is like a group marriage. We all have to become aware of our real and unreal expectations of each other, the hidden contracts we have, the kind of family we can become. Much can be learned by what we call ourselves.

Although officially adopted by her stepfather, it took one young girl two years to start using his name on her school papers. Her real father was dead, her mother had changed names, yet it was two years before the girl really believed that they were a family. Confusion often arises when we have to introduce stepparents and stepchildren or refer to a stepfamily. Our awkwardness, or lack of it, is at least partially related to how confidently we see ourselves as a family.

When there are adolescent children of different sexes, remarriage naturally stimulates sexual tensions. The children are beginning to develop an awareness of their own sexuality and sexual drives, and they are further titillated by the love affair between their parents. In their previous families, sex was simply one of the many aspects of their parents' relationship, and usually very much in the background. But in this new family, sex seems very special for both generations. Furthermore, there is confusion about the application of the incest taboo. Adolescents realize that there is a prohibition, but their sexual feelings are so strong and the "family" connection may seem so weak that they are irresistibly drawn to experimentation. There is also a possibility that they are chosen as delegates for parents who have run into sexual problems once remarried.

That's what we see in the Belden case. Susan and Steven came into therapy for sexual problems. They had been married for six months, and although they had had a very passionate and successful sex life before they were married, the wedding seemed to cool them off. They couldn't understand it. Steven, who had a sixteen-year-old son still at home, was a widower of just a few months when he met Susan. She had a thirteen-year-old daughter and had been divorced for six years. Steven's children—two older daughters and the boy, David—did not like Susan and disapproved of the marriage. Susan's daughter, Pam, and her other relatives thought it was a good match for Susan, who had been alone too long. Initially, therapy focused on Susan's feelings of failure about her first marriage and her concern, exacerbated by the coolness of Steven's two daughters, that this marriage would fail as well.

However, as therapy progressed, sex became a major issue. It turned out that both Susan and Steven were uneasy about sex and felt that their adolescent children were responsible for raising some of the doubts they felt. The therapists suggested that they bring Pam and David into therapy, which they did. The kids were very quiet and certainly did not want to talk about sex, but several times during the session both Susan and Steven expressed some envy of their children and their sexual attractiveness and interest. One therapist jokingly said that the parents seemed to be afraid that their children made a better couple than they did. Although the parents didn't see it, the therapist caught the glance that passed between the children and suggested that they come in for a private session.

Sure enough, the therapists soon discovered that the children were having sex and had been since their parents' wedding night. They were both proud and ashamed of themselves. Initially, their only emotion was excitement, but they were both increasingly plagued by guilt. Not just guilt about a sexual relationship at their ages, but a genuine fear that they were spoiling the marriage and possibly endangering the new family. The therapists asked if they thought their parents knew what was going on. Pam thought her mother might know; David was sure that his father did not. The therapists asked how they thought their parents would react if they found out. Both children felt that the parents would be devastated and envious. They knew that their parents had sexual difficulties because the mother made some not-so-subtle references to the father's virility.

The therapists asked if they had any ideas about helping their parents, especially since they knew that their parents' problems began when they got married. David pointed out that he and Pam had become sexually involved at the same time. Pam wondered if their parents' problem was, in fact, caused by their awareness of the children's relationship. David didn't think that even if they knew about it now, they had known from the beginning.

One of the therapists then suggested that their parents might be scared about being married again, about their children's view of the marriage, about being a family. To which Pam exclaimed, "And we're helping them out in the sex department." It was David who realized that he and Pam were actually "stand-ins" for their parents. Pam wondered if their parents could do more if she and David did less. David, now eager to reinstate the incest taboo, thought it would be worth a try.

The therapists, cautious about the possibility of real change, suggested that the children break off their sexual relationship for two weeks and return to the next regularly scheduled session with their parents. The session's revelations would remain confidential, but they gave the therapists and Pam and David a chance to be more helpful to the parents.

The kids never came back. The parents did—twice. First, to report that they were doing much better and the second time to say that they really didn't need to come any more. They had rediscovered the passionate feelings that had characterized the early days of their relationship, and they were getting along fine with their children. The therapists were particularly interested in their information about the children. Pam and David weren't around much any more. Pam was very involved in the debating club in school, and David had a girl friend. The children's growing independence was a sign to the therapists that they felt their parents would be all right and that this reformed family was strong enough to allow them to make connections in the outside world. Obviously, the parents were also feeling the effects of this family self-confidence.

The Hidden Persuaders

The hidden forces in family life that guarantee the family's indelibility are particularly tumultuous during adolescence. Although these forces of power, dependency, autonomy, love, and separation are ever-present features in family life, the changing nature of the family—its new needs—rearranges these forces in Stage Five. Consequently, as the family regroups around these realigned forces, new systems evolve. The new systems have to be designed to let the adolescent out of the family while saving a space of a somewhat different size and shape if he or she wishes to return.

The Child-in-Us System

Adolescents are still children, but they do not need the same kind of care they needed when they were younger. Many parents find this confusing and difficult to accept. Adolescents do need care, support, and parental attention—when they ask for it. But parents who are dependent on having dependent children may not be able to move into this new role. Some parents are further hampered because they overidentify with their children's feelings of insecurity and underidentify with their need to be treated as equals and to go out on their own. When parents are not ready to let go of their children or of certain childlike dependencies of their own, they work to keep the child in the family.

A divorced woman named Connie resisted such changes and then became overly involved in them. The divorced mother of two teenaged girls, Connie did everything with and for her children. They all went together to parties, movies, ball games, even school dances. They spent evenings studying together. Connie was taking classes in adult education in order, she said, to reactivate her teaching credential. Her friends thought it was more likely that she was trying to keep up with her daughters. Connie seemed to be trying to keep her girls very close, to ignore the fact that they were growing up and had outside friends. This behavior seemed more appropriate for a much younger family and was precipitated by the divorce. When the father departed, the family retreated to a safer time.

The girls had many friends of both sexes, and everyone gathered at their house. Connie was always present. In fact, the girls and Connie often dressed identically or, at least, very similarly. When the friends left, mother and daughters would put on a little play for their own amusement. They would imitate the people who had been there, reconstructing events and conversations. In this way, they kept the rest of the world at a distance—until the older girl fell in love. Although she still spent most of her time at home, she spent it on the telephone—talking to the boy in her life. Connie and the younger daughter teased her a lot, but they got a great deal of pleasure from her adventure. Then the younger girl got a boy friend, and Connie and the more experienced older daughter joined together to rib her. Although the family circle opened up a little, Connie and her daughters were still very interdependent as evidenced by their teasing and involvement in each other's affairs.

In the meantime, the father was also working to open the system up. Referred to by the mighty female triumvirate as Oedipops for his clear interest in his girls' sexual preoccupations and fantasies, he became concerned about seeing triple whenever he was around his children and ex-wife. Although he was quite aware that their tight bond was probably a reaction to his escape from the family several years earlier, he bravely suggested that the girls needed more freedom.

He wanted his daughters to spend more time with him, giving Connie the freedom to find her own friends or lovers. This meant that he had to take more responsibility than he had ever had in the past—more than many men would have wanted. It also meant that Connie had to trust him. And although she didn't trust him as a husband, she did trust him as a parent. Furthermore, he trusted himself as a parent, and so did his daughters. Indeed, this mutual esteem made it possible to create a change in the family system.

The girls felt freer with their father because they knew he could take care of himself. When they were with their mother, they had to invest much of their energy in taking care of her. But Connie herself had changed during her period of dependency on her daughters. Their relationships with their boy friends reassured her that she, too, could meet and go out with other men, that she wasn't a failure simply because she was divorced. The father's offer had come at a very good time for everyone. It fostered a creative change for the family and helped them move from an enmeshing dependency on each other to a new capacity for trust and autonomy.

The Coming-Home-to-Roost System

In Stages Three and Four, autonomy concerned family boundaries, especially the rules and patterns that set the family apart from other families. In Stage Five, the important boundaries are individual ones as both adults and adolescents struggle to define themselves. The major issue involves a struggle between the real and the ideal—who am I, really? And who do I want to be or feel I should be? Adolescents work out this struggle by comparing themselves to both cultural and family models, testing and trying out various styles of behavior and identity. Adults face the issue by comparing their own adolescent ideals, which may or may not have been realized. Although this reevaluation occurs in families with and without children, families with children may face the extra pressure of tremendous intergenerational conflicts.

For adults, the conflict between their real and ideal selves is particularly poignant during this stage. In middle age, we begin to realize that we don't have the time or the talent to do what we had always dreamed of doing. And we externalize these internal conflicts by locating them outside ourselves. Who is more available than an adolescent whose own identity has not quite solidified, who reminds us of ourselves, and who takes us as a model? Because our adolescent children remind us of our own failures and anxieties—and lost possibilities—we tend to express our own rage and disappointment at them. Similarly, we may avoid them because they represent unpleasant thoughts or memories. In other words, the conflict between generations is likely to surface as a conflict between a parent's ideal self and his or her real child.

Jim Vine, for example, was a modestly successful contractor who had always wanted to be a fine cabinetmaker. He didn't seem to have the eye for it or the ambition and had taken over his family's contracting business instead. He had always felt bad about joining the family business rather than making it on his own as a real craftsman. His pride and joy was an elaborately carved and pieced together jewelry chest that he had made for his wife soon after their marriage. It was the only object like that which he had ever created, but over the years he began to act as if it were just one of many he had made and sold as a young man.

When his son, Dick, got a C in woodworking in high school, Jim was irate. He wouldn't let Dick tell his mother about the C because she would be so disappointed. Dick was disappointed himself, but only because he hadn't lived up to his father's expectations. He didn't care about being a cabinetmaker himself. Nonetheless, his father made him feel worthless, which was exactly how his father felt about himself. The father actually had deposited his own low self-esteem in his son.

Unconsciously, he encouraged his son to feel that he couldn't live up to expectations because he himself could not live up to his own ego ideal. Although Jim had always held on to the fantasy that he would one day return to woodworking, he knew deep down that he couldn't or wouldn't do it. So Dick became Jim's delegate to succeed. But Dick wasn't really interested in woodworking, so his failure reminded Jim of his own failure, allowing Jim to avoid facing his own low self-esteem by placing it on Dick's shoulders. This depressing pattern is very characteristic of families at this stage, and it is one that continued to plague this family. There always was an edge to the relationship between father and son, although it lessened over the years.

A Tyrant System

Power is a major force during this stage because the adolescent begins to assert power over himself or herself. Often this is done by denying the power and authority of the parents. In healthy families, the power struggle can be very beneficial. By testing their strengths and exposing their fears, families learn when they feel powerless and when they feel that they can control their lives. A good fight helps everyone learn what really matters to them. In a bad fight, however, the goal is to demolish the opposition, thereby ensuring that no one leaves the family. Families locked in a power struggle are usually very "close."

The Beachwood family was a very tightly knit group. They did not appear to fight at all, but there were very genuine power struggles going on between the parents, between the parents and the children, and ultimately between each family member and the family itself.

There were six Beachwoods. Diane and Frank Beachwood were childhood sweethearts who married when they were both twenty-two. Their first child, David, was born two years later and was closely followed by Andrew. Three and a half years later the twin girls, Peggy and Patty, were born. Frank was an engineer, a company man for twenty years. Diane spent most of her time at home with the children or in the garden. They had saved carefully for the children's educations, but inflation was running ahead of them so Diane went to work when the children were in high school. She got a part-time job in a chic dress shop in the upper-middle-class suburb where they lived.

Then one of the twins, Patty, stopped eating. She was sixteen, and it began with a diet. She just kept losing weight. Her parents became alarmed and took her to the family doctor. He was worried, too, and ordered a series of tests to explain this surprising change in Patty. They could find nothing wrong, but the doctor decided to send her to a teaching hospital in the city where more sophisticated tests were available.

Diane and her daughter went to the city hospital. The girl could hardly walk into the room. The tests continued, but Patty lost more weight every day. Frank and the other children visited and tried to cheer Patty and Diane up, but there seemed to be nothing any of them could do. This went on for two weeks with no visible improvement. Rather abruptly, Diane decided that they had had enough, and she took Patty out of the hospital and drove home. She did seem to be in better spirits, but she still could not eat. She ceased losing weight, however, and seemed to stabilize, although she was painfully thin and very weak. Diane brought her meals, but Patty could not keep them down.

Twice a week Diane took her daughter to see a psychiatrist. The hospital had suggested that the problem might be anorexia nervosa, an emotional illness. Neither Diane nor Patty believed that it was an emotional problem, but they went anyway because they had tried everything else. It didn't seem to help, so Patty stopped going after a few weeks. Diane and Frank read up on anorexia, but they couldn't see what it had to do with Patty. True, it tended to afflict adolescent girls and to start with a diet, but they couldn't really see what problems of female identity Patty might have.

A few weeks later Diane's boss left for three months of summer vacation and put Diane in charge of the shop. That meant full-time work. Diane did not object because she really couldn't do much for Patty anyway. They were company for each other, but mainly Patty just lay in bed all day reading. But just a few days after this change in routine Patty started looking a little better. In two weeks she was getting up and dressed and even walking around the neighborhood a little. In three weeks, she told her mother she felt well enough to take a couple of classes in summer school. By fall, when she entered her junior year, everything was back to normal.

Diane and Frank never were able to explain what had happened. They felt that Patty had probably had some sort of mysterious and elusive virus. However, Diane was not unaware that there might have been more involved. She knew, for example, that her daughter began sneaking food right after she came back from the hospital. She also knew how important Patty had always been for her. Patty was sickly all through childhood, and Diane had often sat up with her, nursing her through one illness after another. The twin, Peggy, was very healthy, happy, and closer to her father than her mother.

By the time Peggy and Patty were about eleven, it was quite obvious that Peggy was going to be a very striking young woman. Patty was not pretty. She was a little dumpy, had continual skin problems, and was excruciatingly shy. Diane had been a pudgy teen, and she identified very strongly with her daughter. She had not overcome her own feelings about being overweight, about being unattractive, about being insecure and frightened of sex and men.

True, she was married and had had four children, but in many respects she had not completely outgrown the awkward, scared teenager she had been. Patty was her obvious delegate, someone very much like her who might be able to resolve those old conflicts about sex and identity.

But Patty was also her father's delegate. Frank was having problems with the twin, Peggy. He was certainly aware that the cool relationship he had with his wife probably contributed in some way to his feelings for Peggy. But he was not aware of Patty's role. Frank was terribly afraid of his feelings for Peggy, but those feelings were so compelling that he wasn't sure he could control them himself. So he projected his need for restraint onto her twin, Patty. Patty became, unconsciously, his protector, his superego, the guardian of his sexual morality, his hedge against incest. The drama of the child who was wasting away took his attention off the healthy, sensual child and gave him a chance to internalize and center his incestuous drives.

So Patty was the delegate of one parent who wanted her to find a physical identity, a sexual identity, with which she would be comfortable, thereby making the parent comfortable, too. And she was also the delegate of a parent who wanted her to deny that sex was a component of identity or that sex ran in families. So her role in the family was to deny what she knew was happening. No wonder she became anorexic. It was the perfect symbol for her role in the family—she was cancelling herself out.

Anorexia nervosa, the starving disease, is overwhelmingly an affliction of well-fed, adolescent girls from families that are closely bound. It is about looks and identity and maturity; the young girl appears to be fighting off the fleshiness of womanhood. The diet that spurs the downward spiral is invariably keyed to the obsession with slimness that is so characteristic of the female adult in industrialized countries. There is a horror of having flesh on their bodies. The anorexic often does not see that she is thin enough. She is still fighting the swollen body of the adult female. But most symbolic of all, menstruation ceases or never begins, and the association between childhood and adult female functioning is not made. The adolescent remains a young girl.

Patty was not free to become an adult until her mother went off to work full-time. Diane liked working and liked being in charge of the shop. She felt that she had some control over her life and began to develop confidence in herself. Furthermore, she spent more time alone with Frank because they now drove to work together. This brought them closer together physically than they had been in a long time. Although they slept in the same bed and ate at the same table, they were closer together in the car than they had been lately in either of those two places. A simple matter, but proximity and the time together, while not immediately saving their marriage, did release them from the need to involve their children in their conflicts. And it released Patty from her childlike body and the necessity to protect it by staying in bed.

But what does this have to do with power and tyrants? Well, it is impossible to prevent people from starving themselves. This is a very powerful position to be in. No one in the family could make Patty eat. Anorexics are very eager to succeed in their program of denial. They may become exhilarated as people who fast often do. Fasting is very impressive to most of us because it shows such power over the body. In a family system it also shows power over the body corporate. The exhilaration may also have to do, as it did with Patty, with the fact that the anorexic often is the "good" child in the family, the one whose needs always have been met last because she never seemed to have many needs.

Patty had always been powerless in the family, especially whenever her mother needed a delegate. Her inability to eat offered a perfect solution. She was clearly suffering, but she was also getting a lot of attention. The family needed her to divert them from old, unresolved identity issues as well as from their fears about the upcoming separation of this baby (she was twenty minutes younger than her twin, Peggy) from the family. Although they squeaked through this crisis, largely because of Diane's job, the family's lack of awareness about their involvement in Patty's illness makes them a high-risk group when Patty and Peggy actually do leave home, Diane's job becomes less demanding, or the next developmental change comes upon them.

The Cutting-Our-Losses System

All forces and systems are set in motion to help cut losses when the apron strings are cut. Stage Five presages and prepares us for the real physical separation of child and family. Things will never be quite the same again. The adolescent has to give up, once and for all, the pleasures of childhood. Although she or he may eagerly look forward to becoming an adult, the infantile gratifications of being cared for, protected, and idealized are hard to abandon. And the parent has to surrender his or her own adolescence as well as this adolescent. The parent will not be able to realize her or his own past fantasies and dreams of glory through this offspring. What seemed to be a second chance to improve our lives or ourselves is really a first chance to see who we are as adults. But that means giving up the status quo, which may not seem safe to either adolescent or adult.

Teenagers turn to their peer group for help and support when they are ready to leave the family. This is a source of great concern to parents, not only because they are worried about their child's reputation and safety. Parents also want to make sure that their child's friends will reflect positively on their own image of themselves and their family. But even more significant from a family perspective is the safety of the family identity. Can it be entrusted to this peer group? Will our values and standards flourish in that environment?

The irrational and even pathological feelings parents sometimes have about their children's friends is certainly due to separation anxiety, as well as fears about their own future lives once the children are gone. But when rage or intensive curiosity is directed toward the adolescent's peers, we can assume that something larger is also at stake. All parents want their children to get into what they consider a good club; in other words, a group that has a slightly higher status but one that's not high enough to shut out the parents. A "less exclusive" club threatens the future of the family, and does nothing to raise the parents' self-esteem. The family will not survive into posterity if these children reject all its values, systems, and ways of being a family.

Furthermore, parents can't shift their loyalties to a peer group in the same way that adolescents can. Their friends are not all going through the same thing at the same time. Their friends' children may not be the same age, their careers may not be at the same stage, their time may not be structured in the same way (on the semester system, for example). Of course, parents still have each other. But when they are anxious about being left alone together or when they are otherwise unable to give up their children, they may unconsciously set up a system that makes separation even harder.

The parents may spend a lot of time and energy condemning the children's peer groups or, worse, offering themselves up as "playmates." Or, the parents may try to convince the child that she or he will fail in the big world and would be better off staying home.

This can be done directly, as in "You can't do anything right. What makes you think you should have your own apartment? You'd probably burn the place down." And it can be done indirectly, as in, "Of course, you can have your own apartment. How much money do you need?" On the other hand, the parents may not say anything at all, but their behavior may convey a similar and very clear message to the adolescent.

For instance, an adolescent goes away for a weekend and returns home to find her parents drunk, sleeping in separate rooms, fighting, scapegoating a younger child, or acting hostile to her because she dared to leave. She learns that it isn't worth leaving to have to come home to that. Another teenager finds that whenever he invites friends over, his parents are rude, cold, and argumentative to him and to them. He learns that it is better to leave his friends out of his family. In both cases, the family is working to keep the child home.

Children who have such experiences naturally worry whether their parents will be all right if they leave. They may fear that the parents will have nothing to do, that their identities are so tied up in their parenting role that they are no longer individuals. They may think that mother and father will separate, that they have been staying together for the children's sake and not their own. Teenagers are very wrapped up in their own identities, their new lives, but they can't, at least unconsciously, completely sever their ties to the family. They want to be able to go home again whether or not they actually do so. And to make that choice possible, the family must be available to them. Thus, their investment in the family indelibility is dependent on their fear of losing their place in the family as well as on their anxiety about facing the outside world alone.

A Social Security System

In previous stages we've used the phrase "social security system" to refer to the way in which affection is distributed around the family circle to make people feel that they belong. In this stage, we're going to examine the way indelibility is dispersed to make sure that people belong. It is an unconscious process that has to do with our identities as women and men and families, and, perhaps, societies. There is some drive or force in family life that begs for repetition. The case that follows is all the more bizarre because it illustrates that identity issues can be passed on even when the identity of the main characters is not known.

Rob Melrose was seventeen when he and his girl friend Marcy found out that she was pregnant. Marcy and her family felt that Rob should marry her. Rob's parents did not share that view, although they were willing to foot the bills for the child's delivery and the adoption process. Marcy was surprised by their attitude, especially since Mrs. Melrose seemed so fond of her.

The Melroses themselves had been married only a couple of years. Mr. Melrose was Rob's stepfather. They liked to get away on weekends and often left Rob alone. Mrs. Melrose joked about their trips, saying things like "What if I get pregnant?" But Marcy was the one who got pregnant. And it was Marcy who had the child and put it up for adoption. Mrs. Melrose made it clear that Mr. Melrose would pay for Rob's college education but not for his transgressions. If he wanted to go to school he'd go alone, not with a wife and child. And Rob wanted to go to college. He continued to see Marcy, but things never were the same. Mrs. Melrose and Marcy remained friendly, and Mrs. Melrose was later godmother to Marcy's two children.

Ten years after this pregnancy, Mr. Melrose, who was twenty years older than his wife, died. The morning of the funeral Rob and his mother were sitting at the breakfast table talking. Rob said that he felt he'd lost a real father although his reaction puzzled him, since he'd only lived with his stepfather for a couple of years and had not seen much of him afterward. Mrs. Melrose looked at Rob thoughtfully and then announced quietly that Mr. Melrose was Rob's real father. Rob was shocked. His mother said that she and Mr. Melrose assumed he knew but wanted to protect their feelings by remaining silent. Actually, Rob had no idea.

Mrs. Melrose explained that she had literally been seduced and abandoned by a charming, attractive, married man when she was in her twenties. When Mr. Melrose came courting, when Rob was about fifteen, Rob never suspected that this man and his mother had had a previous liaison, especially one involving him. Actually, Mrs. Melrose had not been very interested in this man who had done her wrong. But Mr. Melrose had been persistent. He was no longer married, he wanted to make things right, and he wanted to reclaim his son. He was also well heeled and could provide a finer life-style for Mrs. Melrose and a college education for Rob. So she relented. They were married quite happily for about twelve years, and Rob changed his name to Melrose. When he recalled the incident he realized that it had been a clue. No adoption proceedings were necessary. They went before a judge, Mr. Melrose presented some papers he'd signed in a private session, and Rob became a Melrose.

Mr. and Mrs. Melrose frequently talked about telling Rob. They wondered if he knew. Mr. Melrose, who had children by his previous marriage, believed that Rob didn't know because Rob seemed to like him. If Rob knew how shabbily his mother had been treated he'd hate the man who was responsible. And Mr. Melrose loved that boy; he didn't want to risk Rob's hatred, although he wanted to acknowledge the relationship.

Mrs. Melrose assumed that Rob knew, but she did not want to test her assumption. She loved Rob, too, and she didn't want to explain all the white lies she'd told him over the years. She didn't actually worry that Rob would hate her; she did not get that far. She feared that he would leave her, and he had been her entire family for so many years. If he found his father, he would no longer be only his mother's son, and she didn't want to risk losing his love and attachment to her. That's why she had not sided with Marcy. She had had an unwanted child, too, but she didn't want to let him go.

Mr. and Mrs. Melrose did not tell Rob who he was and who they were in so many words, but they certainly "told" him in other ways and actually replayed their own history through their identification with Rob and Marcy. Although they were not aware that they encouraged his sexual impulses, they did leave him home alone frequently, and they knew he had a serious girl friend. Mrs. Melrose's jokes about pregnancy, an unlikely occurrence since she was in her forties, showed her identification as a newly married woman with Rob and Marcy's awakening sexuality. And her attitude and behavior when the pregnancy was announced also indicated that she identified Rob with her husband before he was her husband. Indeed, by discouraging a marriage between Marcy and Rob, she was encouraging Rob to repeat his father's behavior. In effect, the Melroses "told" Rob his identity through their identification with him. This system took up all the family's energy during those years before Rob left for college. Even the fact that Rob did leave, rather than stay and marry Marcy or take her and the child with him without family help, echoed his father's actions. But the identification proved to be more indelible yet.

About three years after his father's death, Rob looked up Marcy. He had found it difficult to talk to anyone about his father, and for many years only he and his wife and his mother knew. But after a time he got curious. He wondered if any of the people he'd known, especially at the time his mother married, had guessed the truth. Marcy had not. She was still angry at him and not particularly interested in the story of his origins. But the interesting thing about his visit to Marcy was that it happened almost exactly fifteen years after the birth of their child, which meant that the child was the same age Rob had been when his real father came on the scene. Rob and Marcy talked about trying to find the child, just to see if it was all right. Rob especially felt that children should be able to find their real parents if they wanted to. But he and Marcy never did anything about it.

Ironically, Mrs. Melrose herself was adopted. She had spent years trying to find out who her parents were. Therefore, one might assume that she would be particularly eager to tell Rob all about his origins, since she understood how it felt not to know. One might also think that Rob would insist on finding his child. However, when we identify with situations in which we were forced to take a passive role, we became especially eager to master the feelings of helplessness we had in those situations. Mrs. Melrose could do nothing about being adopted or finding out who her real parents were when she was a child. But as an adult she could release her frustrations with that passive role by taking an active role in a situation that echoed her own experience. It wasn't that she maliciously, or even consciously, denied Rob information that she had been denied. Rather, it was that she had learned, through identification, a very powerful role, one with a passive and an active side. She had no other model, and she took the active side when she got the chance. And Rob did exactly the same thing.

The underlying dynamics of this unusual case are played out in a more ordinary way in the everyday experience all parents have of catching themselves doing or saying something to their children that they swore they would never do or say. "I will never treat my kid the way my father treated me," we vow. Then, when we do, we say, "I don't know how that happened. That's exactly what my father used to do." We simply do not realize how powerful our unconscious identification with our own parental models and families of origin really is. We do not understand how an abused child grows up to become a child abuser, or how a child who felt abandoned can later abandon his or her own child. We do not see that repetition serves a purpose and that indelibility is an insistent and unconscious reality.

It is very important for parents to give their adolescent children a part of the family identity to carry with them when they leave. It is equally important for adolescents to take something, too. Even if, as we saw in the Melrose case, that "something" is not an act or characteristic that we are proud of or consciously would have wished on our offspring. That need to belong, to be part of some indelible process, is particularly pronounced during Stage Five. It is, in fact, that which gives us the strength and tenacity to find ourselves—as adults, as adolescents, and as families.

Stage Six:
Letting Go and Taking Off

Family systems continue to evolve even after children grow up. New developments in the family life cycle challenge these systems and stir up the psychological forces that the systems regulate. The most dramatic change in Stage Six is in family structure, as old members leave and new members arrive. But this ongoing disturbance of the status quo is punctuated by several chronological events that also have impact on families with children and on those without. These events, ranging from menopause to retirement, mark the developmental struggles of any middle-aged family. They affect relationships between family members and bring out new roles, just as the changes in family form do.

Relationships and Roles

Family relationships change when all members are adults. Family members assume new roles in relation to one another, and these new roles and the interactions they inspire change the family system over a period of several years. In families today we pay so much attention to young children and young adults that we have virtually ignored the roles of adult children and older parents. Yet a grown child may still be treated as a child by parents who cannot relinquish their old parenting roles. Similarly, adult children may not be able to take on adult roles because they are reluctant or afraid to give up their roles as children.

Couples also develop new roles in relation to each other as they are thrown back on one another's resources. Initially, however, they may be uncertain about the focus of these new roles, or the direction of their future relationship. They can never again be the couple they once were, so they have to carve out a new identity for themselves as a twosome. For those with children, their remaining connections to those children prevent retrieval of their pre-parental state. They may have assumed that their roles as grand-parents would fill the gap in their lives, only to discover that they don't know how to be grandparents or don't even want to be grandparents. Similarly, they may have anticipated their children's independence only to find that their children are endlessly depen-dent. And adults without children may have been eagerly waiting to retire, to pay off their mortgage, or to travel, only to find that the anticipation was better than the reality. Furthermore, the care of aging parents adds another dimension to the relationship between middle-aged couples.

In Stage Five, adolescents were searching for themselves, and parents were trying, at least for a time, to maintain the status quo. In Stage Six the pattern reverses—parents search for new roles and young adults settle in, launching their separate lives, families, careers. In Stage Five, many parents identify with their children, hoping to find themselves or resolve old conflicts. In Stage Six, adults turn to the past, searching for role models for their changing lives.

We start thinking about how our parents were grandparents and how our grandparents were grandparents. We fantasize that our retirement or menopause will be similar to our parents'. We think of being, for better or for worse, the in-laws our in-laws were. We think about our parents' old age and deaths as harbingers for our futures. We feel that we will lose our looks, our health, our spouses, our houses, our wits, or our lives in exactly the same way our fore-bears did. So strong is the power of indelibility in our minds, while we are searching for our new selves, that we may have a hard time separating our own identity from those of our role models'.

The conscious, formal, socially acceptable roles of parent, hus-band, grandparent, or adult child are not the only roles that now change. The informal, psychodynamic roles that helped the fam-ily of origin operate are also evolving. The child who was always the scapegoat, the one who was blamed when things went wrong, leaves the family, forcing the family to find a new scapegoat or give up that role altogether. Some parents find themselves trapped be-tween generations, responsible for aging, dependent parents just when they are about to be free of their children. Couples caught in the middle this way have to learn to make decisions for aging, auto-cratic parents without becoming autocratic toward their own chil-dren or parents in the process.

In Stage Six all roles, from scapegoat and autocrat to savior and saint, have to be reshaped, eliminated, or replaced by roles that are better suited to the new structure as well as to the new conflicts in the still developing family. For example, in some families, the antagonism between mates is exacerbated by the departure of children. There is no one left to stand between them, to distract them from their conflicts, to protect them from each other. Couples who seemed to have a close, if stormy, family life will start to drift away from each other and perhaps even separate. Middle-aged divorces are not always the result of having nothing in common after all those years of childrearing. They may occur because parents have too much in common. These couples cannot get along because they fear being consumed by or otherwise destroyed by their partners once the children's protective presence is lost. Some couples who are uncomfortable being together turn to hobbies or work to keep them apart. Others will turn to a pet, treating the animal as they would treat a protected last child. Then there are couples like the Zingers, who actually came together after their children left home.

Nobody, including their three children, gave Fred and Sara Zinger a chance in a million of staying married once the children were finally on their own. That in itself took many years. The eldest, Jon, was home off and on until he was in his thirties. Alice, the middle child, eloped when she was twenty, but Sheila, the youngest, didn't leave until shortly after Jon did. When all the children did leave, the antagonism and bitterness between Fred and Sara seemed to leave with them. After Sheila moved out and Jon spent all his time with the woman he was eventually to marry, something happened. Sara and Fred changed. They didn't seem to be at each other's throats all the time. They had their moments, but it was not the same. They seemed to like each other.

Actually, they had been changing for a long time, as developments in the family life cycle whittled away at their thirty-year-old family system. The children seemed to keep them from being close to each other, from trusting each other, from loving each other. It took Fred and Sara almost a dozen years to realize that they wanted to and could be alone together. Fred and Sara were not able to shake themselves free of the tension that bound them and turn it into a positive feeling until they were well into middle age. Only then could they give up roles they had assumed all their married lives and take on new and more intimate roles with each other.

The conversation that follows was a very typical exchange between Fred and Sara in the early part of Stage Six. Alice just announced that she and her boy friend, Bob, have eloped. The ensuing discussion reveals the roles played in this family.

"How could you do it?"

"How could you take off like that and get married? Without even telling us. How do you think that makes your father and me feel? Or don't you think we have any feelings?"

"You wouldn't have let me."

"What do you mean, 'let' you? You're of age."

"You know very well what I mean. You didn't want me to marry Bob."

"How can you say that? How can you say that we would keep our daughter from marrying anyone she wanted to?"

"You wanted us to wait."

"You are a little young."

"I'll always be too young to marry him."

"She's right, Sara. You don't like Bob."

"You keep out of this."

"What do you mean keep out? I'm her father, aren't I? Or is there something you've been meaning to tell me?"

"Oh, shut up. Don't you care that she's robbed us of the only wedding we'd be part of?"

"Is that what it is? Is that why you hate them for eloping? Because you don't get to go to a wedding?"

"Stop that. I don't hate them. You know I don't. But Jon'll never marry and Sheila can't. At least Alice could do the right thing."

"I've never done the right thing before. Why would I start now?"

"She's right, Sara. She's always been the bad one, just like me."

"Oh, cut it out, Fred. She's not bad. You are, that's for sure, but I'm talking about being hurt. Can't you see I'm hurt?"

"Hurt, eh? So Alice should marry some jerk she can't stand so you won't be hurt?"

"I didn't say that."

"You didn't have to."

This had been Fred's and Sara's main style of communication ever since the children were old enough to set off the fray. One of the children, in this case twenty-year-old Alice, precipitates an issue that Fred and Sara can start to fight about. Although Alice adds a few words, the real fight soon involves just Sara and Fred, as it always does. No matter what the occasion, these two will fight. The children, Fred's mother when she lived with them, even their friends, were foils for Fred and Sara. Alice was not a true scapegoat, even though her rebellious behavior usually set them off. But they did not blame her for the friction between them; they blamed each other. Alice or someone else played the role of catalyst. Sara usually looked like the aggressor, an uptight and righteously ungiving woman. But Fred, who seemed long-suffering and good-natured to outsiders, was suspiciously available to her. Her aggression was often a response to a calculated move on his part to anger her. But, as we'll see, this was all to change.

Being Menopausal

Although much attention has been paid lately to male menopause, it is not a biological experience and cannot really be compared to female menopause. A man's more gradual aging, his loss of hair or an occasional erection, are not nearly so poignant as women's more sharply defined loss of reproductive ability. The real meaning and pain behind menopause is the awareness of aging and loss, and the impact of this realization sends reverberations echoing through the family. Everyone is affected by the deep life-change experiences of their pivotal female member.

Many women have only good feelings about the menopause. They are rid of the problems of monthly menstruation. Their sexuality becomes distinct and special when pregnancy is no longer possible. At last they are able to drop certain aspects of the mothering role and start a different kind of life. They look forward to this evidence that marks their transition to new roles with their husbands, children, friends, careers.

Women with female children often experience an intense period of overidentification with them. If their daughters are young and beginning to explore their own sexuality, many mothers feel threatened, jealous, and uncomfortable with their girls for a while. Unconsciously, the mothers wonder about their own sexuality, especially now that it is not tied to the possibility or the danger of pregnancy. If they can't get pregnant, they may not want or feel that they should have sex. Or they may feel that they should have more sex now that pregnancy is not an issue. They are facing the separation of sex from reproduction, possibly for the first time in their lives. For their daughters, the sex drive may be stronger than the drive to reproduce, and mothers who identify with their daughters may be very ambivalent about teaching them the consequences of sexual intercourse.

Women who become menopausal when their daughters are having children may long to replace their daughters. They envy these children and sometimes make it difficult for them to learn how to be mothers. Instead of supporting and encouraging their daughters, they are critical and try to take over baby care. They don't think their daughters can do anything right. They think that they were, and still are, better mothers than their daughters. Any woman who is not able to give up her role as the mother of young children in order to mother adult children may respond in this way. But menopausal women are more subject to the stress of change than other women and therefore more likely to fall into this pattern.

The juxtaposition of the individual life stages of each family member naturally creates tension between generations, in the family subsystems, and in each individual in the family. This was certainly the case when Sara Zinger had to have a hysterectomy at age forty-two. This event marked the beginning of Stage Six for the Zingers, particularly for the change that was to come in the parental subsystem, in the relationship between Fred and Sara. Women like Sara, who have thought about the menopause but are not yet aware of any physiological change, are naturally frightened by the idea of hysterectomy. Even women who have stopped menstruating find a hysterectomy traumatic. And their fears are felt around the family circle.

Sara certainly did not want more children. She was a working woman, well informed, who knew that the change would not be the end of her life, especially her sex life. Yet even before she felt the effect of lowered hormonal levels, she was in tears. In fact, she awoke from the anesthesia crying. She could not understand it. She did, however, think about her mother all the time. Her mother was no longer alive, but she had had a most difficult menopause, and Sara had heard a lot about it. Sara did not seem to have hot flashes or any of the other problems her mother had complained about, but she continued to be terribly sad. She wondered if she was upset because she expected to be upset, either because her mother had

been or because women were "supposed" to be upset by menopause. If her mother had troubles, if other women have troubles, in
order to be a real woman, she, too, should have troubles.

Fred felt sad, too. He knew that this would not change Sara or
affect their sex life. For all their quarreling, they had always had
an easy if not terribly passionate sex life. Fred did not feel threatened by this sign of aging. After all, Sara was young for the operation so he was not especially concerned, although he knew both
men and women related menopause to aging. He was not one of
those men who find that the possibility of pregnancy makes sex
more exciting. Like Sara, he wondered if he expected to feel upset
and therefore did, even without conscious cause.

In this instance, Fred and Sara actually were looking at their
roles as man and woman for clues to their feelings. But they did
not really consider how their roles as mother and father were affected by the hysterectomy. They did realize that the hidden
force of separation was a powerful aspect of the whole experience.
Menopause is the loss of the mothering role. Even for women who
do not have children, it is the loss of a potential role they have
lived with all their lives. For both mothers and nonmothers, it is
the loss of unborn children, of potential they no longer have. In a
close marriage it is also the loss of the fathering role. Although
this did not appear to be such a marriage, Fred's sense of loss was
an indication that he felt closer to Sara than he let on most of the
time.

However, separation from the womb was not the only issue the
Zingers were facing. On a deeper level, there was an unresolved
separation issue that the hysterectomy intensified. It concerned
Alice. Just two months prior to Sara's operation, Alice had had an
abortion. Alice was then sixteen and had no intention of marrying
the father of her child. She had not even planned to tell her parents,
but she did need their help. Although no one questioned the decision to abort, a sense of loss was to reverberate for several reasons.

First of all, abortion is loss and a painful experience even when
it is the right thing to do. Although everyone tried to forget about
it and it was never discussed, both Alice and Sara recognized that
one of them was losing what the other quite clearly was capable of
using. The abortion made the parallel between the end of Sara's
reproductive life and the beginning of her daughter's quite obvious.
Alice was more supportive of Sara during the months following her

operation than anyone else Sara knew. They never spoke of it, and perhaps they missed a great opportunity, but Alice, though only a young woman, seemed to understand what had happened.

But more significant than the parallel between mother and daughter was the loss of Alice herself. A girl who becomes pregnant may still be a girl, but she is also a woman, and a woman leaves home. Alice was clearly grown up. She had one more year of high school, and then she'd be off to college. But she already had left the fold by having an intimate liaison with someone outside the family. They'd lost her, and they were about to lose the role she played in the family. As we saw in the beginning of this chapter, she was to continue being a catalyst for Fred and Sara's battles during and even after her elopement. But when Alice left home, she was not as available for their negative and devoted attention.

The family had not really recovered from the abortion in another way, either. The loss of Alice's virginity, or at least this obvious sign of the loss, was a blow to the family's self-esteem. Although no one outside the families knew, there was great fear that someone would find out. But even if it remained a secret, the Zingers felt ashamed. They had lost face. A child of this family should know how to prevent pregnancy. A child of this family should be a virgin at sixteen. A child of this family should know all about sex and choose to "save" herself. In a way, Alice's role as catalyst in the family saved the group from examining its tension. Naturally, Fred and Sara fought about the abortion—the doctor, the time, the place, the secrecy. Alice's pregnancy gave them yet another problem to fight about, saving them from facing her maturity squarely.

This blow to the family identity also distracted the Zingers from realizing how that identity was about to change as the structure of the family changed. In this family, as in many families, the beginning of the menopause illuminated other events that accentuated the changing roles, the lost roles, the shifting role relationships, and the new roles of a new stage of development taking place in this family. No wonder that Fred and Sara felt a greater sadness over the event than they expected or could explain.

Being Parents

It is a tradition in many American families for parents to help their children get started, to take care of them through years of schooling and to support them in early marriage and beyond, be-

fore they are financially independent. But that tradition is changing. Many young people spend years in school preparing for their
careers and then get jobs that pay more than their parents ever
earned. Others delay marriage and childrearing until they have
established careers, by which time their parents may be feeling the
squeeze of fixed incomes and in need of help themselves. Young
families are also more likely to have two incomes.

All of this is confusing to parents who are not quite sure how to
relate to their children if they are not helping them. If their own
parents helped them, and if their peers' children are following a
more traditional course, they have no models for another kind of
relationship. Furthermore, the old model offered a transitional role
for parents who still needed to feel needed as well as for the children who needed them. Today there may be no transition. Either
there is a sudden change when a child moves from school into a
high-paying job, or there is no change at all as children continue
their educations, their lack of commitment outside the family, or
their dependency on the family indefinitely.

Some parents encourage this state of dependency in their grown
children because they are uncertain or frightened about their future and the family's future when these young adults leave. If the
children don't seem inclined to follow their own pattern of marrying and settling down, thereby giving the parents a helping role,
these parents may not be eager to give up the children. They may
prefer to keep the children at home until they can develop new
roles for themselves, especially in relation to each other. At this
point couples may be very uncertain about each other, wondering
if they are still interested in each other or fearing that they cannot
take care of one another. They need their children on hand so that
they can prolong the roles of mother and father and avoid the roles
of wife and husband.

Parents may also be worried about a dependent child's ability to
take care of them when they are old. If children can't take care of
themselves, how can they be trusted to take over when the time
comes? This lack of trust is exactly what keeps the children from
becoming independent in the first place. Such circular family systems keep everyone in the family at a time when all should be developing some autonomy.

Children play into such systems because they are worried about
their parents. They are concerned about their parents' survival if
no one is around to watch over them, keep them apart, give them

something to do, provide a scapegoat or catalyst for them. These children are willing to go on playing a familiar role for their parents because they are not really autonomous themselves and may not have wandered far beyond the family's borders. They haven't found new roles for themselves on the outside, and they seem to be needed at home.

Sara and Fred Zinger's oldest child, Jon, was in this category. He had a very special role in the family to which he and his parents unconsciously clung because none of them was ready for change. Jon had been a very precocious child. When he was still quite young, Sara had taken him to a phrenologist as a kind of joke, but when the man proclaimed Jon a genius she took it quite seriously. Later, in school, he was found to have a high IQ and was put into a program for gifted children. He was a shy, docile, and rather withdrawn child. The Zingers naturally fought over his future, but both wanted him to be a professional man. Sara leaned toward medicine and Fred insisted on law. But Jon did not pay much attention to them.

In his first year of college Jon decided to be a writer. Since there seemed to be no specific courses to take, he spent the next several years reading and talking about writing. After graduate school he taught English part-time in a Catholic boys' school and began work on the great American novel. He lived at home most of this time, moving out occasionally to live with a woman or stay with friends. Eventually his parents cut off his college allowance, but Sara gave him money whenever he came to the house. That is, she always asked if he needed it and he always seemed to. She also bought groceries for him, and Fred paid for his medical insurance. They never forgot a holiday or birthday present and were delighted to entertain him and his friends. Jon did not pay much attention to these gestures. He seemed to be bemused and tolerant about being babied.

Actually, though, he needed the gestures. They strengthened his role in the family. Jon was always regarded as totally inept. "He's the genius, and he can't change a light bulb" was the chorus. The family was not derisive about it, but this affectionate teasing reinforced his incompetence. He got attention for his inability to do certain ordinary things that ordinary people did. It made him underordinary rather than extraordinary. It made them feel more comfortable with this person who was really a little frightening to them. He encouraged their denigration because it made him feel that he belonged. It gave him a clear role. But it also reinforced his failure to become competent and independent.

His family did not really want him to succeed because that might confirm his superiority and thereby reveal their inferiority. And he did not want to be a writer as much as he wanted to be part of his family. To them, a writer was someone who could not make a living, someone who was inept, someone who belonged in this family. Jon could be an artist, but he couldn't quite be an adult if he was to play his role properly. Their generous presents and nonstop handouts revealed their lack of confidence in his ability to take care of himself. Their roles as providers and nurturers would be threatened were he to become a man so they all reinforced his failure, portraying him as too inept to grow up. Eventually he did marry Regina, a lawyer who had a secret yen to be the mother of a great child. With his compliance and encouragement she took care of him for several years.

But then he did grow up. The writing did develop into something. Almost by accident he became self-sufficient, and that upset the family system. His parents continued to send him expensive gifts, even after they had retired and were living on a fixed income. But he began spending money on them, too. However, they were not comfortable with such gestures, although they acted proud and pleased, and they tended to fall into the old family routine of making him appear unable to manage. They felt that they should provide, even when it was quite clear that he had more financial resources than they. Jon was over thirty when the following incident took place in a restaurant where he'd taken his parents for dinner.

"But I want to take you, that's why I asked you to meet me here."

"Jon, we really appreciate this gesture. We really do, don't we, Sara? But you shouldn't. Just give me the check."

"That's right, Jon. It's the gesture that counts with us."

"Mother! Dad! It's the check that counts with me. Now let's hear no more about it. It's bad enough that you ordered from the right side of the menu."

Jon slams a credit card onto the check tray, and the waiter takes off with it. Talk turns to other matters for several minutes. Then the waiter returns with the charge slip. Jon checks it and signs. The waiter thanks him, puts the receipt on the tray, and leaves. Sara leans across the table and eagerly places a ten-dollar bill on the tray.

"Here's the tip, Jon. Let me leave the tip. I know you can't afford this whole dinner. It was just lovely."

Jon picks up the ten, folds it carefully, and forces it into her hand.

"Mother, I added the tip to the charge. Now shall we go?"

Jon takes the parking ticket and leaves the restaurant ahead of Sara and Fred, who are whispering to themselves.

"Did you see how much tip he left?"

"Yes, way too much."

"Well, I think that's sweet."

"I think it's foolish, but he'll learn."

So saying, Fred stands back while the attendant holds the car door open for Sara. As he moves on in, Fred slips the boy a dollar bill.

"Thanks, son," he says.

Sara and Fred were clearly uncomfortable with Jon's new role as caretaker. Their expectations of being parents did not include the reversal in roles that Jon was demanding. They weren't ready to be on their own, and they certainly weren't ready to lose their formerly dependent son.

It is interesting to observe, however, that this incident did not precipitate the usual bitter bickering between Fred and Sara. They were united in confronting Jon's independence and even conspiratorial in discussing him, a marked change from the earlier exchange over Alice. The intervening years had begun to soften them. In earlier years, they could not give up their own notion of their duties as parents and providers. Their rigidity about their parental roles reflected their fears of not living up to their own expectations, a failing each blamed on the other. They weren't even aware that they could be or wanted to be different until events opened their eyes and gave them the opportunity. They did have a lot in common, and they did have the resources to support and care for each other.

The Zingers found it particularly difficult to let Sheila go, and they were able to do so only because they had begun to turn to each other. It could not be a real launching. Sheila had suffered from cerebral palsy ever since she was a child. She was bright and capable, but at home she never had been able to receive the training she needed to develop self-sufficiency skills. When she was twenty-two, she left home to enter a special program that taught these skills. Similar programs had always existed, but the Zingers had never considered them as an option in the past. And, although Fred and Sara presented the idea as one that was only suddenly available, the truth was that *they* were suddenly available. Because of what had been happening to them as a couple and to the family structure as a whole, they finally were able to let Sheila go.

It was not an easy decision, nor a clean one. They continued to feel guilty about not caring for Sheila themselves. But they found that they no longer needed her as they once had. Sheila had always been the family saint. They needed a saint, with all that rancor being expressed by the founding members of the family. They were unable to recognize that Sheila needed something more than they could offer until they finally learned how to fulfill each other's dependency needs, instead of concentrating their energies on various third parties. Sheila continued to be worshipped, but now she was also respected for her ability to take care of herself. This was a role change for her and brought about a change in her relationship with each of her parents. The Zingers and Sheila could relate to one another more equally once the parents stopped giving her the care that even she knew others were better able to provide. This family system had always hinged on the lavish attention Fred and Sara gave their children, although they actually, if unconsciously, resented giving that attention. It also hinged on the children's acceptance of all that care, and the children had resentments, too. In this stage, that system finally began to break up, as the changes in each individual generated changes in the system itself.

Being In-Laws

We get most of our ideas about being in-laws from our own in-laws and from our parents as in-laws. Being an in-law, like being a stepparent or even a grandparent, can be a confusing experience. Most of us have not prepared ourselves for the roles, and we find that they are not popular roles. A mother-in-law is not a mother. We do not treat our son-in-law as we treat our son. Yet our daughter or spouse may expect us to. Our child's spouse may have expectations entirely contrary to our own. There are cultural stereotypes to contend with. The family system has to expand to include the new in-laws as well as the new in-law roles for the original members.

As the family grows older, the circle defining it spreads out, forming concentric circles that give members and their mates and children autonomy under the family "umbrella." But there is always the family identity to consider. A major subject of family drama, in fact and in fiction, is the person who finds a "significant other" in a mate everyone else sees as an unacceptable other. The family identity is threatened by the lout, the gold digger, the simp, the snob. Whether the difference is class, religion, conscience, or wit, the family must find a level on which to meet this addition. We have more trouble with the role of in-law when the new in-law or in-laws do not seem to fit into our family. The more rigid the family identity and the roles family members play, the more difficult it is to accept and relate to in-laws.

We said that the Zingers did not like the boy Alice eloped with. They did not like the boy who made her pregnant, or the boy who first kissed her, or the boy next door. As far as they were concerned she had terrible taste. Bob, her husband, turned out to be greedy and self-centered, just as they thought. For a while, Fred and Sara fought about Bob and fought with Alice about Bob. They were very cool to Bob himself. But after a few years, when their need to fight all the time had died down, they came to accept Bob and to leave Alice alone. Neither Bob nor Alice had to play the catalyst for Sara and Fred anymore because they were learning that they were actually more comfortable with fewer dependents. Again, they had strong ideas about the proper parenting role, but they weren't really comfortable with these ideas. Their dependents reminded them of their own dependency needs. And their weak parental subsystem, which resulted from their own sense of inadequacy as parents, prevented them from supporting one another.

It is common to extend a child's role to his or her new spouse. Therefore, Regina, Jon's wife, was seen as a bit inept, although in fact she was anything but. However, she, too, was different. She didn't seem to want a house and family the way other women in the family did. She did not seem to mind supporting Jon for years and years. She always said she'd be working anyway, so what difference did it make. Neither Sara nor Alice could understand that and tended to slyly depreciate her domestic or social skills. Her

successes, such as becoming a partner in her law firm, were duly
lauded but viewed as routine or even accidental. It was all done
gently, but then it had been that way for Jon, too. By identifying
the in-law with the family member change was less obvious.

An in-law may also be identified with a fantasy family member,
such as the daughter, son, mother, or father we never had. If the
newcomer fits the fantasy there won't be any problems. But if she
or he doesn't, the entire family will have a rough time. One mother
of an only son had been looking forward to his marriage almost
since she found out her baby was not a girl. She imagined great
companionship and fun, neither of which she'd ever been able to
share with her very resistant son. She hoped for a daughter-in-law
who loved poetry and music, someone with her sensibilities. Of
course, her daughter-in-law loved movies, sports, and wild parties.
The young woman had everything in common with her husband—
and nothing in common with his mother.

Being in an Empty Nest

When all the children leave home and the nest is empty, some
parents have no idea who they are or what to do with themselves.
Their identity, both as individuals and as family members, has
been so tied up in mothering and fathering that they are lost. They
feel worthless and useless. They feel robbed of their roles and of
their children. The pain of separation often reminds them of other
separations, particularly from their own families of origin. Although they mourn the loss of their children, they are also mourning the loss of themselves. The children will be all right; they have
everything to look forward to. The parents are not sure that they
have anything to look forward to.

Some parents simply cannot believe that their children are not
coming back. One man was found working on an addition to his
large home on the very day of his youngest child's wedding. Guests
who tracked him down discovered that he really believed his children would be spending much time there with their children and
spouses. He seemed almost desperate to put on the finishing touches
before the reception. In another family, the new grandparents began remodeling the day after their daughter-in-law gave birth to a
baby boy. They turned their den into a children's playroom, complete with two bunk beds, assuming that there would be another
grandchild soon. Until their son became a father they hadn't real-

ized that he really had left home. They immediately and rather maniacally began making plans to get him, or part of him, back.

Recently, it has become fashionable for well-educated and informed women to deny that they are at all affected by an empty nest. They do not want to be labelled "just mothers," and they recognize that our society looks down on mothers who cannot gracefully let their children go. However, almost all women are socialized to become mothers at a very early age. Often this role is so central to a woman's sense of worth that even other areas of competence, such as career or community work, do not compensate for the loss of the children. In essence, it is forced retirement. Women must put away the mothering skills and the knowledge about child development that have been so much a part of their life-long work. To have no sense of loss in a culture as child-centered as ours is as unrealistic as building a bunk bed for a child who does not even exist. We are still a people obsessed with children and with turning out proper children. No wonder it is hard to let go!

On the other hand, parents, and women in particular, know that children grow up and leave home. Indeed, empty-nest theoreticians do not give parents credit for foresight. Watching children grow up and away is an inherent aspect of raising a family, although that does not negate the fact of loss and the very real depression families may experience over separation. But these feelings are not necessarily either unexpected or devastating. In fact, some women and men have very positive feelings about launching their children. It frees them to pursue other interests, to deepen relationships with other people, especially spouses, and perhaps to have different and more successful relationships with their adult children.

A more serious criticism of the empty-nest syndrome is that it is presumed to afflict only women. However, men also derive part of their identity and sense of worth from their parenting role. Even fathers who were not home very much when their children were growing up can suffer from the empty-nest syndrome. Although fathers, like mothers, may expect or want the family to remain the same, their sense of loss may be intensified because they feel they missed out on fathering while they were building careers or working. When they are finally ready and able to put some of that energy into their family, their children are leaving home. Thus, men's nurturant qualities, which may not even surface until middle age, are never fully examined or expressed.

One of the most difficult role reversals in Stage Six is that between

Being Children

middle-aged adults and their aging parents. This is particularly true if parents have always had financial or psychological power over their progeny. When such a parent becomes ill, infirm, widowed, or impecunious, the balance of power in the family shifts. Even if the children do not have greater financial resources than the parents, they certainly have the advantage of more time and better health. The parents will despair of losing their power and position in the family, and the children will despair of trying to take care of these unhappy people and assume responsibility for their well-being.

For each generation it means a change in a traditional role. The parent has to hope that the child can take care of her or him; the child has to hope that she or he will be allowed to do so. There are resentments on both sides, even in families that are very willing to switch roles. Older people who have always taken care of themselves resent their children's care because they resent needing it. The middle-aged resent having to give this care just when their own children have become independent.

Fred Zinger's mother, Grandmere, as she liked to be called, ruled the family with her fortune. She was a bossy, officious, arrogant, and rich woman who had opinions about everything. She had always run Fred's easygoing father's life, and she was more than willing to run Fred's. Naturally, this caused scrapping between Fred and Sara. But Grandmere was more than a mere catalyst; she was the power broker. She was always threatening to cut someone out of her will.

No one knew how much money she had, but she certainly thought it was an impressive amount. The children often wondered whether she had any at all since she lived a rather austere and penurious life. But Fred told of great wealth in his childhood, and he assumed that it was still around somewhere. He wasn't at all sure that he wanted it, nor was Sara, but somehow they had been seduced into thinking that Grandmere's money mattered. Grandmere herself had long ago equated money and love. She felt she could hold on to her family's affections by promising them a pot of gold at the end of her life.

She was in her late sixties when she came to live with them. She hated it. She insisted that she could get along by herself. She had

had a slight stroke and, although she wasn't paralyzed, her eyesight and memory were impaired. She hated being dependent and never ceased asking them when they were going to let her out of prison. She accused them of treating her like a robot and spent hours looking over her "papers," which they knew she could no longer read—or change. Fred was used to her tyranny so this behavior did not surprise him. He did determine, however, that he would never live with his children. That was probably why he responded as he did whenever Jon wanted to do anything for him. He could bear being resented by his mother and even his wife, but he did not want to be resented by his son.

Grandmere still had a place in the family. First she used her money, then she used her infirmities to remain a source of great irritation, giving Sara and Fred something to bicker about and maintaining a role she had played with her husband and her own parents long before. When she finally was admitted to a nursing home, five years prior to her death, Fred visited her every day, dutifully listening to her rant about being treated like a robot there and insisting that she would be all right if he'd let her out. Fred's attention to her created even more bitterness between him and Sara. But when she finally died they did not cast about for a new battle scene. In fact, it was just a year later that they let Sheila go. Certainly Grandmere had worn them out, but other changes in their lives and their growing sense of dependence on each other contributed to their willingness to lose this tyrant.

A note on Grandmere's end. She choked to death. It all happened very fast. Fred was feeding her and did not realize what was happening for several crucial seconds. By the time help arrived it was too late. Fred had anticipated her death for so long, yet he never expected to be a participant. He had worried about finding her dead in her bed, or getting a call in the middle of the night, or coming home to the news. But he didn't expect to be there. He wondered if he'd been feeding her too fast—if perhaps she was right, that he did treat her like a robot.

He went over and over the experience in his mind and with Sara. Sara felt sure that Grandmere had choked on purpose. It would be just like her, according to Sara, to refuse anything more from Fred as a final revenge, a last tyrannical act. Although Sara didn't see it at the time, her interpretation had some corollaries among other Zinger dependents. Grandmere wasn't the only one who was resentful about being overprotected. Alice's elopement was a defiance of her parents' need to be needed by her. So was Jon's night out with his parents. So was Sheila's pleasure about moving away from home.

Sara and Fred were overplaying their roles of parent caretakers with everyone, and they were too entrenched in the activity to recognize that their bickering might be a sign that they had some resentments of their own. Although they were acting the part of superparents and superchild (Fred to his mother), they did not really feel that they were very good at it. They didn't realize that less care would have been enough care and would have freed them to find themselves and each other sooner. And when they finally lost all their dependents they realized that they could get along better without them.

Being Adult Stepchildren

When the parents of grown children divorce and remarry, their adult children are often confused. "This woman my father married is not my mother, but I cannot treat her as an equal either." "If my parents get divorced in their old age, how will they manage alone, and how much responsibility should I have in their lives now? I've been treating them as a couple for so long I'm not sure I know who they are as separate people." These changes in the older generation upset our equilibrium. Whom do we trust, depend on, love now? Who makes decisions and what happens to our family's identity? How do we describe ourselves and our relationships to each other?

The ways in which we answer or resolve these questions establish the framework for a new family system. Some of us also may have to take on new roles, since it is unlikely that the new system or any new people in it will be carbon copies of the old. These roles may be hard to define, especially if, for example, we must deal with a structure that isn't as formal as remarriage. It is difficult to be righteous about our children's living arrangements if their grandparents are living the same way. Changes in parents' lives and relationships affect both middle generation adults and younger adults, as well as the relationships among all of them.

Being Grandparents

Grandchildren and grandparents are trapped on either side of the middle generation, the power center in most families. The middle people have the most to say about how money is spent, how decisions are made, how rules are upheld. Ironically, the middle people also have to shoulder the responsibilities and pressures that make them feel powerless. Worries about the children, making a living, and caring for their parents leave them little time for themselves. Their power over the others only diminishes their power over their own lives. Of course, in some families, especially as people live longer, the older generations continue to have power, at least in some areas.

Generally, however, both the youngest generation and the oldest one find the semblance of power that they miss elsewhere in their relationship to each other. Through their grandparents, children can relive the omnipotence of infancy. They get to make decisions because grandparents will take care of all their needs and gratify their impulses in a way that their parents no longer can. And grandparents find that they are able to satisfy these needs better than they could satisfy their own children's, giving them confidence and a sense of accomplishment. This raises self-esteem for both generations, making each feel beloved and worthwhile.

However, when grandchildren become adolescents and begin to break away from their families, they sometimes patronize formerly favored grandparents, which can be very demoralizing to those grandparents. Sara Zinger's parents both died before the Zinger children were very far into adolescence, thus escaping any such taint. Instead, they were canonized. The children had all had a very special bond with these grandparents, especially when compared to Grandmere. The children visited their maternal grandparents every summer and as often as possible during the year. After they died, within months of each other, the whole family spoke of them in one breath. They were perfect, simply perfect. No one had anything bad to say about either one of them. No one had anything real to say about them, either. They were idealized, and that served a purpose during the long years of Grandmere's "incarceration." The family could put up with Grandmere and their own martyrdom because they knew that she really was impossible. Her awful behavior emphasized the other grandparents' wonderful qualities, even when they were no longer around for actual comparison.

Naturally, Fred and Sara had hoped to emulate her parents' role as grandparents when their turn came. But it did not turn out that way. They discovered, somewhat to their own surprise, that they really did not want to be grandparents at all. Alice did not have her children for several years, and when they finally came, they were so difficult. They didn't behave, they weren't quiet, and Alice didn't even notice. Fred and Sara were simply not very interested in being doting grandparents. Once Sheila was gone, Sara went back to work. She did not have the time to care for Alice's kids. This caused great conflict between Sara and Alice. Alice expected Sara to be like her own grandmother, and she wasn't. Sara wanted to be a good grandmother and mother, but as time went on she became more interested in her role as a working woman and wife.

Actually, Fred was more cut out for the role of grandparent than Sara, having greater interest than she in interpersonal issues and family ties. But by the time Alice's children were in need of a grandparent, he was too old. At least that is what he said. The children tired him; he felt uneasy with them. He remembered that Sara's parents, even his own grandparents, had been much younger than he and Sara were when they became grandparents. Perhaps age did make a difference. He certainly did not seem to have much patience any more. And he was rather afraid of turning into Grandmere. Furthermore, he had other interests now. Since Sheila was gone and he and Sara had become so close, he no longer yearned for the close relationship with these children he once thought he wanted. It was all very different from what he had expected, and he felt mildly surprised and disappointed. Even though he chose the role of distant grandfather, he felt that he didn't know his lines.

Some men, however, find that they are very interested in taking care of their grandchildren. In fact, they are a little resentful that their wives are expected to take an active role with the grandchildren while they are regarded by their children and perhaps their wives, too, as tag-along or support personnel. Men are not given much encouragement to take on caretaking roles, even though in later life they often are better suited to these roles than women.

Some grandparents act as though they are parents to their grandchildren. Either because they overidentify with their children's parental role, or because they do not trust their children as parents, they unconsciously blur the boundaries between generations. In both cases, old, unresolved power struggles and dependency needs, usually dating back to the grandparents' own families of origin, reassert themselves. This is a hard pattern to crack when it is part of a family's history since all the role models followed the same pattern. However, parents who resent this kind of intrusion on their roles may be able to break the pattern by *not* fulfilling their parents' expectations.

For example, a new mother who knows that her mother expects her to know nothing about baby care can make a special effort to care for her baby whenever her mother is present. In this way, she can let her mother know that she wants to assume *complete* responsibility for her child. It's very easy for grandmothers to take over in such a situation, if so inclined, because their daughters are tired, unsure, and perhaps used to being dominated by their mothers. Furthermore, all new mothers make some mistakes and feel a little incompetent at first. It is hard to persevere when mother is watching, waiting to take over.

One new mother who was determined to maintain her own autonomy and give her mother some autonomy as well, made private lists of chores that her mother could help her with whenever she knew her mother was on her way over. They were very detailed lists, broken down into categories such as laundry or shopping, and they outlined the procedures the daughter wanted to follow. For example, first she'd tell her mother that she needed help with the washing, then she'd ask her mother to hold the baby while she gathered together the dirty clothes, then she'd take the baby back and ask her mother to separate out the white and colored clothes, then she'd tell her mother where the soap and bleach were, and so on. She always made sure that her mother had a chance to hold and be with the baby, but she changed the baby's diapers, fed it, and comforted it. She was in charge, but her mother got some rewards, too. After a while it wasn't necessary to be so rigid, but having a plan gave the daughter confidence. It also helped her mother become a good grandparent. Of course, not every new grandparent has such a good teacher.

Not Being Grandparents

People whose children do not reproduce, for whatever reasons, lose a role they may have looked forward to as well as a little family esteem. Their children's choice may seem to represent a rejection of their own lives. If they assumed that they would be grandparents, they may resent the fact that their children have cheated them out of a role. Uncertain about their role in relation to adult, nonprocreating children, they may see their children as irresponsible and continue to treat them as children. On the other hand, they may reject their children as selfish and misguided and isolate them from the rest of the family. Fred and Sara Zinger did a little of both.

Part of the reason Jon and Regina Zinger married was that neither of them wanted children. Fred and Sara did not realize or believe at the time that this was a serious decision, even though the children assured them that it was. Jon and Regina did not think that they were cut out to be parents. Both were ambitious and enjoyed their freedom, but they were not child haters and did not feel that children would keep them from having two television sets and a house in the country. They were motivated by personal feelings about parenting. They were very insecure and felt there were others who were more suited for the role. They were quite aware of the blow it would be to their families, but that was not reason enough to change their minds.

Although neither Sara nor Fred had much interest in being grandparents to Alice's children, they went through a very typical routine with Jon and Regina about children. It was as if they could not help themselves. Whether it was in order to be able to talk to their friends about their grandchildren or to be affirmed in their own parenting roles, there was no stopping them. Sara spoke glowingly of the joys of motherhood, not necessarily relating them to her own experience. She often said that the births of her children were the highlights of her life. She maintained that no one wanted to miss the experience of having children. Fred confined himself to wistful and rather fanciful remarks about babies, children growing up, other people's babies and grandbabies. This went on for years, although there was clear evidence of Fred and Sara's real attitude toward grandparenting in their troubles with Alice and her children. Jon and Regina patiently explained again and again that they did not feel the experience was for them.

Love was the hidden force that motivated Fred and Sara's irrational insistence on the joys of parenting and grandparenting. Do Jon and Regina really love us if they choose such a different lifestyle? Do we love them enough if they turn out like this? This all relates back to the social security system discussed earlier in this book. Family members want to feel that they belong to the family and to each other, not just for now but forever. We can't be indelible if no one exists to remember us. We can't be indelible if our genes aren't marching into the future.

Being Retired

Retiring involves a role loss of major proportions for both the individual and the family. Men are still more likely to feel that their identity is tied to their work, but more women are making this connection, too. To retire is to lose some sense of self, even when we look forward to the freedom we will gain. Some retired people simply do not know what to do with themselves. It's more than just a matter of who we are and what we will do with our lives now. It involves basic questions—what time do we get up in the morning if we aren't going to work, and what do we wear and do during the day? We've lost a routine that buttressed our role. We've lost the co-workers, the clients, the associations and groups to which we belonged.

We also lose a role in the family when we retire. We lose our authority. To provide is to have a certain amount of power. Retirement may mean a reduced income, which will affect everyone and thereby reduce power around the house. Women often survive domesticity better than men, whether they worked or not, because most women have been raised with the concept that household tasks expand to fill the time available. Also, women have more experience with friendship than most men, and friendships can be particularly rich and rewarding in the later years. Women are more inclined to maintain work friendships, dropping into the office for lunch with some former associates or keeping tabs on everyone by phone. Women are also more likely to make new friends later in life, partly because many only begin working after their children leave home, and partly because they are naturally more assertive in later years. Men tend to keep friends from school and from their early working days. Business-related socializing no longer exists, and the social contacts of the couple or the family are reduced. Therefore, since they are no longer bringing in income or outside contacts, many men and women may become more dependent on their families for stimulation and a sense of purpose.

Sara Zinger had this experience when she retired from the welfare department where she had worked before she had her children and then again for twelve years after Sheila left home. Like many people, she did not really like being around the house. She was not even interested in spending much time with her family. She was interested in and willing to provide for their physical needs. She had worked part-time as a caseworker when the children were growing up, and although it was not steady work, she was a steadier source of income than Fred, who seemed to be laid off or up much of the time. She was also a wonderful administrator for her own family, looking after their welfare, making arrangements for everything, seeing that everything went smoothly. She never was the mother, the emotional caretaker, that Fred was. He was the one who listened to the children's problems and took care of the family's mental and emotional health. Sara was the social and financial manager.

When Sara retired she was finally able to take advantage of Fred's nurturing qualities, a side of him that she had previously regarded as inept or unmasculine. Her concern about the latter may have reflected her own doubts about being a self-sufficient, well-organized, and perhaps unfeminine woman. When she came home to stay their relationship solidified into a pact in which each had something to give the other. Fred got a chance to be the mother he had always wanted to be, and Sara was able to accept the mothering she had always really wanted. Sara was only able to become dependent on her family once she had retired.

The underlying theme of retirement is separation—separation from a former identity, from a provider role, from friends and associates, from routine and purpose, and certainly preparation for the separation from life and all one's loved ones. But there is another theme involved. Retirement calls for a new autonomy, a new sense of identity and of family, a new purpose. Many people spend several years after they retire trying to establish a new identity. They mourn the loss of their old self and presume, for a time, that their lives are over. Then, they discover that it's not the end of everything. They still are healthy, they still have family and friends, there still are new roles to be taken on. One man, whose wife had died when they were both in their early sixties, retired on schedule at sixty-five and felt that there was really nothing for him to do without his wife or his job. But three years later he married an old friend who had lost her husband, and together they built a new life around the eight children and twenty-seven grandchildren they had together and their mutual hobby of photography. Fifteen years later they were still going strong.

Being a Couple

Autonomy is a particularly important force for couples who find themselves alone together in late middle age. For some, it may seem impossible to be a couple again. The sense of being special, of complementing each other, which they felt in early marriage, is gone. They cannot recapture the people they were then. Habit, rather than attraction, has kept them together. After many years of noncommunication and little feeling for each other, they may even find it difficult to raise issues that would upset the balance, even though the balance rests on boredom. Other couples will change a little. For example, one will begin to mother or father the other, and they will become like parent and child, thereby reviving two familiar roles but rejecting their potential for new roles and a new identity.

Couples also have to consider their own individual growth over the years and the way this will affect their relationship in Stage Six. Once past fifty, men tend to become more passive and women more aggressive. Men usually reach a peak of aggressiveness and assertion in their thirties and forties when they are building careers and providing financially for their families. In contrast, women often are most assertive and outer-directed once past forty or forty-five. Even women who do not have children tend to nurse their careers, husbands, or other family members up to this point. In this sense, male and female menopause are very similar—both involve a "change" of life.

Our strong, cultural stereotypes of mothers-in-law and little old ladies in tennis shoes are related to this dynamic. Some women who feel this surge of energy and strength do become more aggressive, even intrusive, in their families and communities. Although this rush often follows the menopause, the cause is more likely to be cultural and psychological than chemical. Women who are eager to get out on their own are freer to do so with childrearing behind them.

Men may be more inclined to fight feelings of growing passivity than to enjoy them. Some men will turn to alcohol, psychosomatic illness, younger women, or religion to express their soft sides in covert and socially acceptable ways. In some families, men carve out a role for themselves as the dominant grandparent. This happens particularly when there is a precedent in either the man's family or his wife's, giving both of them as well as their children a model for such a role. It also can happen when the grandmother is preoccupied with a job or some other interest, leaving a gap that the grandfather is able and willing to fill. Widowers may have a particularly easy time filling this role since there's no competition. Men who have always been more passive in their marriages can come into their own in Stage Six as their spouse's roles change, lending more support to their developing role.

Fred and Sara Zinger actually did take on new roles and become a new kind of family in a way. Everyone expected that they would go on bickering and interfering in their children's lives in order to have plenty of material for their conflicts. Or they would divorce. But they did neither. They developed an independent and quite different family system in which they actually began, for the first time in their lives together, to trust each other and to depend on each other. This couldn't happen to them until they were free of all other distractions. And that process was not really complete until Sara had retired.

People sometimes choose professions that reveal something about their personalities and needs. Sara was attracted to a caretaking job as a social caseworker partly because she wanted to be taken care of herself. But she didn't know that consciously. Only when she retired and gave up all her caretaking cases—including her own children—was it possible for her to become the object of others' concern and care. Her family, of course, counted on the fact that she would care for them without demanding any care for herself. And the whole family system operated with such equilibrium that cases were continually provided for her. First there was Sheila. Then there was incompetent Jon and the rather lackadaisical, soft-hearted Fred. And Grandmere! Sara had to be the reliable, steady, if distant, head of the household—until her hysterectomy.

In the evaluation process that often accompanies a development event, Sara became ever so slightly aware that she wanted to be taken care of. She had a hint of what Fred could do for her during that difficult time, just from his identification with her and his commensurate and empathetic sense of sadness. And there was the support she got from Alice. All this set in motion a semiconscious awareness that she did not want to take care of others all her life. That was when she began to see Sheila differently. She felt that nothing could be done about Grandmere, but it became clear that she was holding on to Sheila more from habit and the need to maintain the status quo than from need on either Sheila's part or the family's.

It was really quite evident that Sheila belonged in a special care facility. Oddly enough, Sara knew lots about such places and had even worked in one once. Even though Sheila's care increased the family tension and added to the amount of bickering between Sara and Fred, they could not let her go. The status quo is a stout foe. Sara had been aware for some time that she wanted things to be different, but she was not aware enough to free herself from the established system.

But it wasn't just Sara's realization that change was possible that made change possible. Fred saw it, too. He had always been half afraid of Sara, as he had been of his mother. It was his mother's death that changed him the most, although each developmental event in this stage made him more aware of his own identity. When his mother died, he didn't have anyone to take care of; Sheila was away and Jon was his own man. Fred began to see that his lack of ambition added up to something. He was a very comforting person, a reassuring person, and there was someone around his house who needed reassuring at about that time. Sara had just retired. She didn't know what to do with herself. But Fred knew. The movies. He had joined a senior citizen club that showed old movies every afternoon. They started going almost every day, seeing movies that they had first seen when they were courting over forty years before. In a way, they were courting all over again, but they were different people, people who knew each other and themselves much, much better. The next few years brought them closeness and peace, which no one would have predicted.

Basically, Fred and Sara became a self-sufficient couple, dependent on each other. The dependency pattern that was so well developed in the family, as one welfare recipient gave way to another, became unnecessary. They were no longer frightened by intimacy, by being alone together. It was too bad that they didn't change earlier. But perhaps they were not ready then. Developmental events have the power to change us only if we are open to change. Each family will meet the tasks of each developmental stage in its own way, depending on the family personality or identity, its history of problem solving and role playing. As a couple, the Zingers obviously were more comfortable with the roles of husband and wife than with mother and father, grandmother and grandfather, daughter- and son-in-law, but they did not know that in the beginning. Many families have strife precisely because they do not know how hard they are working to keep things the same, maintain the old equilibrium, hold the boundaries and the forces in check, and be loyal and true-blue even when real freedom and love depend on letting go and taking off. For Fred and Sara the struggle was to get away from both their children and their parents. Their middle years were a quest for autonomy from both generations.

For all Stage Six families it is vital to avoid fixation on outdated roles. Family life is continually evolving, even though we haven't paid much attention psychologically to that fact in our society. Families that are still interacting as they did ten or twenty years earlier need to evaluate the ways in which they have not changed to see if perhaps something should have changed. If there are children still at home, perhaps the question is not "Why doesn't that kid get out and get a job?" but "Why do we need that kid at home?" If there is a retired person around talking about the great triumphs of yesteryear, perhaps the question is not "Why does she insist on living in the past?" but "Why won't we let her into the family now?" If our spouse is always talking to the dog, perhaps the question is not "Why does he pay more attention to that dog than to me?" but "Why do I want him to pay attention to that dog rather than to me?" Sometimes we have to direct our questions to our role in the family before we can bring the other roles up-to-date.

❀◆❀

Stage Seven:
Curtain Calls

Family systems remain fairly static during endings. They have to. Whether the ending is part of the family life cycle such as a natural death, or a nondevelopmental crisis such as a divorce, the family clings to the status quo. The omnipresent, underlying forces of family life must be kept under control until the family can rally its resources to meet the change. This is true even in less dramatic endings; for example, remarriage, the loss of a job, a move to a new home or city. We will not be leading the lives that we led before. In order to handle the new situation we carry our familiar ways of coping, our family systems, intact into the readjustment or mourning period.

But there is change, change that makes it possible for the systems, the forces they govern, and the family identity itself to remain the same—and, consequently, indelible. And the change surfaces in a family's roles, the ways in which they act out familiar patterns. The roles themselves do not necessarily change; different people play them. A father might become a mother or a combination of father and mother. A follower could become a leader, a victimizer a victim, a good guy a bad guy. Roles shift to meet the family's needs. After all, everyone knows the various roles and unconsciously recognizes how they fit into the whole.

The person who gets the part is not as predictable as primogeniture or sex lines might lead us to expect. One divorcing father solemnly told his five-year-old son that he was now the man of the family, the leader and protector for his mother and sisters. But although the boy was named after his father and was devoted to his father, he was too young to really "get" the role. That went to the middle child, a nine-year-old girl who was her father's favorite and had always been the leader in the family and out.

Family members often share an important role, especially during the adjustment period. Divorcing couples, for example, can share childrearing, money, even work, after they have severed their marital bond. Families that lose a breadwinner may all have to work in order to get by and hang onto the status quo.

Occasionally, one family member will develop an unconscious—and sometimes even conscious—alliance with another family member who has died or left the family and will carry out that person's wishes after she or he is gone. For example, the dying mother of two daughters who lived some distance from her named her sister as executrix of her will. She insisted that the sister remove all her beloved household possessions immediately after she died because she suspected that her estranged husband would try to claim them. She wanted them to go to her elder daughter, who had a home for them.

After the woman died, her sister did nothing. She just couldn't seem to act even though she knew what she was supposed to do. The elder daughter couldn't take over because she didn't know the contents of the will at that time. But the younger daughter did. She demanded a copy of the will from her aunt and made all the arrangements, getting the movers in the day after the funeral. This daughter had always been her mother's designee, at least unconsciously. The aunt was aware of this bond, and she may have been unable to act because she recognized the prior claim. Although the mother had made her sister her official executrix, her daughter and unofficial executrix took over the role.

Each ending is also a new beginning, despite the very real loss we have to encounter. Our lives and families may never be the same again, but they will be surprisingly similar. Roles are reallocated simply to ensure that the family endures. We take this continuity for granted. Many of us harbor our own deathbed legacy fantasy in which we literally pass on what is important to us. But we don't always recognize that our role exists in context and that we are passing on a piece that fits into and makes possible a larger entity, which has a far greater chance for continuity than we do alone. The whole family system rides on its roles as each younger generation becomes the older generation ad infinitum.

This chapter focuses on a family that illustrates its indelibility through several endings: death, remarriage, divorce. The Franklins were certainly not aware that anything had been preserved in their lives. The endings were painful and sad, and they were as distraught and unhappy as any of us would be. Yet life did go on and time healed their wounds. Life and time, of course, are not just states of being. Time does heal because a family has a chance to reassign and test out the roles that were lost. And that's what happened to the Franklins.

The Franklin family system revolved around one person who made all the plans and decisions. This dominant leadership role was held by the mother or matriarch, Miriam Franklin, who was herself the daughter of a very powerful man. The role and the system were supported by her husband, "Frank" Franklin, a very passive, distant person. He was very proud of Miriam, as he had not been of his own mother, a very submissive person. The system was further supported by the eldest daughter, Molly Franklin Temple, who was actually her mother's slave. She was totally dependent on her mother, afraid of the world, and very loyal to her family. She was married to Hugh, an outsider like her father, and they had two boys, Hugh-too and Sean, who rather looked like his grandmother. The final support in the Franklin family system was the younger daughter, Ailene Franklin, a single woman in her twenties. Ailene's role was to deny that there was ever any conflict in the family, even though the existence of only one spokesperson, Miriam, naturally left several others out. Nonetheless, the Franklins characterized themselves as a happy, busy, close family. That is, Miriam characterized them that way.

When the Franklins learned that Miriam had cancer, they fell apart. It wasn't just the loss of the mother that frightened them, it was the loss of everything. Miriam was the center of their family. She was the one who listened to everyone, who gave advice and comfort to all. Who would take care of them? Without her they were finished.

Miriam

Miriam Franklin was fifty-three when her doctors confirmed what she had suspected. The lump was malignant, inoperable, and terminal. They recommended chemotherapy to slow down the cancer and ease the pain. Miriam tried it but found it too debilitating. She had things to do, including preparing her family for her loss. Since she did not tell them right away, that became a pressing concern. Furthermore, she had work to do in the time she had left.

She had been editing a collection of Japanese children's stories and poems. It seemed imperative that she finish it.

Miriam was extremely powerful and charismatic. Everyone listened to her, no matter what she was talking about. She was intelligent and entertaining, but, more importantly, she was truly magnetic, and her family was both proud of her and in thrall to her. She was absolutely dominant in the family circle. Both her aging mother and her two daughters were completely dependent on her. She had very clear ideas about dying and, although she was frightened, she was also brave. She approached her impending death much as she had lived—running the show. So when she did tell her family she had pretty much decided how things would be.

Tom Franklin, "Frank" to everyone, was stunned by the news. He was fifty-five and looking forward to an early retirement. He could not imagine life without Miriam, and he was shocked that she had kept her illness a secret. They had been married for thirty-two years, and he thought he knew all there was to know about Miriam. Perhaps he hadn't wanted to see any changes in her. Possibly, that was why he let her go on calling the shots during her illness—they could maintain the illusion that nothing had changed. Of course, Frank had never been one to speak up or out. Friends assumed, correctly, that he was the strong, silent type. They knew he was silent, and he'd have to be strong to live in Miriam's shadow for so many years. Although he was a very successful aeronautical engineer, his work was never a topic of conversation. Talk and friends at the Franklin home reflected Miriam's artier vein. Frank was always behind the scenes, the person whose devotion and diffidence contributed to Miriam's strength.

Frank had some trouble maintaining that role during the last eighteen months of Miriam's life. He became very agitated. He would start talking—babbling, really—in the middle of other conversations. He did not talk about Miriam or himself, but his friends and family feared that he would not survive without her. Generally, his monologues concerned Supreme Court cases that had just been tried or, in his opinion, should be tried. Since that was hardly his field, friends were a bit mystified. He seemed so angry. He seemed obsessed with the injustice of what was happening to Miriam and to himself, although he never said that directly. Indirectly, however, he was expressing anger and fear about losing Miriam, and all the underlying psychological forces of family life were getting out of control. Since the Franklin system was one of deferral to Miriam, it was unusual for him to take the initiative about anything. His outbursts indicated that the system was beginning to crumble under the strain. But it did not crumble because the family rallied to cut Frank off.

Frank's agitation, his lack of passivity, threatened the status quo, and the status quo was very important to the family at that time. So Miriam and her daughters, as well as friends who were used to interacting with the family, managed to defuse Frank's feelings, making them seem passive and submissive even when they were anything but. They deactivated his agitation by making it appear "normal" and "natural" and therefore of no consequence.

Of course he was upset, they reasoned. Of course he was fixating on some outside source of authority (the misguided Supreme Court). It was natural to take your frustration about the unfairness of life out on someone or something else. In other words, nobody heard Frank. His reactions were not really taken seriously. Since everything important was said by Miriam, it was as if he weren't talking. He was patronized, or matronized, and left on the outside as always.

Thus, Frank had no power to address his family in a new way, just as he had no power to address the Supreme Court. The system was so ingrained that they could not hear him even when he was shouting. His own indirectness in upbraiding the Supreme Court instead of some authority closer to home contributed to the way he was treated. He did not elect to express his pain in a more immediate way. The Supreme Court is, after all, a distant body.

Even if this had not been a crisis, Frank's outbursts may not have been heard. In that event his rantings would have been regarded as aberrations and he would have been ignored or not taken seriously because his concerns were "abnormal" or "unnatural." The system called for his submission, his role as an outsider, and it got that during Miriam's illness and for some time after she died. Although Frank wanted to break ranks and express his fury and despair more directly, the family context did not allow room for that.

Such devotion to the power distribution in a family system is not untypical during crises. Even those who feel that they or others are changing find that this is no time to stage a coup. The powers that be will hold fast, as will those who keep them in power.

Molly Franklin Temple, on the other hand, played her role to the hilt and never had any conflict with the system that demanded her abject loyalty. That's what she wanted to be. Molly was thirty, the mother of two boys, eight and six. Her husband, Hugh, was also very loyal to Miriam, who had been like a mother to him as well. Molly was grief-stricken and couldn't face her mother for the first few days after she got the news. It was truly as if she was going to die, too. She was so undifferentiated from her mother that she believed she could feel the cancer in herself. But shortly thereafter she began spending a great deal of time at her mother's. Actually, she had always spent a lot of time at her parents', and she was relieved that Hugh encouraged her frequent visits. They lived close by, and Molly began dropping in every night after Hugh came home from work. Eventually, she quit her part-time teaching job in order to help her mother out in the mornings as well.

The odd thing about Molly's visits was what she did while she was there. Although she helped with meals and did little chores around the house, the most remarkable thing she did was the laundry. Every day she would just "throw a few odds and ends into the machine" or "really do a clean sweep of the linens" or "run a big (or small) wash." Because she'd usually just done a clean sweep, there was often nothing that needed washing, so she'd bring something from home.

This curious centering on a mopping-up operation had an interesting connection to Molly's family role. After all, slaves do the work, especially the dirty work. Concentrating on dirty linen seemed to reassure Molly of her loyalty and place in the family. She was a trusted slave. The fact that she was expected to do a lot of work by the rest of the family did not seem strange to her or to them. She had always done the work in order to continue being cared for and dependent upon the family and on her mother in particular. Part of this work was the work of holding the family together. Although Miriam was the dictator and decreed that the family would be close, together, happy, or whatever, Molly was the one who always did her bidding. Molly was the proof that they were close.

The fact that Molly did more laundry than necessary did not go unnoticed by Miriam and Frank. Privately, they called it her "Lady Macbeth syndrome," presuming that she felt guilty about the amount of time she spent with them, away from her husband and children. Doing the wash was almost ritualistic. They felt she was cleansing more than the clothes which, thanks to constant washing, were not very dirty. Although Molly maintained that she was helping her mother, a fact that her mother didn't deny, an outsider might think that Miriam was actually helping Molly. Miriam's role was to care for others, and Molly enabled her to continue that role by letting her comfort, direct, and support Molly.

Ailene Franklin, four years younger than Molly, did not believe that her mother was really going to die. Her role in life and in her family was to deny anything unpleasant, to be the optimist, to cheer and distract the family.

Ailene lived in the Dome community about an hour out of town. The community was a collective of seventeen adults and eight children who lived in six geodesic domes they had built themselves on some property one of the group had inherited. The community was made up of potters and farmers. What they couldn't grow, they bought with the proceeds from their pottery sales at weekend fairs and swap meets around the area.

Ailene was neither a potter nor a farmer but rather a dabbler in photography who had visited the community one weekend with a friend and offered to photograph the domes, the group, and the pots. They offered her the use of their kiln dome for developing when it was free, and they invited her to live with them while she worked on this project. The project went on and on. Ailene learned how to throw pots and grow vegetables, fell in love with a couple of community members, and became indispensable to the group for her cheery disposition and ability to distract them from any problems. Although Ailene's real family could not understand what she saw in this group of misfits, she was not upset by their reaction. The community gave her a sense of place that was strong enough to withstand such criticism. Of course, that sense of place and her role were very similar to those held in her family of origin, although this was a larger stage. She continued to be the optimist, protected by the community's strong ideology of collectivism and communal spirit.

In her family of origin, the ideology was the family's belief in one strong person who in turn would protect and speak for the others. Ailene was most comfortable in situations where she would be protected and spoken for in exchange for loyally diverting her protectors from their worries or conflicts. Thus, she diverted her family from confronting problems by entertaining them—literally breaking into song whenever her mother's wishes seemed threatened. Whenever her father tried to move closer to his wife or one of his daughters, Ailene would push him away by insisting that he play a game with her or watch her perform a little dance she'd just learned or engaging him in some farfetched fantasy about what she'd be when she grew up. When she did grow up, she continued that role. If Ailene sensed trouble, she made those around her into her audience.

She responded to her mother's news with a series of lectures, insisting that diet caused cancer. If only her mother would become a vegetarian, eating the fresh vegetables the community would happily supply, the cancer would be driven out. Miriam acquiesced, not because she thought vegetables would help her but because she was sure that eating them would help Ailene. She tried to convince Ailene that the cancer was already there and spreading rapidly, not to be discouraged by a change at this late stage. But Ailene could not hear her most of the time. She was too intent on denying the obvious, holding onto her role against the forces of dependency and fear that were tugging at her. Ailene's refusal to acknowledge death was in the great family tradition. Her role was nurtured and preserved by the whole group to help them maintain some emotional control, although none of them was consciously aware of that. They could all laugh at crazy Ailene who wouldn't face the facts, rather than facing the facts themselves.

Oddly enough, Miriam, spokesperson for the family, always independent and forceful about what she wanted and how things would be done, was unable to tell her own mother that she had cancer. Her mother was old, nearly eighty, and lived far away but was alert and healthy. But Miriam, who had a hospital bed set up in the living room where she could keep track of everybody and seemed to accept her own death with great courage, could not find the strength to tell her mother that she was dying. She evidently felt that everything would fall apart if she told this one last person. She had managed to prepare everyone beautifully, and in many ways she felt prepared herself. But her defenses against the terror she must have felt on some level did not seem strong enough to work against her mother's grief.

Miriam's acceptance, her realism, her careful attention to the feelings of others, were not relevant to her relationship with her mother. Although she was perfectly autonomous, almost to a fault, in her present family, there was an unresolved issue of autonomy in her family of origin. Miriam's own mother had been absolutely inseparable from her parents. It was a pattern that Miriam, mostly through rejection of her mother, had changed. She took her powerful father as a model. But in doing so she had to ignore her own dependency needs.

It did not seem possible, at least from what she saw in her family of origin, to be both dependent and autonomous. Those forces came into conflict for her when she needed care of a different sort than she had ever needed before. She needed the kind of care her mother had gotten from her mother. She longed to be babied, even as she was being strong and rational and brave. She hesitated to seek that solace from her mother because she never had, because she might not have received it even if she asked, because she didn't want to be disappointed, or because she didn't know how to ask. Furthermore, if Miriam had been able to approach her mother she might have slipped out of role, and the family system was not open enough to allow that, especially at this time.

In all of us, as in Miriam and other members of the family, the hidden forces of power, dependency, and autonomy rise to the surface in endings, spotlighting role assignments. The family continued to treat Miriam as an independent and strong woman even though her inability to tell her mother about her condition indicated that she felt vulnerable in at least one area. This is not atypical of families at all. Many of us have seen or been in families where a very old or ill person is still regarded as the autocrat she or he once was. It isn't at all appropriate, but families don't know what else to do unless the person holding the role relinquishes it—and perhaps not even then. Everyone is hesitant to get locked in a power struggle or role conflict with someone who is sick. It might kill them. More significantly, though, it might kill the survivors. They realize that they would not know what to do with the role if they had it. They fear change and struggle fiercely to hold on to the old, familiar patterns.

Thus, none of the Franklins, including Miriam, could acknowledge Miriam's needs. If they could have, the transition to life without Miriam might have been easier, but then they would not have been the Franklins. The Franklins continued to treat Frank as low man on the power pole even though he wanted to assert himself. They allowed Molly to become almost a parody of herself as she took on an increasingly heavy housework load, and they tacitly supported Ailene's denial of the loss they were all facing. They worked to keep the psychological forces at bay.

After Miriam

Before Miriam died she left written and oral instructions with each member of the family concerning her burial, her poetry, her possessions, their lives, feelings, and actions, complete with alternatives to cover any unforeseen developments. In her compulsive attention to these details Miriam tried to guarantee that she would not leave her family. And it worked. Even after her death they kept her very much "alive."

They followed her instructions to the letter. The memorial service and burial were conducted just as she had requested. Her possessions were divided as she had wished. Her clothes and jewelry were given away; her books went to the local library. But Miriam was preserved in more important ways. The family did not use certain possessions—a chair she often sat in, her car—that were strongly associated with her. They cared for her plants as if she'd be returning to inspect them. Kitchen utensils were used in her idiosyncratic ways. However, the family had some regrets about what they had given away. Although they had followed Miriam's wishes, Frank and his daughters realized that there were items they had wanted to keep—things that meant more to them than to her.

But it was the references to Miriam that most firmly established her presence beyond the grave. "I wonder what mother would have to say about that?" "Miriam never liked her." "Remember the time mother. . . ." We all want to be talked about, and fond references to a beloved person are quite natural. However, they sometimes invoked her more morbidly, as someone who was still running the show. They all used her to "decide" certain issues, to bolster their cases, to support their particular preferences. Of course, Miriam herself was not completely responsible for this extraordinary power she continued to have over her family. Although a forceful personality when alive, the family's continued dependence on her preferences and opinions was a means of fulfilling their own need to depend on someone beyond themselves, to have someone in the family who would take care of them.

Gradually, however, Miriam's influence over the family's problem solving waned. It took close to two years. Certainly, she had not been forgotten, but someone else began to exert the influence that was once hers. The family had found a substitute. Frank had taken over much of her role; he became the dependable one, nurturing and advising the rest of the family. He was not dominant in the way Miriam had been, but he was central in many ways to the family's operations and activities.

Miriam had wielded power in the service of dependence, using her strength to ensure that the others were dependent on her and bolstering her strength on their dependency. Frank, on the other hand, gained power by being available and dependable. Everyone in the family, particularly his daughters, Molly and Ailene, realized that Frank was solid, thoughtful, and reliable. He did not have Miriam's charisma or magnetism, nor did he develop these characteristics. But his new role in this family was strikingly similar to hers, and he would never have taken it on had she lived.

The family needed a strong, sage central character, even if that meant losing the role that Frank had previously played, that of an outsider. (And, as we shall see, that role reappeared a little later in a new guise.) Frank, however, became very much an insider, *the* insider, in fact, who tied the family together and ensured their survival. They were not the same family, but they were still a family, and many things about them remained the same. After Miriam's death the family entered a new phase, a phase in which they shifted roles but kept up some of the same patterns.

The widow or the widower is not necessarily the one who takes over in such a situation. Frank could have remained the outsider, and one of the daughters could have become the central figure. Neither of these daughters, however, was a likely candidate for Miriam's leadership role. They were born to follow. In some groups it is harder for a follower to become a leader than for that follower to promote and develop a new leader. Frank had no experience being a leader either in this family or his family of origin. But he had no experience being a follower either. Given his daughters' expectations and his wife's example, he was able to fall into the leadership role and learn it as he went along.

In a similar situation, when a strong woman died, leaving two children and a husband, the two children shared both their mother's leadership role and their own roles as loyal but not totally dependent followers. The father, who had always been the family scapegoat, continued to be the scapegoat. Nothing was lost in the dynamics of their family interactions.

Mourning

There was a rule about denial in the Franklin family. They denied or tried to ignore the unpleasant, the painful, the disturbing. They never talked about how they would be affected by their loss, they ignored any chance to prepare themselves, and they encouraged Ailene to convince them that it wasn't really happening. Even Miriam's way of preparing them—her lists of instructions —were a denial of the fact that she would not be around any more. And once she had gone, they denied that fact in many little ways. They mourned her death, they were sad and depressed much of the time, but they also carried on as if she was still there some of the time. This was their way of keeping her role active until they could find someone else to play it. In another family, or with a different kind of loss, the role might have been shared, dropped, rewritten, or lost during this period of adjustment. For the Franklins, denial was a natural defense during the reallocation period because it was already in their repertoire. But it is actually the replacement, however and whenever he or she takes over the role, that ensures the family's survival.

Ghosts

Some families do not seem to find a replacement. Instead, they behave as the Franklins did during their denial stage—they keep the deceased person alive. They insist that she or he is "watching over" what goes on. They take no action without consulting the dear departed. No one sits in his or her place at the dinner table. The rules, values, opinions of this person continue to be followed or espoused. The ghost of the dead person becomes the replacement. Needless to say, unless the missing person was very inert, the family system becomes moribund. It is hard to solve even everyday problems if one of the key family roles is played by a ghost. This is a particularly prevalent response when one is the last living member of a generation. The widow or widower feels near death, too, and finds it easier and more comforting to share the company of familiar ghosts than to take on new or dual role assignments.

Identification

Sometimes, a family member will really believe that he or she has "become" the departed person. Frank Franklin took over Miriam's role in the family, but he never thought that he was Miriam. Molly was actually the family member most in danger of over-identifying with her mother, even for some time believing that she could feel her mother's cancer in herself. Occasionally, a family member will take on the symptoms of the sick person, especially a terminally ill person, and believe that he or she is going to die, too. But overidentification also can be an issue after death, as it was—twice—in the Cahuenga family.

When his father died of a heart attack, Carlo Cahuenga made the arrangements, stood by his mother, and informed all the relatives. Carlo was very calm and philosophical about it. His father had had a heart condition for several years so his death was not unexpected. Right after the funeral, Carlo had what appeared to be a heart attack. They got him to the hospital right away, and acute indigestion was diagnosed. He spent the night there and came home to adopt the role of his father in earnest. Just ten months later the family gathered around another gravesite. Steve Cahuenga, Carlo's younger brother, had lost his four-year-old son. The boy, Jeremy, had died of leukemia. Steve looked pale and wasted at the funeral, and during the graveside ceremony he fell into a long slow swoon. It took almost ten minutes for his frantic family to rouse him. He was weak and listless for several months afterwards, as if adopting the illness, if not the role, of his son. Identification with the dead was this family's patterned response to loss. It was an attempt to avoid separation, to replace the lost person with themselves.

New Faces

In Chapter Five we saw the connection between loss and pregnancies. Sometimes, an unexpected or accidental pregnancy seems to follow a loss somewhere in the family. We see this rather frequently in teenage pregnancies. Although there are many connections between teenage pregnancies and other family dynamics, a recent loss in the family is certainly high on the list. The loss might be the death of a parent or grandparent, but it could also be a loss of another kind—a parent or sibling leaving home, the loss of a job or home, the loss of a neighborhood, school, friends, or relatives after a move. The loss affects the whole family, and they often cast about for a replacement. Although a new baby, a new spouse, or any new addition to the family constellation does not replace the missing person in terms of role or personality, she or he may replace someone else, such as the youngest or the newest family member, easing the way for a shift or reassignment of roles.

This particular type of replacement is certainly not a conscious process for most families, and seems almost biological in nature. It has even occurred in larger contexts. Several years ago in the small mining community of Aberfan, Wales, there was a disaster that later revealed a very strong connection between loss and birth rate. A stockpile of coal slid into a school, killing 116 children and twenty-eight adults. An entire generation of children in that community was virtually wiped out. But in the next two or three years, there was a dramatic increase in the birth rate.

At first, Welsh census takers and officials assumed that the births were occurring in the families that had suffered a loss. But on closer study they found that this assumption was not entirely accurate. Many of the newborns were found in families that had lost a child or an adult, of course, but by no means all. Indeed, many of these people were past the age of childbearing. Rather, the increase was observed in families that had remained intact during the tragedy. In fact, the birth rate was 50 percent higher than it had been in the same community five years previously, and was in sharp contrast to surrounding communities, which had steadily falling birth rates.

Community consciousness appears to be influenced by such losses. The need to replace those who were killed is unconsciously sensed by all those who live and work together. Indeed, the post–World War II baby boom in this country is seen by some as a nationwide response not just to the soldiers who returned home but to the soldiers who did not. The family is just as responsive to the need to perpetuate itself as is the human race.

Families reallocate roles in many ways during endings. They may simply shift one role as the Franklins did, or they may develop a more complex pattern of role realignment. Shifting roles may be coupled with various replacement styles, or there may be no shift at all, just direct replacement. In many instances, the system and the roles themselves remain the same. The Franklin family did not end when Miriam died. Although certainly something died in each of the family members, and the loss of Miriam had a very profound effect on the whole family group, the family system did not break down, the underlying forces remained stable, and in many ways there was not much change in the family's dynamics.

Of course, some families *do* change, and others *do* fall apart. But in general only minimal change will occur. And by observing and sharing in these processes, children, who are often more sensitive to positive family feelings than adults, gain confidence in the process of continuity and learn to repeat the patterns that lead ever onward. The Franklins certainly went on.

When Frank Franklin decided to move in with Anna, he believed he would be starting all over. He was sad about the end of his first family, but after all, his daughters were grown and his wife had died. It was time he had a new life.

Frank

Two years after Miriam died, Frank Franklin told his family that he was going to live with Anna. Anna? Who was Anna? Everybody was surprised—and horrified. What did he mean "live with"? They soon found out. He planned to move into Anna's house and live there with her. The sexual implications of this arrangement were too overwhelming for them to even consider. Molly and Ailene were shocked that their father could dream of living with someone he wasn't married to. Ailene tried to be cheerful about it; after all, she lived with a whole group of people who didn't "own" each other through marriage, but even she found it difficult. Molly felt betrayed. She had a vision of her father moping around the house when she was not there, faithfully upholding the memory of her mother. Both daughters felt that this was the absolute end of the family. They had lost their mother; now they seemed to be losing their father. Even the family they'd become since their mother's death was over. How could they explain to themselves or others that the family patriarch was living in sin?

Frank explained that they had considered marriage, but since he planned to retire soon they really needed Anna's widow's pension to make ends meet in these inflationary times. She would lose it if she remarried. Besides, her three grown boys didn't much like the idea of her remarrying, even though they lived in other cities and rarely visited her. As it happened, Molly and Ailene didn't like the idea of marriage any better than the idea of living in sin. In fact, Anna would not have been their choice for their father at all. She wore very bright clothes and too much makeup. She had streaked hair, no taste, and a high, squeaky voice. Friends and family felt that in looking for someone who would not remind him of Miriam, Frank had gone overboard. Of course, Anna turned out to have a heart of gold, but those differences in class and style became real barriers to her acceptance by those who had known Miriam.

The family had been able to provide caring and love for everyone, even after Miriam's death, as long as roles could be reassigned within the boundaries of the remaining family. But in truth something had been missing. And Frank Franklin had acted to correct that. He was replacing himself. He had found an outsider.

Anna filled the space that Frank had always occupied in the family before Miriam died. He had found someone who could support his new dominant role—someone who would not really threaten that power; someone who could always be pushed aside if necessary; someone who could take care of the family materially and make few personal demands. Anna was perfect for this job. She organized every family gathering, paid the bills, did the shopping and handled the day-to-day routine. And her role freed Frank to do all the advising, supporting, persuading, and sympathizing. She truly did not seem to mind being regarded as support personnel.

Because Frank now had a new role, neither he nor anyone else in the family realized that his new relationship mirrored his marriage in many ways. And Anna seemed to derive as much satisfaction from her role as Frank had when he played it with Miriam. For Anna, the dynamic was also a duplication. In her family of origin she had been the adoring and somewhat ignored younger sister of a boy much favored by their mother.

Molly and Ailene reacted to Anna in somewhat the same way they had reacted to their father when their mother was alive. Frank remained the center of the family. They solicited his help and advice in all matters; they depended on him and revered him. And they totally ignored Anna. It was as if she did not exist. They did not seem self-conscious about that or even very aware of it. Although they were upset that this arrangement between their father and *that* woman continued, they were able to live with it by ignoring it. Once again their pattern of denial, a strong family defense, rose to protect them from an awareness of loss. They were able to meet the change in their father's status by keeping familiar roles intact.

Frank, in choosing Anna, may have sensed how well she would make all that possible. She was already an outsider. As the daughter of a divorced woman with a favorite son, Anna had always been on the outside. Her family of origin prepared her for this role. But to the Franklins she was also an outsider in terms of class and background. Frank must have known at some level that this type of person would, in the long run, be more suitable than someone who was a substitute for his dead wife. Not only did he want to continue playing the new role he'd found himself good at, he also recognized that someone who was like Miriam would arouse rivalry and jealousy of a more bitter nature than Anna could inspire. But to ensure that Anna remained an outsider, he never urged marriage. They talked about it occasionally, but the conversations were never resolved. The idea of marriage just hung there over the years, even as their commitment to and dependence on each other grew. Unconsciously, it probably was important not to make their relationship legal.

Frank Franklin died twelve years later, when Anna was in her sixties. Anna was not able to keep the family together as he had. There was no role shifting that included her. She did follow the familiar denial pattern of mourning, keeping Frank's clothes, books, pipes, and so forth, in perfect readiness for close to three years. But she found that none of Frank's children or grandchildren particularly appreciated her efforts, and after a time she didn't appreciate them herself. Holding on to Frank kept her in the family until she could recover from his loss. However, once she truly separated herself from him and realized that she had not died, too, she moved into a circle of her own friends and relatives and left his family behind.

Molly and Ailene and the rest of the family were very depressed after Frank died. This truly did seem to be the end. They were a rudderless group. Neither Molly nor Ailene really wanted to compete with their mother's or Frank's record as leader. In a way, they maintained their state of low energy by not taking on or sharing leadership. There was no one in their generation to be the strong, central figure this family so needed. But they managed to get by as a leaderless group. It wasn't until the next generation, when the grandchildren had established themselves, that the leadership pattern reemerged and a new leader became available. Molly and Hugh's second son, Sean, was to support his parents and his aunt both financially and emotionally. He turned out to be personable, capable, strong, and very charismatic—much like his grandmother, Miriam Franklin.

Hugh could not bear to think about divorce, even though it had been approaching for several years. To leave his family would put him out in the cold and shatter his ideal picture of what family was. He worried about the son, Hugh, who was so much like him. He felt it would be the end of all of them.

Molly and Hugh

Hugh and Molly Temple were married for twenty years before they finally got divorced. Hugh-too, their first son, had just entered college. Sean was a junior in high school. The children were not surprised that their father wanted a divorce. They were both aware that their parents led separate lives. They noticed that their mother spent all her time at her mother's and then later at her father's. Even when she was home she wasn't really home. She slept late in the morning and stayed up all night. She played bridge in the afternoons, fed the family in the evening, and then headed for her parents' home. Their father spent more and more time at his tree ranch (watching the trees grow, Molly said). He'd go there in the morning and then work late at night to make up the time. The boys saw that there was little communication or feeling between their parents.

Hugh had accepted Molly's bond with her mother because that seemed natural enough to him. But it was one thing to have a wife who loved her mother and quite another to have a wife who doted on dad. That made him uneasy and resentful. He was jealous. There was something so exclusive, almost sexual, about it. He felt that if Molly had an exclusive relationship with any male it should be with him. Or even with young Hugh, whose loneliness and awkwardness in puberty reminded Hugh so sharply of his own adolescence. The whole situation brought back memories of his own parents, who were always more interested in each other than in him.

Molly and her father were like his parents, and the similarities revived his sense of not belonging, of being in the way. His parents were not mean, just thoughtless. They would go out to dinner, visit friends, even sit at home, without giving him a thought. As an only child who was left out of the family much of the time, he felt he was always an interruption in his parents' perfect relationship. And his current family circumstances revived many of those old feelings.

It brought back something else, too. When Hugh was an adolescent, from about fourteen to seventeen, he had had constant allergies—sinus problems, hayfever, colds, and respiratory infections. His parents, teachers, and doctor felt that he was especially sensitive and susceptible. There was a history of allergies in his family, and he was also rather delicate. After he left home and went to college, the allergies faded away. Everyone thought, as he himself did, that he had outgrown them. But at age thirty-six they returned. He could not shake a cold, his sinuses had to be drained and redrained, he was often watery-eyed.

Certainly as an adolescent, Hugh's feelings about being an outsider were acted out in his nose. The swollen mucous membranes and congestion of blood in the sinuses, so characteristic of a cold or of being cold, seemed directly related to feeling left out in the cold. And the watery eyes, characteristic of a cold, too, but not unlike weeping eyes, seem to register a loss. In his teen years that loss was the imminent separation from his parents when he went off to college. In his middle years that loss was the imminent separation from Molly and his children. He was already "out in the cold" again in this family. It was as if the allergies were trying to tell him something. After he and Molly separated all the allergies disappeared.

Molly made the mistake of marrying a man like her father instead of a man like her mother. Her parents' marriage had worked because they were so very complementary, but Molly was not her mother, even though she found it difficult to separate herself from her mother. Hugh was attracted to Molly partly because she had the kind of close bond with her mother that he had so wanted with his. He expected to be that close to Molly, to her family, and to the children they would have. Molly expected that, too. She didn't realize that she could not have the same kind of marriage that her parents had. She didn't realize that a slave is not necessarily able to be a nurturer and caretaker. Within the family system she responded to orders, not to needs. But Hugh didn't give orders. Only her mother did and, while they were babies, her boys. Later, her father did, taking her even further from Hugh. She needed someone dominant and nurturing.

Molly's difficulties as a caretaker were rather transparently obvious in her cooking. She was always in a rush to fix dinner since she sandwiched her preparations between her afternoons out and her evenings with her parents. (Breakfast and lunch were quite beyond her.) Her dinners were often cold or undercooked and unfailingly unappetizing. Her inability to nurture and, perhaps, her own intense need for nurturing were reflected in these pathetic little meals for which she neither received nor expected any acknowledgment. When her mother was alive, Molly and the boys, if they were with her, would often eat another meal at Miriam's house.

Molly was terrified at the thought of losing Hugh, even though she actually had lost him long before. She did not want to take care of herself, and she didn't want to go back to work. Furthermore, however tenuous their connection, she had no one but Hugh. The ironic implication of their marriage was that it was like a divorce anyway. They lived in the same house but had had separate bedrooms ever since Hugh-too had gone off to college. They never had sex anymore and rarely even had dinner together. They shared a roof, but only sporadically a life. They both complained bitterly about each other's lack of interest in the relationship, yet the idea of legitimizing their separateness frightened them. As with many divorcing couples, they thought of divorce as the end of everything. They didn't recognize the ways in which they were already divorced or the ways in which their lives would not change.

Hugh continued to support Molly after he'd moved just a few blocks away. Sean and Hugh-too, when he was home from college, spent almost as much time at their father's as at their mother's. Hugh had rented a slick sort of bachelor's pad that embarrassed him but suited the boys fine. They liked to drop in at all hours, sometimes bringing friends along, to drink and eat, listen to music Hugh couldn't understand and, occasionally, study. Hugh often wasn't there. He continued to work late and was as much a shadow in this new home as he had been in his home with Molly. In fact, the boys, with their various outside interests, left him outside much as Molly had. But he had a role. He provided, both financially and emotionally, a place for the family to gather.

Molly did not miss the boys very much. She had always been home so infrequently herself. They were always in and out, and they always let her know where they were. Molly did not approve of the time they spent at Hugh's. She felt Hugh did not give them much supervision, that he left them on their own too much. He felt that they were certainly old enough to take care of themselves and accused her of trying to restrict them. They would sometimes have screaming fights over the boys, which is exactly what they did before they divorced. The only difference was that they now fought over the phone since they rarely saw each other. And their fights were not just a continuation of a family pattern but an expression of closeness as well. Fighting takes some passion, some intensity. It had always been Molly and Hugh's strongest form of intimacy. It wasn't until they stopped squabbling many years later that they were truly separated from each other. At that time Hugh remarried, and Molly firmly decided that she would not.

Many of us fail to recognize that the acrimony and bitterness following many divorces is a form of holding on. It may not seem like holding on, but ill feeling is better than no feeling at all, especially for people who are alone and striking out on their own. The tension between them survives because it is the tie that binds them. Just as a negative family identity can hold a whole group together, recriminations and accusations can hold a couple together. It becomes the only method people have to express what remains of the caring and special identity they once had.

One man, who counted among his old friends only those who refused to speak to his ex-wife, could neither speak to her nor look at her. He picked up his children every weekend on the corner rather than risk running into her. He conveyed some messages through the children and had his secretary call her regarding money or custody matters. He clearly felt guilty and sad about the end of his marriage. Unconsciously, he wasn't ready to face his loss or break free of his dependency on his wife. They had married very young, and he had gone straight from his overbearing father's house to his own house with very little idea of who he was.

Gradually, he began to find out who he was and what he wanted, but by then he had a wife, three children, and a sick father to support. When he finally felt strong enough financially to make a move toward independence, he found he couldn't take his marriage with him. He managed to get through a lengthy divorce, but he felt so guilty about abandoning this woman who was even less secure and autonomous than he, that he couldn't really let go.

It wasn't until his father died three years later that he was able to face his ex-wife. By becoming the head of his family of origin as the eldest son, he gained enough confidence to run his own life. And as any family therapist might predict, when he freed himself he also freed his ex-wife. She had been developing some autonomy of her own without him, but it wasn't until he did not need her anymore that they were able to be independent, civil, even friendly toward each other.

Because they had been leading such separate lives, Molly and Hugh were able to carry on the roles that they had played before the divorce. Although there were changes, in that Hugh had a separate home, the emotional and psychological tone of the family remained the same for several years after the divorce, until the marriage really ended. The separation of these parents from each other, from the family identity, and from their children, was echoed in the separation of the children from their parents.

Sean and Hugh-too were in the stage of seeking their own separate and individual identities. They were learning how to stand up alone and in groups other than their family. Both parents and children had similar individual tasks. All family members were trying to become autonomous and independent at the same time. This was a case where a very fused family, generally unable to separate from each other, à la Molly and her mother, was able to pull apart and gain support from each other while doing so. They were fortunate in that their proximity during the transition period to a more autonomous group enabled them to continue in their old roles and systems until they were able to take on new ones.

For some families endings like divorce mean a constriction of the family circle that throws individuals into panic. Boundaries close in. Suddenly, there are less people to rely on. Suddenly, we have to call on our own resources, many of which have been dormant for years. This can be exciting and exhilarating, but it is also draining, and, in the beginning, dreary and frightening. As the circle narrows, people feel the fears of infancy (when to have mother out of sight was to be totally abandoned). The security of being married, like being a child in a family, looks better than we know it to be. We feel we do not have what it takes to stand alone. Having no ties, limits, demands, or roles is threatening. But it is also a time when peer groups take over some of the roles our former family played.

One of the reasons why Molly Franklin did not feel abandoned by her husband or sons was her bridge club. Molly was a very good bridge player, and the women in her club were all older than she. Several of them had been divorced. They considered her a protégé, both as a talented bridge player and in the role of a divorced woman. They played every day, and Molly worked very hard to be a good player in both roles. She was devoted to the group and, in a way, they served her as her family of origin had. Collectively they were dominant, powerful, protective. They provided her with the role of devotee or willing slave. She found in them a chance to belong in a way she had not belonged to anyone except to her family of origin. Life with Hugh and the boys had never been so secure; there was no leader in that group. The bridge club had lots of leaders, and the group itself led her along. She was very comfortable with them.

Peer Groups and Endings

We sometimes overlook the importance of extrafamilial groups during endings. We know that teenagers, like the Franklin boys, gain support from their peer groups when it comes time to leave their families. We see that a man whose father just died throws himself into his "family" at work with a relentless obsession. We hear it said that we really find out who our friends are during a crisis. It's not just that we find distraction and escape in our work and our friends. It's not just the sympathy and support they offer. When our inner world is crumbling and we are struggling to maintain the family equilibrium, it is like climbing on a life raft when we discover that the roles we take in other contexts are still there. The support we get from friends, co-workers, and other peers gives us the confidence we need to play our roles, even new roles, in our families during difficult times.

Changes in role relationships with peers may indicate impending role changes in our families. For example, a woman who was always available to her friends learned how helpful and supportive friends can be during her mother's terminal illness. Instead of always giving help, this woman learned to accept help from others. This experience enabled her to accept support from her family when she ran into financial difficulties a short time later. Always the one who cared for the family, a real pillar of strength, she would never have asked for their help had she not had practice in doing so in her peer group.

Peer groups also support old rules. Very often, our friendships and work relationships echo our family relationships, especially family of origin relationships. The woman above was a savior to both friends and family until events taught her a new role. People who were scapegoated as children are very likely to be blamed for problems at work. Leaders in the family will be leaders outside the family. During endings, we often get a sense of continuity from the roles we go on playing in peer groups. We may be uncertain about our continuing effectiveness as the family leader, but we are reassured to see that we are still the leader at the office or in our social group. This gives us a sense of stability when we most need it, thanks to a crossover effect between peer group and family.

We can see this kind of stability in older people who move into nursing or retirement homes. The homes—and their residents—constitute a new kind of family for many people. These are the people they live with, eat with, and interact with. These are the people they confide in and sympathize with. These are the people who often seem to understand their feelings about themselves and their situation better than their own relatives. But adjustment to this new family is predicated on adjustment in peer groups prior to this one. That is, a person who has always been a leader will be a leader, and the person who has always been a loner is not likely to become gregarious and sociable in a retirement community.

One man, whose mother was very shy and retiring, arranged to have people come to her when her health failed. Taking advantage of both public and private social services, as well as friends and neighbors, he was able to provide the kind of help his mother needed in order to remain at home.

A woman came in every morning to help her get bathed, dressed, and fed. A physical therapist came in twice a week to help her exercise a healing hip injury. She was taken to a social meeting once a week by friends, and every Sunday another friend took her to dinner. She had an appointment once a week to have her hair done and, most important, to have a manicure since she had always been very vain about her still beautiful hands. A county health nurse checked on her every week, and a private agency delivered a hot meal every evening. Hr son saw her twice a week and talked to her every day on a special phone that did not require dialing at her end. Because her eyesight was failing, both the phone and talking books (books on cassette tapes) were available to her as a public service.

The son spent a great deal of time arranging these activities to maintain his mother in her accustomed family role of quiet, behind-the-scenes manager of family life. Although she was no longer the manager, all the activity in her behalf made it possible for her to maintain the illusion that she was running the show. Of course, her son actually had taken over much of her role, and he was caring for her as she had cared for him when he was a little boy. She became even more retiring as he grew more adept at nurturing. These subtle role changes helped maintain their family system—a system that could only incorporate one individual's needs or demands. The son rightfully intuited that his mother, as long as she was alert and well enough, had neither the family nor the peer group experience to end her days happily in a group setting.

For some older people, however, such settings are ideal. Lonely in their own homes, isolated from friends and community activities by decreasing mobility, and living some distance from children or other relatives, these people find renewed opportunities for "family" in condominiums, retirement communities, and nursing homes. First, they have age, situation, and often health concerns in common. Then, special interest groups form around cards, golf, books, crafts like painting or needlepoint, religion, dancing, diets, music, and children, grandchildren, or even great-grandchildren. And perhaps most important of all, friendships develop that enable these people to play family roles with each other.

Once again, roles will be allocated to meet the predictable needs of any family—maintaining group stability and developing support systems to meet the individual needs of all members. To do this, each group member will draw on his or her previous family experience, from nuclear to blended, to single-parent to couple, and the roles those families required, from parent and child to martyr or clown.

We all have a tendency to undervalue such peer groupings, perhaps because there is a general belief that "family" runs out when children are grown. Few of us appreciate or even recognize what we bring to every small group that we belong to, even temporarily. Yet we always carry with us the roles, rules, systems, and problem-solving techniques of that first and most important small group we ever belonged to, our family of origin. We will always have a sense of group equilibrium, and we will unconsciously strive for it in whatever group we find ourselves. We will always find ourselves in other groups. Whether we are widowed, divorced, remarried, alone, or in a group after children are grown, we will still be part of a family, maybe more than one family.

Furthermore, peer groups play a very important role in modern families. Although it is true that the idea of family has a different meaning in different families and in different classes, the definition of family is changing across the board because roles within the family are changing. And as we experiment with role reversal and alternative groupings, we gain much support for these new roles from peers and from the social context in which we find ourselves.

Meeting Ends

Families meet endings in much the same way that they meet other changes. We try to maintain the status quo while using everyday problem-solving techniques to get by. And our techniques are likely to work now because we are all working toward a common goal—preservation of the family that was. We are all in conflict with the ending itself, rather than with each other, as in other stages or crises. We are united against a common enemy, namely, loss and fear of loss. Other underlying psychological forces, such as power, autonomy, love, and dependence very much affect our family's mourning. They account for the pain, anger, relief, despair, and uncertainty of endings. But they do not greatly change our family systems and patterns of interaction. Instead, these forces work to ensure our indelibility as we unconsciously mobilize resources to perpetuate ourselves, or at least a memory of ourselves as stamped on our group identity. We often find a shifting, sharing, replacing, and continuation of key roles in the family's—even the separated family's—systems. Although families do change, with new people in old roles and old people in new roles, basic family systems do persist, a fact that is often overlooked in the grief and confusion of most endings. This persistence results in the generational repetition of roles, rules, and numerous psychological and behavioral patterns.

The Franklins, for example, continued to operate without an outsider after Miriam died until Frank found an outsider in Anna. After Frank died they went on, somewhat halfheartedly. Because the leadership role was more important to them than the outsider role, they suffered more and felt more unlike a family without it. Much of their energy was tied up in the search for a role replacement until they found that replacement in the grandson, Sean. But they did survive their endings.

Today, many people feel that they will not survive their endings because there is no future generation on which to pin their hopes; a lack of family commitment in society itself. We think such pessimism results from the scant attention paid to the family —how it really works and why. Even in childfree, blended, single-parent, and other alternative families, there are dynamics that continue the line internally. Families may not look the same, but they operate in many of the same ways their forebears did. We don't walk away from our family, whatever its form, any more than we walk away from the larger society of which we are members. Families are persistent, insistent, and indelible in many ways that have not been appreciated or even acknowledged. Our society has been so concerned about the end or death of the family that the ways in which the family perpetuates itself and continues to provide a "home" for adults and children alike, have received too little study. We would not deny that the family today is in turmoil, that it is changing, that there is no perfect or foolproof model of family right now. Yet this very turmoil indicates that the family cannot be dismissed. The family dialectic is as relevant to the family in general as it is to individual families. Our small groups are always caught between the inevitability of change and the resistance to change. As long as we need both the growth and development of change and the comfort and security of stability, family in some form has a future.

Epilogue

⚙◇⚙

The Future of the Family

It is impossible to end a book about the family without saying something about the future of the family, especially since many people believe that it has no future. Joan Didion once wrote an essay about her daughter's birthday that introduces the subject very well. "I would like," she wrote, "to give her more. I would like to promise her that she will grow up with a sense of her cousins and of rivers and of her great-grandmother's teacups, would like to pledge her a picnic on a river with fried chicken and her hair uncombed, would like to give her *home* for her birthday, but we live differently now and I can promise her nothing like that."

Didion's nostalgia for that world of cousins by the river is shared by our culture. There is a great hunger for the world that Didion pictures—a stable, tightly knit world, a place of tradition and connection that we see vanishing before us. Because families today are becoming provisional and ever more fragmented, we suddenly look back with very romantic eyes. That family in which papa was the breadwinner and mama stayed home with the children looks as if it shored up, even fostered, stable values. It is praised for being, as Christopher Lasch has put it, "a haven in a heartless world." In retrospect, the nuclear family seems golden.

But from at least the middle of the nineteenth century there has been a prevailing vision of the family that both glorified its past and called its future into doubt. The very founder of sociology, Auguste Comte, raised grave questions about the survival of the patriarchial family more than a century and a half ago. He was not sure that the family could withstand what he took to be the anarchic forces of the French Revolution. The same uncertainty was carried into the New World as families separated from their roots to put down new roots in new lands, and as men and, later, women separated from their families to find work in our large industrial cities. The Civil War, which pitted brother against brother, was a further source of doom prophecies for the family. In each decade of our cataclysmic century the family's end has been prognosticated.

In 1927, the behavioral psychologist John B. Watson predicted that by 1977 marriage would no longer exist in the United States. He was convinced that the family was headed for a complete breakdown and that, by the seventies, children would be totally out of control, primarily because of the effect of the automobile on American life.

Ten years later, Pitirim Sorokin, a sociologist, predicted that divorce and separation would become so pervasive that there would be little point in distinguishing between marital and non-marital sex. "The family as a sacred union of husband and wife, of parents and children will further decrease until the family becomes a mere overnight parking place mainly for sex relationships."

Later still, by the 1940s, prognosis had turned apocalyptic. Carl Zimmerman, also a sociologist, predicted that American urbanization would lead to the fully atomized family. Having found analogies, especially in our affluent hedonism, between the families of late classical life and those of the contemporary world, Zimmerman was convinced, as were many in the forties and fifties, that the decline and fall of the family was but a prelude to the fall of western civilization.

More recently, that noted historian of the family, Philip Aries, made this tentative appraisal:

> One can imagine the extreme situations. Either the conjugal family keeps its current role, or ephemeral unions completely replace it. Personally I lean toward a third hypothesis. The indissolvable, monogamous community will persist, but only during the woman's voluntary period of fecundity and the education of the children. Let us say, for about 15 years. Before and after this period there will be no stable community, no family.

What interests us and motivates this commentary on past and present prophecies is how fully any diagnosis about the family is tied, and has always been tied, to the way we look at the larger society of which it is a part. Whether the focus is the French Revolution, the frontier, the industrial revolution, the horseless carriage, sexual liberation, or the growth of technology and the alienation of man, any reading about the family is based upon the external changes we perceive in the larger social order. We see the family changing primarily in context.

At least, changing its form. "Court Lets Man Who Is Now Woman Keep Four Children" reads one headline. "Gays Demand Right to Marry" reads another. "Divorced Father of Three Kidnaps His Children." But many more stories—the vast majority, in fact—are less sensational and just as different from what has gone before. Futurologist Alvin Toffler speaks of a blueprint for future families, a world of childless marriages, professional parenthood, postretirement childbearing, corporate families, communes, geriatric group marriages, homosexual family units, and so on. But right now, today, we are living with blended families of stepchildren and stepparents, serial monogamy in one exclusive relationship after another, with and without legal marriage, and family networks that are extended not vertically through generations of blood kin but horizontally through friendship and remarriage.

In other words, the prophets tend to get it wrong. The automobile certainly changed American life and American (and other) families, but it did not mean children out of control. Although some children are indubitably out of control, they tend to be the ones who do not have cars or hopes of getting cars. That situation has more to do with our inability to solve the problem of poverty than our ability to drive. Although our sexual habits have definitely changed, the family is not the overnight parking place for sex; rather, the overnight parking place is for sex. And, although science has raised more questions than it has answered about the quality of our lives through nuclear, medical, and technological revolutions, we are still talking about what all these changes mean to the family.

Perhaps one problem for the prophets is their focus on the external features of a constantly changing society. There appears to be an historical tendency to look at the form of the family for its content. But we would make a case for the psychological content, the content for survival, that has not been given much attention. Just as important as the external changes, which mirror the changes in the larger social order, are the internal forces for family life, which do not change that much.

The family is basically a very conservative institution. There has been a tendency to look at the differences among families, particularly to compare present families with families of the past. Less attention has been given to the similarities; it is there that the patterns, roles, rules, and forces that we have examined in this book reveal that the family has more staying power than most social scientists and, indeed, families themselves have realized. Certainly something accounts for the fact that we continue to live in small groups of mutually dependent people.

Because we are living in a time of rapid change, we do not recognize that we still believe that "blood tells" or that our particular family group is somehow special. Joan Didion herself wonders, elsewhere in the essay we mentioned, if she was "born into the last generation to carry the burden of *home*, to find in family life the source of all tension and drama." She asks what a woman from a more recent generation can possibly make of *Long Day's Journey into Night*. There are probably plenty of generations throughout time that could make nothing at all of it, yet the Greeks would surely understand. As with all periods of time, those that we study are those that reflect or offer something to our time. That younger woman may not fathom O'Neill, but she will have some reference points of her own from her experience in her family of origin. It, too, is family, and if our time tends to see her experience as the end rather than a phase, that is human nature.

Today, many of us look around and find nothing familiar. We are not living the lives our parents lived, and we are not modeling ourselves after them as we (and they) believed they modeled themselves after their parents. And when our own children do not turn out like us, we are dismayed that we who miss a sense of generational bonds could in some way be responsible for a further loss of continuity. We feel a loss of something inexplicable, that sense of place that Joan Didion describes, that idea of home that connects one generation, one family member, to another. But what we fail to recognize is the way in which our children are like us—repeat our pattern—in being different from their parents. That is the continuity.

We overlook this link not only because family forms are so unfamiliar today, but also because of the disorientation we attribute to moving all the time, not having a place to return to should we choose to do so. Yet that is part of the fantasy, too. In this country especially, people have always been highly mobile—moving out West, moving up on the social scale, moving to the suburbs, moving to another, often better job in another place. This longing for the form or the place from the past that will tell us where we belong seems to reflect a longing to belong. And much of this feeling is caused by our inability to recognize all the ways in which we do belong to the specific group of people with whom we grew up.

The truth is that we do not see all the ways in which our early family struggles over power, autonomy, dependence, love, separation (and probably many more psychological forces) influence our later sense of context. We do not see that we find groups that allow us to play out the same struggles all over again. We do not realize that we play certain roles in order to gain equilibrium in whatever group we live with. We certainly do not see that families of all sorts go through a developmental cycle in which issues of identity and conflict resurface again and again. We do not see this continuity because of all the discontinuity around us. We have tended to focus on the outer realities and overlooked those persistent inner realities.

This book is really an attempt to give people a chance to look at that inner reality of the family, which we believe changes very little from generation to generation and, in many respects, from family to family. All families go through stages, all have identities of their own, all battle forces they don't understand, all have experiences together that are indelible. The family as our most influential social unit has persevered despite the changes in society. The family has changed and it continues to do so, but it has not disappeared. And we believe that the hidden forces, the identification process, family systems, and a fundamental psychological need to maintain the status quo account for the family's persistence as an institution.

In revolutionary or transitional times, it is typical to want to change the family dramatically and to attempt to do so. That would seem to be the contemporary American situation. Perhaps all this talk about the death of the family is a national conspiracy to mask our death wish for the family. In the sixties and early seventies the family was criticized from every quarter. It was called paternalistic, child-centered, restrictive, and inflexible. Everyone could see that the nuclear family was not an appropriate, or even extant, example anymore. Working women made a tremendous difference in the shape of the family. The impact of day-care centers and other influences, from psychology to birth control, has made the family less private and, in the minds of many, less responsible. Yet even there we see signs of indelibility. The welfare mother who is the daughter of a welfare mother or even the granddaughter of a welfare mother is no stranger to continuity. The high divorce rate has not discouraged marriage. Instead, marriage continues to increase as divorced people marry again and sometimes again. People who do not have children do not renounce their relatives or refuse social interactions that are surprisingly similar to family bonds.

Although we are still in a period of transition, and the death of the family is still a hot topic, we are beginning to see that family still exists. Betty Friedan, who got us over the feminine mystique, has recently advocated more concern for the well-being of children and adults of both sexes. She suggests flex-time and childcare in the business world, for example, so that both mothers and fathers could be parents and workers. Alvin Toffler, author of *Future Shock*, now foresees a society of electronic cottage industries in which families of all forms and ages work at home to produce products and services that are available to others through our instant communications and sophisticated technology. Isaac Asimov, the scientist and author, has envisioned a world in which children would become very precious because there would not be many on whom to pin our hopes. Because we would have to limit reproduction, children would belong to everyone, and people everywhere would work to see that they were supported and protected.

Each of these predictions could be said to be the result of our present economic uncertainty, for we are more acutely aware than ever before that resources and time are running low on a worldwide basis. Women and men both have to work just to get by. Working at home with the help of children and other relatives may be necessary if we don't have the fuel to get to the office. Reducing the birth rate may be another necessity in times of dwindling natural resources.

But to us the salient feature of these stories is the faith they illustrate that family will continue in some form or, more appropriately, forms. Although tremendous questions loom in the future—how children will be cared for, how families will be affected by genetic and biologic engineering, how we will manage our environment in the near future—there seems to be a trend developing toward acceptance of the family as a changing, not a dying, entity. And we believe that this is not only true but extremely positive. A new family (or families), is long overdue. We can have opportunities, as the family opens up, to form families that are less rigid and constricting than the mandatory nuclear family was becoming, families that better suit how we live and work with each other now.

We will not predict, but we certainly do hope, that people in the future will take their internal family life into account whether they are up against the mundane everyday problems of being with others or the vast imponderables of a changing society. It won't make them instantly immortal or lastingly successful, but we think a little reflection on patterns and roles and repetitions can give individuals a chance to intervene in and change their lives if they choose to do so. It can also give them an idea of what they belong to, a sense of continuity, and a hint of indelibility.

✿✿✿

A Selected Bibliography

Ackerman, Nathan, ed. *Family Therapy in Transition*. Boston: Little, Brown and Company, 1970.

———. *The Psychodynamics of Family Life: Diagnosis and Treatment of Family Relationships*. New York: Basic Books, Inc., 1958.

Anthony, E.J. and Benedek, T., eds. *Parenthood: Its Psychology and Psychopathology*. Boston: Little, Brown and Company, 1970.

Barnett, Joseph. "Narcissism and Dependency in the Obsessional-Hysteric Marriage." *Family Process* 10 (1971): 1:75.

Bebbington, A.C. "The function of stress in the establishment of the dual-career family." *Journal of Marriage and the Family* 35 (1973): 530–37.

Bernard, Jessie. *The Future of Marriage*. New York: World, 1972.

Boszormenyi-Nagy, Ivan and Geraldine M. Spark. *Invisible Loyalties*. Hagerstown, MD: Harper and Row, 1973.

Deutscher, Irwin. "The quality of postparental life: definitions of the situation." *Journal of Marriage and the Family*, February 1964.

Dicks, Henry V. *Marital Tensions*. London: Routledge and Kegan Paul, 1967.

Didion, Joan. *Slouching Toward Bethlehem*. New York: Farrar, Straus & Giroux, 1968.

Duvall, Evelyn M. *Family Development*. 4th ed. New York: J.B. Lippincott Company, 1971.

Epstein, Helen. *Children of the Holocaust*. New York: G.P. Putnam's Sons, 1979.

Erikson, Erik. *Childhood and Society*. New York: W.W. Norton & Company, 1963.

Fabe, Marilyn and Wikler, Norma. *Up Against the Clock*. New York: Random House, 1979.

Ford, Frederick R. and Herrick, Joan. "Family rules: family lifestyles." *American Journal of Orthopsychiatry* 44:1, January 1974.

Glick, Ira and Kessler, David. *Marital and Family Therapy.* New York: Grune and Stratton, 1974.

Gould, Roger. *Transformations.* New York: Simon and Schuster, 1978.

Guerin, Philip J., Jr., ed. *Family Therapy.* New York: Gardner Press, Inc., 1976.

Gutmann, David. "Individual adaptation in the middle years: developmental issues in the masculine mid-life crisis." *Journal of Geriatric Psychiatry* 9:1 (1976): 41–59.

Henry, Jules. *Pathways to Madness.* New York: Random House, 1965.

Johnson, A.M.; Falstein, E.I.; Szurek, S.A.; and Svendsen, M. "School Phobia." *American Journal of Orthopsychiatry* 11 (1941): 702–8.

Keniston, Kenneth. *All Our Children.* New York and London: Harcourt Brace Jovanovich, 1977.

Kübler-Ross, Elizabeth. *On Death and Dying.* New York: The Macmillan Company, 1969.

Levinson, D.J. et al. *The Seasons of a Man's Life.* New York: Alfred A. Knopf, Inc., 1978.

Lidz, Theodore. *The Person: His and Her Development Throughout the Life Cycle.* rev. ed. New York: Basic Books, 1976.

Liebenberg, B. "Expectant fathers." *Child and Family* 8 (1969): 265–77.

Lifton, Robert J. *The Broken Connection.* New York: Simon and Schuster, 1979.

Lindemann, Erich. "Symptomology and management of acute grief." *American Journal of Psychiatry* 101 (1944): 141–48.

Melges, F.T. "Postpartum psychiatric syndromes." *Psychosomatic Medicine* 30 (1968): 95–108.

Minuchin, Salvador. *Families and Family Therapy.* Cambridge, MA: Harvard University Press, 1977.

———, Rosman, Bernice L. and Baker, Lester. *Psychosomatic Families: Anorexia Nervosa in Context.* Cambridge, MA: Harvard University Press, 1979.

Money, John. "Sex, love and commitment." *Journal of Sex and Marital Therapy* 2:4, Winter 1976.

Moulton, Ruth. "Some effects of the new feminism." *American Journal of Psychiatry* 134:1, January 1977.

Murstein, Bernard I., ed. *Theories of Attraction and Love*. New York: Spring Publishing Company, Inc., 1971.

Napier, A.Y. and Whitaker, C.A. *A Family Crucible*. New York: Harper and Row, 1978.

Rapoport, Rhona. "Normal crises, family structure, and mental health." *Family Process* 2:1, March 1963.

————, Rapoport, Robert N. and Ziona Strelitz. *Fathers, Mothers and Society*. New York: Basic Books, Inc., 1977.

Rhodes, Sonya. "A developmental approach to the life cycle of the family." *Social Casework*, May 1977.

Rosenbaum, S. and Alger, I., eds. *The Marriage Relationship, Psychoanalytic Perspectives*. New York: Basic Books, 1968.

Rossi, Alice S.; Kagan, Jerome; and Hareven, Tamara, eds. *The Family*. New York: W.W. Norton and Co., Inc., 1979.

Sager, Clifford J. *Marriage Contracts and Couple Therapy*. New York: Brunner/Mazel, 1976.

Sanguiliano, I. *In Her Time*. New York: William Morrow, 1979.

Sarnoff, Charles. *Latency*. New York: Jason Aronson, Inc., 1976.

Satir, Virginia. *Conjoint Family Therapy*. Palo Alto, CA: Science and Behavior Books, Inc., 1964.

————. *Peoplemaking*. Palo Alto, CA: Science and Behavior Books, 1972.

Skolnick, A. *The Intimate Environment*. Boston: Little, Brown and Company, 1973.

Solomon, Michael A. "A developmental conceptual premise for family therapy." *Family Process* 12 (1973): 178–88.

Stierlin, H. *Separating Parents and Adolescents*. New York: Quadrangle, 1974.

————. "Shame and guilt in family relationships." *Archives of General Psychiatry* 30 (1974): 381–89.

Toman, Walter. *Family Constellation*. 2d ed. New York: Springer Publishing Co., 1969.

Wenner, N.K., Cohen, Mabel B., et. al. "Emotional problems in pregnancy." *Psychiatry* 32 (1969): 389–410.

Whelan, Elizabeth. *A Baby? Maybe. . . .* New York: Bobbs-Merrill Company, Inc., 1975.

Wooley, P. *The Custody Handbook*. New York: Summit, 1979.

Zinner, J. and Shapiro, R. "Projective identification as a mode of perception and behavior in families of adolescents." *International Journal of Psychoanalysis* 53 (1972): 523–30.

Index